The
Big Rumpus

The
Big Rumpus

A Mother's Tale from the Trenches

Ayun Halliday

SEAL PRESS

THE BIG RUMPUS: *A MOTHER'S TALE FROM THE TRENCHES*

Published by Seal Press
An Imprint of Avalon Publishing Group, Inc.
1400 65th Street, Suite 250
AVALON
publishing group incorporated Emeryville, CA 94608

Interior design by Paul Paddock

Library of Congress Cataloging-in-Publication Data is available for this title.

ISBN: 1-58005-071-9

9 8 7 6 5 4 3 2

Printed in the United States of America by Berryville Graphics
Distributed to the trade by Publishers Group West

For India, Milo and Greg

For India, Milo and Greg

Contents

1 Prologue: The East Village Inky

25 The Daily Grind
Trenchdweller
The Stacks
Nitpicking
Holy Flurking Snit
Because I'm the Mother, That's Why

85 The Way We Were
NeoNatalSweetPotato:
Dispatches from the New World
Waiting for Milo

165 Human Anatomy
Topless Lunch
The Chopping Block
These Parts

233 Hot Dates
December 25
February 14
April 15

285 The Extremes
Spare Us
Mashnote to Milo

Acknowledgments

I would like to thank all the people who are mentioned in this book, even the ones I haven't seen since elementary school. I am particularly indebted to Spencer Kayden, Karen Christopher, Sarah Cooke, Jesse McDonald, Carol Eggers, Rob Helms, Emil Wilson, Amanda Sullivan, Richard Wofford and Anna Brackett. Although Stephen O'Rourke was left on the editing room floor with a description of the sub-zero night we went to see the Macy's Day balloons inflated behind the Museum of Natural History, he continues to be an important part of my family's life. Bill Coelius, while not named, is clearly identifiable as the dinner guest who says all those bad words in front of the children.

My motherly burdens have been leavened by the midwives at the Elizabeth Seton Childbearing Center, the staff of St. Vincent's NICU, Dr. John Snyder, Jane's Exchange, everyone involved with Open House Nursery School and the children and adults who enliven the littered surface of the Tompkins Square playground.

The staff of the Boerum Hill Food Company was kind enough to let me treat their restaurant as an office while writing this book. Eat there when in Brooklyn!

My family has weathered my attempts at autobiographical anthropology with bright, shiny faces. Thanks to Betsy and Art Harris, Reed Halliday, Paula Kotis, Beth and Sam Kotis and Robert Brockway.

Thanks to Bee Lavender, Ariel Gore and the hipmamas for putting the ball into play and keeping it rolling. Chris Dodge is another who has boosted my heinie to the top of the mountain time and time again. The NeoFuturists provided an excellent training ground. Leslie Miller, my editor at Seal Press, is a compassionate, capable butcher who made this book's gestation and delivery a time of great joy.

My profound gratitude to everyone who has read the *East Village Inky* over the years, as well as the independent booksellers and reviewers who have helped get the word out.

Whereby would hang my tale without India ("Inky"), Milo and Greg Kotis? I cannot thank them enough, but suspect I should remember to try.

The
Big Rumpus

Is that me when I was a little baby? Where's my shoes? What's that Z for !? Where's Milo? Oh he wasn't borned yet, I know.

Prologue:
The East Village Inky

Is that me when
I was a little baby?
where's my Shoes?
What's that Z for !?
Where's Milo? Oh·
he wasn't borned
yet, I know.

the east Village
— INKY ·
in which the mother
of a 3 thumbed baby
blah blah blah blah
BUY THIS
ZINE! → $2

EVEN
ALL
Y'ALL

Prologue:
The East Village Inky

I remember when I couldn't wait to be old. I spent an entire afternoon in the sunless passageway between the neighbor's chain-link fence and our garage, covering every brick I could reach with colored chalk. Squatting to retrieve the yellow stub from the dirt so that all my flowers wouldn't be pink, I had no trouble believing that I was creating an art gallery. Crowds of adult art-lovers would march up our driveway, eager to pay for the privilege of squeezing into that narrow space behind the garage. I would sit by the forsythia bush, depositing their admission fees in the red plastic cash register I had received for Christmas.

By the time my mother called me for dinner, doubt had started to creep in. What would I do in winter, or when it rained? How would people buy the art? I couldn't very well expect my parents to let me disassemble the garage brick by brick. Even if they were willing, I had no experience with heavy demolition, and the only tools I was permitted to use without help were in the sandbox, under a board, because the neighborhood cats did bad things in there if we left it uncovered.

My mother called again. I grew up in the kind of neighborhood where women cooked carefully planned meals for their families and where children emerged from bushes, holes and private narrow spaces when summoned, shortly after their fathers' cars turned into the driveways. I had big plans for what would happen to me when I was old. I had a big imagination and no sisters or brothers to tell me that I was a total stupe.

Some might say that I held on to my childhood for a good long time. I studied theater and applied my degree to a career in waiting tables. I traveled around Europe, Asia and Africa with a dirty backpack on my shoulders. The plays in which I performed started at midnight and had no special effect more involved than clicking a flashlight on and off. I got married in a rented loft in New York City wearing striped stockings and a cheap dress, through which, I later learned, my underwear was plainly visible. I wrote poems that I didn't finish, considered plastic milk crates furniture and had a lot of friends like myself. My first child wasn't born until I was thirty-two. I'm not an idiot, but I genuinely believed that the baby would spend a lot of time curled at my feet like a kitten. Being pregnant was like decorating my parents' garage in colored chalk, except that now I was the mistress of an East Village apartment only slightly larger and worlds more expensive than their old wood-paneled station wagon. The unsuitability of my situation didn't bother me. I had great plans for the surprise package in my uterus. I took pot-shots at Barney the purple dinosaur and those ugly toys that play tinny electronic versions of "Twinkle, Twinkle, Little Star." There was no reason why the baby couldn't be my confederate.

Even after she was born, I continued to imagine that I would have no problem partaking of all my established amusements. I would bring her with me! She would learn to turn her nose up at all plastic representations of characters who didn't join *Sesame Street* until years after I stopped watching. Osmosis would lead her to like what I liked. I like to read books with lots of words and no pictures. That's fun for me. I gravitate to activities that involve holding a pen. I like to sit in auditoriums filled with quiet, respectful people watching other adults on big screens.

Babies don't like these things. You can sneak it past them for three or four months, but once they figure out how to crawl, forget it. The older the baby gets, the less willing she is to indulge you. She will use every weapon in her considerable arsenal to prevent your further participation in the very pursuits that once comprised the most meaningful part of your existence. The baby would like to remind you that she is now the primary reason you were put on earth. She will roll over, cry, shit, coo, clap her hands, even grab your pen and jab it into her own eye, if that's what it takes. She does so without guile. As advertised, her gummy smile is irresistible, inspiring fierce pangs in the one who birthed her, but her conversation is far from choice. The little melon farmer will strand you. You have lots of time on your hands but painfully limited options for how to spend it. Your mind gets a bit soft.

I've never been much of a stickler for the housekeeping duties that come with adulthood, but the baby had me in such a choke hold that I felt nostalgic for the days when mopping the floor didn't require hours of strategic preparation. This couldn't be me, absent-mindedly swiping puréed yams and cat hair from the floor into my mouth while waiting for my husband to come home from an exciting day temping at Citibank. I feared that a large and utterly tedious beast would devour me before my firstborn child could mount the tenement staircase, pronounce her own name or eat anything with a texture more robust than wallpaper paste. If it hadn't been for the magazine, I don't know what I would have done. The magazine saved my heiner.

It wasn't one of those glossy mainstream monthlies that publish the same two articles in every issue on disciplining your toddler and decorating the nursery for under two thousand dollars. It wasn't a slick newcomer hyping money management as hip and fun. It sure as bugfuck wasn't *Martha Stewart Living.* I guess one might call it an anticorporate, consciousness-raising, feminist call to arms, although I feel rather immodest saying so since I write the thing myself. It's not really a magazine but what is known as a zine, a self-published, highly subjective personal periodical with questionable proofreading and a laughably small circulation. But my god, I'm thirty-six years old. Most of my fellow zine publishers are disaffected high schoolers urgent with the desire to explain why sexism, racism and the eating of animals are wrong.

I'd always wanted to start a zine. I just couldn't seem to come up with a compelling subject. To put out a zine, you have to find a sustainable passion, something that will drive you to create issue after issue, stapling them together long after everyone else in your house has gone to bed. It wasn't until my daughter Inky turned one that I realized I had something to write about after all. Why, I was no dif-

ferent from Judy Garland in *The Wizard of Oz*! The thing I'd gone
looking for was right in my own backyard, except I didn't have a
backyard; I had a rusty fire escape that I was afraid to sit on with a
baby. I could write about that! Though I sometimes feel like I'm
building a sports car out of an empty refrigerator box, making
"vroom vroom" noises under my breath as I daydream about
driving it down to Mexico by referring to my outpourings as a magazine, not a zine, I can be both self-important and nonchalant.
Some people to whom I give complimentary issues aren't sure what
to call it, given its humble appearance. They ask if I'm still making
my "little newsletter" or "that pamphlet." One woman slightly
younger than I am and thrice the adult always introduces me to her
friends with the conversation-stopper "Ayun makes a zine." The
way she says it, it rhymes with "swine." Her friends wrinkle their
noses politely, as if they've been told that I play with dolls. She con-
fidently mispronounces my name, too, in the spirit of camaraderie.
I'm too sheepish to correct her. I momentarily wish that my name
were Barbara and I were redecorating an old farmhouse that my
husband and I had just purchased upstate. I don't stay embarrassed
long though. That zine keeps my wig on straight when the pedes-
trian lunacy of raising small children is almost more than I can bear.
People who think that it's laughably unsophisticated should see my
art gallery.

For my inaugural issue, I took ten sheets of 8 1/2-by-11 paper out
of our computer's unreliable printer, checking first that no hastily
xeroxed flyers for our old low-budget theatrical endeavors were on
the flip side. I scrounged around for a black fine-point marker and
found one among the dead soldiers camped in mugs on our desk. I

felt as fluttery as a sophomore with a speaking part in *Oklahoma!* The moment I touched the pen to the paper, Inky woke up, so I put her in her little blue backpack and we walked around our neighborhood for hours. The opportunities for rubbernecking in the East Village are endless. I didn't have the money or the disposition to reserve a table at the newly opened restaurant with the heavy buzz, but unlike the other lost souls roaming the sidewalks, I could press my nose to the plate-glass window and gaze until I'd had my fill. The baby gave me carte blanche. Leather-clad couples enjoying seventeen-dollar plates of postcoital polenta impressed each other by cooing at the little face peering in. It sure beat sitting around at home, staring at the congealed blobs of baby food I was too fried to sponge off the walls. We went on safaris in search of intriguing graffiti, outrageous T-shirt slogans and colorfully costumed madmen. Once we saw a severed chicken foot right in the middle of Avenue A. We saw a pile of what I've come to call "poo-poo" with a spoon sticking out of it. Poor man's pudding.

When the weight on my back began to sag, I raced back to our 340-square-foot apartment eager to reunite with the paper and marker. I scribbled furiously while she slept, as if the public was starving for want of our published adventures. Just in case multitudes came to the East Village to retrace our steps, I supplied addresses. I doodled pictures of the shit with the spoon, homeless punks panhandling in front of the pizza joint and a squirrel eating a Toblerone bar it pilfered from a stroller in the Tompkins Square playground. I drew myself in my baggy overalls, gasping as I dragged bags of groceries and a megapack of diapers back from the new K-mart in Astor Place, while Inky clubbed me over the head with the toy we kept tied to her backpack. It took me forever to figure out how to draw that thing, a little geometric structure made of wooden beads and elastic. Every kid in the city seemed to have one.

My printing dwindled to specks of pepper as I tried to squeeze everything I wanted to say into the margins. I was as serious about this as I'd been that day beside the garage, and it was more fun than the time I helped myself to the forbidden hose to make mud pies in February.

When I had covered my ten sheets of paper, I took Inky to a store that sold vintage postcards, Mexican wrestling figurines and pajamas printed with hula girls and flying toasters. The owner hated children, whose tiny grasping hands posed a constant threat to his merchandise, so his unexpected courtesy toward Inky felt like a benediction. "Yours isn't horrible at all," he confided as he broke my ten. He jerked his head toward a customer crabwalking through the narrow aisles after a galloping, squealing toddler. "Those are the ones that give me hives."

I interpreted this to mean "Yours is wonderful and always will be."

In the safety of his vintage photo booth, I shucked Inky from her backpack and fed three unwrinkled bills into the slot. It was one of the half-dozen occasions since my wedding on which I'd worn lipstick.

In the resulting photo strips, Inky looks gorgeous, plump cheeked, her sparse, slightly ratty hair following the lines of her perfect skull. She is so little, nothing like she is now, an impetuous, lippy four-year-old, dressing herself in a tutu and pink cowboy boots to comb out her pet washcloth with her silver-handled hairbrush, a monogrammed relic of my childhood. Inky's baby brother, Milo, is a dead ringer for the child in those photo booth strips, though his mother is more worn and knowing than that gal in dark lipstick. Four years in the playground with no sunscreen has taken its toll. In those black-and-white mug shots from 1998, I look expectant and, thanks to the lipstick, passably glamorous. A silly striped kerchief that I found in the gutter is perched on top of my head. Not long before, I had cropped my long hair into a pixie cut, the first since fourth grade. I fretted that short hair veered close to matronly on all but the most elfin of bodies, but Inky left me with little choice, yanking my long locks from her backpack perch like she was disciplining an unruly Great Dane. My 'do rag was odd, but it kept the soccer-mom look at bay.

The two best photos became the cover of my magazine, which I called the *East Village Inky* in a fit of inspiration. Because even the most deserving of little magazines are not printed for free, I called my good friend Little MoMo and asked if she could help me print my magazine —for free — after hours on her corporate employer's deluxe copier. I assured her that I would do all the xeroxing and collating if she could just entertain the baby. She agreed and not just because the first issue featured a small sketch of her squatting before a wild-eyed sidewalk vendor on the night she purchased a phone-shaped purse that dials out if plugged in to a wall jack. Little MoMo has been on our side since she attended Inky's unexpectedly arduous birth, when she called another close friend midlabor to announce over my mournful wails, "We're gonna get this little fucker out of there!"

I have a problem with margins, the severity of which was discovered when Little MoMo had to spend several hours trying to align my ten originals facedown on the copier's glass so that the copies could be stacked up, chopped in half, collated and stapled together without the center binding obscuring the last word of every line. My transgressions were far from uniform, and some pages had to be reduced. I had not been able to stop myself from scribbling right up to the edge, even though I knew from experience that I was supposed to leave at least a quarter inch of white space. This shrink-when-necessary technique seemed to work well, until MoMo discovered that it interfered with the chopping. She sliced down the middle of one two-sided copy to create four pages. We flipped the pages over, and a center cut made on the front side decapitated the first line of text on the back.

I struggled to amuse Inky, who had decided that this would be the only occasion on which she would snub her beloved MoMo. With the designated child wrangler taking over the controls of the Xerox machine, I was demoted to baby-sitter. I kept glancing at the wall clock, anxious that MoMo, who already had been here eight hours before we arrived, might throw in the towel. Copying the zine was shaping up to be impossible. I feared that Inky's mirthful shrieks might attract a security guard, who would discover our scam and make MoMo lose her job. Most of all, I worried that I'd have to start over, recreating the *East Village Inky* with rulers and proper margins.

Inky's father, Greg, was called in to help. Little MoMo and Greg have joined forces many times to bail me out. They got me through that bewildering interminable labor. Sometimes I feel like they're my parents, taking charge while I sheepishly make faces for the baby in the corner. After more abortive attempts, Greg came up with the solution of binding the issue with rubber bands: Readers could joggle the pages back and forth to see all the copy. By Greg's rigorous standards this was not much of a solution, but it was literally the only workable option given the raw material. He was hungry, since it was almost eleven P.M. After seven years together, he knew I was mostly grasshopper and would settle for something no self-respecting ant would consider. I thought the rubber band solution was great. I insisted on taking Greg, MoMo and Inky to celebrate at the restaurant of my choice. They were so exhausted they could barely chew, let alone engage in witty adult banter. It was a shame, since Inky had given up the ghost, sprawling beside me on the booth, a napkin spread over her head to protect her from errant forkfuls of rice. I've always been a messy eater. Of course, the bill for dinner far exceeded the cost of printing the magazine at a copy shop, though one hardly could expect a Kinko's drone to work so hard figuring out a way to turn ten densely covered originals into a stack of legible copies. They have their own zines to worry about—anarchist screeds, punk rock manifestos and semi-arch homages to 1980s sitcoms that budding intellectual snobbery had prevented me from watching.

The next morning I laid out on the warped, dirty floors of my apartment all the stacks of chopped-up xeroxed paper and assembled them to make a whopping fifty copies of the *East Village Inky*. This felt like a great achievement, given that Inky had a baby's fondness for paper, rumpling great handfuls while sucking a couple of pieces into a repellent, pulpy mass. Several times I untaped her disposable diaper to find a few flecks of homemade confetti planted in the compost.

Rereading my copy, I thought it was pretty good, despite the irritation of having to shift the pages back and forth within the rubber band binding. There were a couple of spelling errors and a poorly drawn hand I'd whited out and never bothered to replace, but I always can turn a blind eye toward my imperfections when fixing them would require much work. Satisfied, I popped Inky into the backpack and struck out for the playground, half a block away.

That was scary. I was about to take the plunge and identify myself as something other than a mother. I'd developed a pretty easy camaraderie with the other parents who used Tompkins Square for their children's recreational needs. Still, maybe our affinity was limited to talking about how much we hated people who could only talk about their children. I had felt a similar flush of friendship for the European tourists Greg and I had hung out with for a day or two on the beaches of Southeast Asia a few years earlier, and where were they now? Taking a deep breath, I approached Inky's cronies' mothers, carrying some little xeroxed invitations I'd whipped together the night before. Above a drawing of a baby astride our tumbledown brick building, I printed, "Roof party to celebrate the first issue of the *East Village Inky.*" There was barely time to explain before one kid snatched a ball out of another's hands. I was grateful for the distraction. It delayed the embarrassment of outing myself as a thirty-three-year-old who thinks forty small handwritten pages can be rubber-banded together and called a magazine.

People were excited at the prospect of a party. We hadn't yet begun the endless round of toddlers' birthday celebrations where the tofu mommies' best intentions were snuffed out by the weight of chocolate icing. I said that I hoped this would be the opening gambit for us to get to know each other outside of the playground. By the end of the afternoon, I had handed out all my invitations, giving one to anybody whose kid's name I knew. Everybody promised to try to make it, except for one little boy's mother who begged off, saying, "I'm sorry. I can't take him up on a roof. It just freaks me out too bad, what could happen to him on a roof." I knew exactly what she meant, but I could not squeeze more than two or three adults into my apartment. She had a reputation for being a bit overprotective. Her son was a shovel-loving sweetie who had been rerouted at thirteen months from an overseas orphanage. If I had had to work as hard as she did to become a mother, I too might have steered clear of the tops of tall buildings. Instead, I believed in a magical force field that would keep the children from harm, the way I once believed a diaphragm would protect my lady egg from marauding bands of sperm. I told people to bring their strollers so we could restrain the children if necessary. I didn't want anybody to walk or toddle or crawl over the edge in the split second it takes a nursing mother to grab another beer.

The night of the party it drizzled off and on, but that didn't stop them from coming. Huffing and puffing after carrying strollers up six steep flights, they arrived to eat grocery-store-brand chips and to admire our stellar view of the Empire State Building. I pointed out that if you stood near the stairs and craned your head to the left, you could glimpse the top of the Chrysler Building. Those who braved the edge could observe the final flowering of the lively Saturday night drug trade on East 9th Street. Everyone received complimentary copies of the *East Village Inky* #1.

"What is this?" one mother inquired politely, gesturing to the zine I offered in return for the wrapped gift she had brought assuming that it was Inky's birthday. I was equally confused. I thought we were all clear on the relative ages of our children. Didn't she remember that her child was exactly seven months younger than Inky, whose first birthday had passed without a party because we were traveling in Scotland at the time?

"Oh, it's just something for you to read on the toilet," I trilled, dancing away to a far corner of the roof. How could I possibly have a child? I was a child, hoping that the grown-ups would make a big fuss over how creative I was.

After a while, enough people were at the party that I could forget why I was throwing it. It was fun to join the adults in making a protective ring around the children. Inky was the only one who was asleep, fastened securely into her backpack. The others sat upright in their cutest outfits, eating Cheerios and quartered grapes from paper napkins. They were the celebrities. Everybody knew them and made a big fuss about what they were wearing. An eight-month-old blonde received a lot of attention over a jeweled bindi dot and braids the size of matchsticks. One little boy was doing laps around the roof, Greg hot on his heels. "Which are his parents?" Greg panted as he passed by. "Can you tell one of his parents to keep an eye on him?"

Actually, I didn't feel I knew the little speed demon's parents well enough to do that. They were probably tired of him. Playground scuttlebutt had it that they were tired of each other, not that we knew either of their last names. On their way out, the father graciously informed me that I had no taste whatsoever for giving

Martin Scorsese's latest movie a pan in the zine. Man! At least he was an attentive reader. I hadn't seen a movie in months when my mother flew in from Indiana, offering to baby-sit so that Greg and I could go on a date. Under the circumstances, my pump was primed to like that movie, but that movie, as reported in the *East Village Inky,* was a steaming piece of j.

I talked a lot about movies in that first issue. I included a review of every movie I'd seen since Inky had been born, accompanied by sketches of her nursing in a theater seat and wailing in her car seat as I leapt guiltily from the passenger side of Greg's Dodge Shadow to meet a friend under the marquee of a Cineplex in Chelsea. I also talked about Habib's Place, the three-table falafel joint on our block, where the owner played Billie Holiday and Louis Armstrong and sometimes hired a jazz band to play on the sidewalk. Sitting near Habib's front window on a summer night, I felt as if I were living in a romantic movie about New York instead of in an over-priced hovel the size of a suburban sandbox. I wrote about stores where you could buy green-tea ice cream at four A.M. and the dirty Russian Bathhouse on 10th Street. I wrote about how Inky had been pulling my hair so badly I went to cut it all off in one of the three chi-chi parlors on our street. One stylist had cried when I entered, "Phew! What stinks like Lysol?!" I did. It was me. There was a time when I would have tried to suppress that information, but motherhood had killed off discretion about my body. Before my appointment I had dabbed myself with lemongrass oil, thinking that it would help me resemble somebody used to blowing sixty-five dollars on her hair. Instead, I smelled like the stuff house-keepers more conscientious than I used to disinfect toilets.

According to a hip young haircutter in platform shoes, that was worse than smelling like the toilet itself. In the rubber-banded zine, I came clean, announcing that more than once I had mistaken the fancy pomade the stylist sold me for my deodorant stick, ending up with beautifully sculpted armpit hair and a relatively inoffensive head. Hell, nobody wants to read about a perfect mother. I drew a picture of a massive woman I'd seen wheeling a screaming toddler up Second Avenue in a stroller, a cigarette balanced on her combative lower lip. Printed on her T-shirt was the legend Fuck All Y'all! All right! It sure beats World's Greatest Mom.

There was plenty I didn't mention. I never wrote about the isolation and despair that had led to its creation. That first birthday we went to Glasgow for a close friend's wedding and figured that we would have even more fun if we participated in an avant-garde performance workshop the bride's theater ensemble was teaching. We could take the whole trip off our taxes on a Schedule C. We had passed ourselves off as working artists for years, the kind of working artists who buy their own props and costumes, who write plays that make copious use of flashlights because the theater can ill afford lighting equipment. In return for cleaning the theater's restrooms and xeroxing our own programs, we got a rock-solid identity unsullied by anything so mainstream as a commercial production. I had performed right up to my due date, despite the discomfort of the audience who'd paid twelve dollars to watch me slam my enormous pregnant body into the black walls. That's how committed I was to downtown theater. After Inky was born, I wrote and performed a puppet show about the two weeks we spent in the Neonatal Intensive Care Unit of St. Vincent's Hospital. Of course, with a six-month-old baby accompanying me to every rehearsal and work session, I couldn't afford to be caught up to my elbows in wet papier-mâché, so the puppets were played by yams. We were always about making it work. I thought taking Inky to this performance workshop across the pond would more than work, that the presence of an innocent, spontaneous child would inspire my new best-friends-to-be, the international artists who'd signed up to take this playful and utterly inessential month-long workshop.

To my chagrin, everybody thought I was a really good mom. They thought I was a dedicated wife, showing up with Greg's lunch every day, which I started to do when I realized that I couldn't attend the workshop in good faith. Inky's chattering and wriggling disrupted the other participants' process, not to mention my own. I spent hours wandering with my papoose through the iron-colored mist, feeling ostracized, lonely and very very sorry for myself. I believed that nobody knew my name. I pumped Greg for details about the other participants, hungry to be involved, however tangentially, with some kind of adult community. During their lunch break, I held my breath, hoping that Inky would do something cute so that people would be nice to me. When people were nice to me, I felt pitied and ran away like Cousin Ribby, the most neurotic of my childhood pets, a cat terrified of humans. I picked fights with Greg. I counted the hours until he would come home for the night. I wished Inky would sleep all day. I wished I could sleep all day. I wasn't allowed in the pubs with a baby. I spent many unhappy, boring hours protecting my host's books and CDs from Inky's little paws. I came back to New York in despair that this little daughter

whom I loved so dearly was going to cut me out of all the fun stuff I bitched about before she was born, like painting the stage at two in the morning, arguing about aesthetics and hanging out in unfriendly bars after poorly attended, poorly performed shows. I was an only child from a repressed and fractured home. As an adult, I'd had a taste of belonging, but then I had a baby and got kicked out. The people who kicked me out were nice about it. They smiled and thought I was a really great mother, but they had stage floors to paint.

I had to take the bull by the horns. Instead of shaking a stuffed bumblebee in Inky's face for the tedious hours between her naps, I could take to the streets. I could chronicle the minutiae of our lives. Spotting a pile of shit with a spoon sticking out could be a genuine accomplishment. I would set a roaring example, like Fred Smith, a retired Wisconsin farmer who spent his last years erecting enormous cement sculptures of patriotic tableaux on his land. My family drove by the Wisconsin National Cement Park for many summers, and then a friend and I finally pulled over, looking for some kitschy hipster fun. Fred was long dead and the neighbors who regarded his creation as a folk art treasure had trumped those who thought it was an eyesore. His property had been designated a national landmark and had received a great deal of exposure on Japanese TV. The ranger gave me a pamphlet about Fred's life and his eleventh-hour artistic impulses. Unlike me, Fred was a Midwesterner of few words. Asked what drove him to create hundreds of giant statues on his land, the farmer replied with something on the order of "People like to look at them and then they like me too." That's valid.

I wonder if dairy farming is so far removed from raising a little child. Both anchor you to a never-ending round of chores that tax your body while doing little to stimulate your mind. You have no choice if you want the living creatures in your care to thrive. They're sweet and without guile, but you begin to crave the company of those capable of speaking in the abstract, people who can understand and maybe even appreciate a book without pictures. You feel like you're alone a lot, although you're hardly ever alone because you're never far from your littlest loved ones and their unrelenting bodily functions. At least the herd doesn't try to follow the farmer into the shower one day. Still, I can imagine how making Thomas Jefferson, Paul Bunyan and hundreds of Indian braves out of cement and broken bottles starts to seem like a crucial enterprise. Any attention is just gravy, but you'd be lying if you said you prefer your turkey without gravy.

What rescued me remains as unpolished as one of Fred Smith's pioneer families, eternally traveling in a cement-covered wagon. I was thrilled when I discovered that a few hundred people out there were willing to pay two dollars to read about what I depict as a life of tedium and frustration. The best part is hearing from readers, which happens fairly frequently thanks to the miracle of the Internet. Many of the *East Village Inky*'s fans have little kids and as such are attracted to the keyboard as a stalling technique. Every minute hunkered in front of the computer e-mailing a stranger is snatched from motherly chores. It is gratifying to hear from women whose children are as old as I am, especially when they give me the lowdown on what life is like "after the last Mr. Potato Head piece has been vacuumed up," as one writer put it. They say that their kids were and, in some cases, still are every bit as anarchic as Inky is. A teenage single mother told me that she thought of her kid when she saw Inky running around in a crown, her father's athletic socks and a pair of black nylon briefs that got mixed up with our clothes at the Laundromat. A childless lesbian wrote to tell me that her girlfriend thinks I'm a hottie! Does she realize that sometimes I apply four or five coats of correction fluid to give myself a flattering expression? Oh sure, the zine is handwritten because I didn't want to waste those precious naptime hours figuring out how to use the computer, but I'll spend forty-five minutes on a tiny illustration, striving for that elusive balance between self-mockery and a hairdo that looks far more insouciant on the page than on my head.

Mostly, the text comes easily, since my muse rarely shuts up. She's right there, spoon-feeding me more material, like guns are bad and a crazy man shooted John Lennon with a gun and Oko Nono cried, did you hear about that? Inky says it; I write it down and enjoy doing it. I draw what she was wearing. Sometimes I think I steer her toward some of her wild getups in hopes that someone will email me, laughing that her kid does the exact same thing. It's so heartwarming to know that we're not the only family whose pet has formed a passionate sexual attachment to an inanimate object. Our cat screws a filthy rag doll three times a day. I'm always a bit uptight when Inky has new playmates over to the apartment, afraid their mothers will see the horrid remains of Jambo's doll on the living room floor and assume that it's one of Inky's toys. In the zine, it's played entirely for laughs and Greg is a good sport about the way he's depicted in opaque glasses, seated on the toilet, preoccupied by Stalin and Iron Age weaponry. Once a male reader wrote that he was very pleased to see a picture of Greg wielding an atlatl and he didn't know why the more mainstream press exhibited zero interest in atlatls. I didn't know what an atlatl was until Greg asked me to draw him holding one. I decided that it should look like a boomerang with a spear sticking out of it. I didn't hear from any women about the atlatl. I figured that they had all gone offline to make macaroni and cheese. It's good just to know that they're out there, in Bumblefuck, Idaho. We might not see eye to eye on the best place to raise our children, but we are all in the same boat.

I used to think that this expression meant that we all shared one boat, that your paddles are made lighter by the presence of others. That's not what it means. Even on a good day, my paddles feel like they're filled with buckshot. I'm willing to bet that every other mother's do too. Shortly after you give birth, most of the activities that defined your identity are suspended to let you mix apple juice, deal with somebody else's snot and develop a lot of highfalutin ideas about television. You're not being paranoid or melodramatic if you feel like you're the only grown-up in your boat. The kids never leave the boat either, but what help are they with the paddles? Their arms are hardly bigger than celery stalks. Also, as delight-fully surreal and repeatable as their beginning syntax might be, their conversation cannot sustain you through the tedious stretches. If it weren't for those little kids waiting for you to harpoon a fish so that they can tell you they don't like fish, you'd go right over the gunwales. You can't leave them to fend for themselves, even though they are the ones who got you into this mess. You're stuck choking down soggy peanut butter and jelly sandwiches in that leaky skiff. The inviting blast of an ocean liner taunts you as it glides by, its portholes twinkling like a string of white Christmas lights. Damn the passenger list of merrymakers in bias-cut gowns and party hats. It's always New Year's Eve nineteen-thirty-something on the ocean liner. Too bad you're missing it. Then in the middle of some dark night, when you're up, dog tired, struggling to keep your sleeping children out of the bilge water, you notice another crappy little boat a few yards out. And another. And another. The ocean is fairly crawling with boats as crappy and little as yours. Each one holds a mother tethered to a baby, a sleeping toddler or a jacked-up three-year-old still gibbering from an ill-advised late-afternoon sugar fix. We're all in the same boat, all right. It smells like mildewed life pre-servers. There are millions of these boats in the sea. We shout to each other across the waves. Nobody will get offended if you have to interrupt her midsentence to seize your daughter by the ankle before she dives after a birthday party favor she dropped overboard, possibly on purpose.

The *East Village Inky* is up to Issue 13 now. Many things have happened in its pages—pregnancy, meningitis, the birth of my little boy and the collapse of the World Trade Center, but I think the real secret to its success is that not a lot happens. That's why I keep writing it. If my life ever turns into a whirlwind of parties, inter-national travel and lucrative writing assignments, I'll stop pub-lishing and let *Vanity Fair* take up the slack. Just think, I could sit on the toilet reading all about myself. Now I write about Inky barging in to demand a snow shovel and an Easter bonnet when I'm on the toilet reading about the thinnest, richest murderers in Palm Beach and the Côte d'Azur, none of whose lives resemble my own. I draw Milo crawling hot on Inky's heels, determined to get at least one handful of cat food. *The East Village Inky* comes out in marathon run-on sentences because I never can stop myself from relating an anecdote about my childhood and recommending an out-of-print book mid-description of how we get up and down the subway stairs. The regularity of my quarterly publication schedule is rare in the zine world. Usually as lackadaisical as possible, in this case I find the pledge of punctuality reassuring. Every issue represents another three months in which my family's luck has held. Nobody has had a serious accident or been diagnosed with a terminal disease. Nobody has gotten divorced or needed to summon the fire department. The bad men have kept to the shadows. Somewhere down the line we'll probably see an obituary for Jambo, but bless his black heart, I think he's the only major character the *East Village Inky* can stand to lose and still stay in business. Every nonevent that I can squeeze between the margins is proof that life is sweet. Hard, but sweet, like a misshapen butterscotch found under a seat at the movie theater. Hey, if it's still in its wrapper, what the hell? Pop it in your mouth and brag about your good fortune.

The Daily Grind

Trenchdweller

My shift starts the moment that a kid forces me awake. The sky is pink from the recently risen sun. It's not too bad if Milo is the culprit. He can be overpowered with a breast like hitting the snooze button. If he's in a bad mood, I just slip him a couple of mother's-milk shooters. He sleeps it off for twenty minutes, wakes up feeling as fresh as a new diaper, rolls onto his belly and farts. His belly is no more complex than a whoopee cushion.

Inky's a bit trickier. When she was an infant, the two of us used to hang out until eleven o'clock in the morning, dozing and nursing in the loft bed Greg nearly castrated himself building. *(Fathers, remember to drill safely! Assume the proper handyman's position! Do not wedge a block of wood between your thighs and drill into it backward.)* But now I'm never ready for her to be awake, because, although she knows that I need coffee, she has yet to figure out why. I can't help thinking of Io, the Greek maiden whom the gods turned into a calf and bedeviled with a pestilential cloud of flies. Whenever she stopped running, the flies bit her mercilessly. She had no choice but to stay on the move. This, as Hermes and even Prometheus observed, was torment. You know it's bad when even the guy chained to a rock so a hungry eagle can devour his self-regenerating liver feels sorry for you.

From the moment she wakes me in the morning, I am Io and Inky is the flies. The flies want vitamins, breakfast and a stack of books read aloud. They need to know what we're doing today. They petition to watch television shows that don't come on 'til 4:30 in the afternoon. The flies don't like to listen to National Public Radio.

I do. As soon as I hear that sprightly *Morning Edition* theme, I feel virtuous. Good for me—I'm up early, pouring cereal and wondering what horrible news story will rumble just below the surface of my day. Inky drags the folding step stool out from its spot between the oven and the wall so she can reach the counter. She's got her agenda. An old lady in the grocery store watching Inky chase the bulk tofu around with tongs told me without malice, "Oh my dear, it's a wonderful thing to have a child who wants to help." Intellectually, I knew that she was right, but there are so many mornings I wish Inky would take a break and let me take care of business. She doesn't seem to realize how finely calibrated an action it is to get everything out of the refrigerator before Milo attaches his mouth to a bottle of Vietnamese hot sauce that draws him to the side door like a siren. I need absolute silence and cooperation. Instead, she's shouting about raisins and a novelty spoon we haven't seen in more than a year. She seizes a half-gallon of milk and pours it three inches shy of the handful of Cheerios in our chipped wedding china. (I remember spending the night at a childhood friend's home and panicking when her mother served me Cheerios for breakfast. I didn't know if I could choke back a whole bowl. They were so plain. I liked to pluck out all the marshmallows in my Count Chocula and move right on to the cinnamon toast. Now I give my own child a beggar's choice: Cheerios or Raisin Bran, with extra criticism if you refuse to take it with bananas.) The milk drips onto the sticky floor, Milo sobs as his beloved hot-sauce bottle is pried from his fingers and I miss the news. It's okay. They repeat the news every half hour, and I won't switch the radio off until 10:30, at least an hour later than we should leave the house for my emotional well-being if not for a pressing engagement.

Sometimes, when I'm jamming my children into their snowsuits or slathering them with sunscreen, I remind myself that I once trudged all the way to the top of Mount Kilimanjaro. That's quite an impressive credit, but god, it was boring getting to the top. I hate walking uphill, and all my companions were so much sportier than I. They bounded ahead, leaving me plodding grumpily, a commercial jingle repeating itself in my brain. The view from the peak be damned. I couldn't wait to get back to civilization, where there were cafés and used bookstores and life was so much more interesting. Waiting for Inky to pick her way down the front steps in pastel-pink cowboy boots, with Milo strapped to my back and a veritable cinder block of diapers, juiceboxes, crayons, bubbles and matchbook-sized Beatrix Potter books slung across my shoulder, I think about how fun it would be to climb Kilimanjaro again. Alone. I picture myself struggling to the top with both children, while fit couples in Gore-Tex and native women carrying firewood on their heads pass us by, nimble as mountain goats. Inky stops midway down the steps, shouting, "Watch me, Mama!" She executes some new trick that looks like a whole lot of nothing to anyone old enough to tie her own shoes.

"Mmm," I say. "Wow." I wonder if it's worth backtracking for the umbrella I left upstairs. I don't think I can stuff another thing in my bag, not even a collapsible umbrella the size of a college diploma. How much does that umbrella weigh? More than a baggie of pretzels but less than Au Jus, the rubber baby doll I refused to pack, saying that we would lose her if we brought her, that if Inky kept bugging me about it, we would just stay home and not go to the playground at all. The thought of herding this sideshow back into the building for an umbrella almost brings tears to my eyes. We can do without it, even though the sky is heavy with clouds the color of dryer lint.

I think my head will explode. Progress grinds to a halt as Inky stops to bark questions and brandish a Chinese menu she discovered in the mail slot. She finds a penny. There is something in her shoe. I can imagine how satisfying it would be to seize her by the wrist and march her double-time to our destination, no nonsense, no talking, no stopping to examine fallen leaves and the neighbor's garbage. I used to fantasize about escaping to a hammock strung between two palm trees along the Gulf of Thailand. Now I run mental newsreels in which I am the scary enforcer, a nanny to be reckoned with, the kind of mean nun to whom I'd never entrust my sweet babies. Please don't tell.

What's it like being the unpaid caregiver of little children?

Fucking grueling, mate. The pain of childbirth is a white-hot constellation of torture, almost impossible to describe, remembered impressionistically at best. It inspires respect. Taking care of the little criminals day in and day out is another matter. Cutting their food into crouton-sized cubes, wiping their spills and their heinies, washing their hair, forcing them to give the ball back, maneuvering them through the grocery store, clearing their mouths of golf balls, dice and Monopoly houses, goading them to pick up their toys, strapping them into the car seats they loathe, reading those hideous Richard Scarry Busytown books incessantly . . . that's like being eaten alive by ants. Not even red ants, just regular ones. Fashionable young ladies clopping down the street in platform shoes and Hello Kitty mini backpacks look at you and see a dumb old pack mule. They may exclaim over the saucy little girl capering at your side or the baby beaming on your back, but there is nothing remarkable, exciting or inspiring about your condition. It's the curse of working in the service industry.

Even though I have held close to a hundred jobs since I got my start in seventh grade, baby-sitting for fifty cents an hour, I am not a worker. A Ukrainian friend of mine whose widowed mother put three daughters through college on the money she earned as a cleaning lady prides herself on being a hard worker. She would make a wonderful Chekhovian peasant, and not just because she's a fantastic actress with a pack-a-day voice who thanks every director who hires her with promises to work her *dupa* off on behalf of the production. She is as deeply rooted in her work ethic as a tree in a faded aristocrat's cherry orchard. Not me! The only time I work hard is when I'm having fun. I had fun some nights as a waitress.

There were days when I had fun as a massage therapist, pressing the flesh of wealthy women who'd never worked a day in their lives. I had fun imagining their lavish apartments. One of them kept trying to fix me up with her son, despite the fact that I was married and pregnant. Her son, also a client, was as scintillating as a bag of hammers, despite frequent skiing trips to Europe and a family fortune founded on yogurt. I liked the idea of inviting this dullard and his under-tipping mother over to my minuscule East Village apartment to eat Indian food off a folding table inches from my bed. I wondered what they would make of my husband, the aspiring off-off-Broadway playwright and temporary secretary. I would brag to them about my work ethic, and they would shudder with distaste. I was just like they were, except I couldn't afford a chalet in Switzerland and twice-weekly facials. Actually, I was better. I enjoyed my leisure. I sat on our measly fire escape, drinking iced coffee and scribbling in my journal, eavesdropping on the diners in the backyard of Yaffa Café three floors below. God, I loved the clatter of those forks and knives. It was the perfect background music for *ma vie Bohème*. I drew comics that never grew past half a page and spent hours painting the intercom with four shades of blue acrylic, only to have it come out not quite right. I read for entire afternoons, sent illustrated postcards to people I barely knew and prowled the Puerto Rican discount stores looking for god knows what. Something cheap, funny and strange. Much of the time I was frustrated, because it seemed like nothing was happening and my apartment never got any bigger or less expensive. Still, I ate in restaurants. I drank draft beer at New York prices in unfriendly bars with people I didn't like and wouldn't remember

meeting within hours of parting. I argued about aesthetics with the others in my theater company. Oh sure, I had a job, but what a job! Making naked people feel better in small incense-filled rooms.

Staying at home to raise my children is like getting off the graveyard shift at Burger King with fifteen minutes to make it to my second job in the coal mines. Of course, once a week I am summoned from the mine shaft to accept the Nobel Prize, but goddamn it, I earn those. My meals, my baths and any activity involving a pen are accomplished as best as they can be with people wriggling on my lap; rooting for my breasts; requesting the millionth retelling of lurid, accidentally overheard medical anecdotes; exacting promises, puking, peeing and knocking over glasses of soy milk. I never rest, and when I do, I'm crabby. Every room I enter, I scan for appetizing handfuls of pocket change and doomed Steuben figurines. Eating in a restaurant or boarding an airplane I feel electrified, prepared to spring, squat or burst into song, even though the children are behaving better than the uptight adults treating us to the hairy eyeball. I go to bed wondering how many times Milo will awaken convinced that his Milk Monkey has abandoned him in the cruel, cold forest: seven? Eight? If more than eight, Inky's going to face a tough crowd when she slips into my bed at six-thirty A.M. to prod the slack remains of my abdomen with toenails that belong on an animal. My snappish response is hardly fair. It's not like she can cut her own nails. She can shinny up the bathroom sink, open the medicine chest and paint her fingers with five coats of gold polish in the time it takes me to navigate a collection agency's voicemail system, but it'll be a few years before she can reliably operate nail clippers. Greg is no help in this department. He's afraid he'll cut her fingers off. He's also unwilling to operate barrettes. He gets mad when I tell people that he never clips the children's fingernails, because, like me, he's frazzled by the constant demands of parenthood. The way we've always broken it down, Greg is Paycheck Monkey and I am Milk Monkey. Milk Monkey purchases the birthday presents for all of the little monkeys' friends and knows which pair of tights goes with which outfit. Paycheck Monkey deals with insurance and repairs on the car that Milk Monkey is too scared to drive in New York City, especially with her precious babies in the backseat. Both Monkeys change diapers, dump macaroni in boiling water and complain about the litter box. It's the standard division of labor for most two-parent families we know.

There are exceptions. I know several stay-at-home fathers. They are fussed over by almost every woman in the playground. The children tend to dig them, particularly if these daddies can play guitar. In my experience, they all play guitars. They wear little Bob Dylan–style caps. They aren't expected to make dinner. They're pretty sociable characters. The mothers of their children show up on Saturdays, smiling unhappily because they feel left out of the playground clique. The majority of the fathers I know put in long days at a jobs they hate so that their wives and girlfriends can stay at home, storing up complaints and implementing firmly held beliefs about nursing on demand, keeping the television off and using no cleaning product stronger than baking soda.

I think the thing that gets to me the most about the stay-at-home-mother gig is the constant side work. I hated that when I was waiting tables too. I liked interacting with the customers. Why did I have to be saddled with such lumpen tasks as refilling the salt shakers, folding napkins and scouring the glass coffeepots with ice, salt and lemon? Every day I must remind Inky to brush her teeth, wipe Milo's face with a washcloth after meals and sort dress-up clothes, rubber vegetables and puzzle pieces into their respective blue plastic bins. I find myself wishing Mary Poppins would blow over to teach me that nifty finger-snapping trick. Speaking of Mary Poppins, I could go get myself a nine-to-five job. Maybe if I could bring myself to delegate some of this drudgery to a baby-sitter, I could sit at my desk romanticizing staying at home with the children all day. Perhaps it would be therapeutic to seek out positive role models like Marge Simpson. So what if she's a cartoon? She seems to take things in stride, despite having three children and no baby-sitter. I'd like to hang out with Marge. But sometimes I get scared when people want to fix me up with other stay-at-home mothers. I feel like a firefly. Sure it's great to spend time with others of my kind, but I worry that the breathing holes the thoughtful non-insects have poked into the lid are not big enough to provide me with a means of escape or even admit much oxygen. I don't want to wind up dead at the bottom of a jar that once held mayonnaise.

When I was pregnant with Inky, I was concerned about how one hooked up with other stay-at-home mothers. None of my close friends had children. A few of my friends' friends did, but pursuing these relationships felt like inviting yourself over to the rich kid's house just so that you could swim in her pool. These women never had sparked my interest before they had children, and now that I think of it, I must not have impressed them too much either. Better to start clean. At a prenatal appointment I noticed a flyer for a mothers' group that met one afternoon a week at the birthing center. That sounded promising, like continuing education. I didn't become friends with a lot of massage therapists until I went to massage school and became one myself. What a relief to know I wouldn't have to waylay strange women on the bus, offering to give them my phone number so that our babies could play together. The mothers meetings would provide me with ready-made companions and they were tuition free, just a few bucks to cover the cost of juice and cookies. I wondered if I could go to one the day after the baby was born.

When Inky was placed in Intensive Care, suffering from an ailment that, thanks to botched lab tests, remains shrouded in mystery to this day, I collected a couple of phone numbers from women whose newborns were in similar peril. Maybe we would stay friends forever. Jeremiah's mother and I made plans to be playground buddies. She was the kind of mother I aspired to be, funky, freewheeling and completely disdainful of the kind of wisdom espoused by *Parents* magazine. Her apartment sounded as pathetic as mine. We agreed that it was worth putting up with cramped conditions, horrible plumbing and mice to be in the East Village, like living in a drawer of the Olde Curiosity Shoppe. "Women have been raising the young of the species in tipis for thousands of years," we assured each other. "The idea that you have to move to a big suburban ranch home the second you have a baby is just a crock of horse shit!" When I told one of the nurses that Inky and Jeremiah were going to hang out together in Tompkins Square, she remarked, "That kid won't make it to the playground." I was afraid to ask what she meant. Was she implying that he was going to die in infancy or that he would be profoundly disabled, requiring feeding tubes, colostomy bags, a respirator? What would happen to my new friend? She had been managing fine with a healthy two-year-old, but how would she get by in a tiny fourth-floor walk-up if Jeremiah needed a wheelchair and maybe a special hospital bed? She really would need a suburban ranch home with a driveway in which to park a specially equipped van. The documentaries I'd seen in which elderly mothers tend to their brain-damaged adult children never take place in cruddy apartments no bigger than four handicapped-accessible bathrooms. I would never see my friend again. That was a glum prospect. The other mothers I'd exchanged numbers with were nice enough, but we hadn't discovered much in common besides bad hospital food, sick children and the fact that we'd all given birth around the Fourth of July.

After Inky was sprung from the hospital, we spent nearly six months traveling, visiting relatives and performing in what I didn't realize was my swan song on the stage. When we returned to New York, I kept busy taking Inky to revisit my old stomping grounds. Every time the weekly mothers meeting rolled around, I seemed to have other plans. I stuffed Inky in her sling and away we went to see my childless friends. When the weather warmed up, I headed to the nearest playground, half a block away in Tompkins Square. By the time the tulips for sale in the Korean groceries flower buckets gave way to sunflowers, I felt no need for mothers meetings. The playground crew had morphed into one organically. It was a grand mix of black, white, Asian, American, European, West Indian, pierced, tattooed, rockabilly, dreadlocked and even regular. There were women whose diaper bags could have fed the Donner Party for a week, who could be counted on for an extra diaper, sunscreen or entire pocket-sized packs of tissues. I was frequently the one who brought the same bagel every day for a week. I liked to have something in case my kid got hungry. Inky preferred begging for handouts to what I brought anyway. "Doesn't your mommy ever feed you?" one of the mothers laughed, winking at me. "Well, don't worry, Inky. You just come to Rose. Rose always has some extra Veggie Bootie for her Inky. Now, where's your sippy cup? You don't have one? Ayun! Here, Inky, take a juicebox and tell your mother to stop losing your sippy cups."

"Hey, Rose," I called, lifting my head an inch or so off the springy asphalt. "Could you brush her hair when you get a minute?"

Now that I knew other women with children, I started getting the lowdown on every mothers meeting in town. I had had no idea there were so many. It was like Alcoholics Anonymous! At pretty much any hour of the day, you could find one just a short subway ride away. I seemed to be the only person who'd never managed to make it to one. Most of my playground cronies had stopped attending by the time I met them. It was so much easier to roll out of bed whenever and lug your stuff a couple of blocks than to try to get the kid in a clean outfit and out the door in time for a meeting with a set starting time. Some of them had signed up for music classes in which the young students banged maracas on the floor in counterpoint to "The Itsy Bitsy Spider." The children seemed to love them. Stay-at-home mothers end up participating in a lot of underwhelming activities for the good of the children. After hearing my friends' impressions of the curriculum, I figured that Inky would enjoy dining out with her parents and listening to some new CDs just as much if not more than attending a music class with a shockingly hefty enrollment fee. She didn't need to meet any more people, and, frankly, neither did I. My needs were well met by the open-air support group into which I had tumbled. A woman who occasionally brought her little boy to Tompkins Square was forever zipping away to meet one of her Mommy-n-Me groups in Central Park or Barnes and Noble or some other playground way the hell across town. "You should join us," she urged. "It's a really great bunch!"

"Ugh, don't believe it," one friend remarked after she left. "I've been to a couple of those, a bunch of women sitting around yakking about their children."

"Well, isn't that what we do?" a more diplomatic mother asked as she removed a nubbin of sidewalk chalk from her toddler's mouth.

"Yeah, you guys never quit!" a baby-sitter interjected, helping herself to her charge's doll-sized cream-cheese-and-jelly sandwiches. "It's blah blah Inky this and blah blah Abby that and potty training this and breastfeeding that."

"Silence, Nanny!" I snapped. "You should be grateful we let you sit near enough to overhear our conversations at all!"

"Oh, yes, I know you're only nice to me because of Abby."

"Speaking of Abby," said a woman whose nursing toddler refused to let go of his toy doll stroller. She used her chin to indicate the top of the baby slide, where Abby clung to a rail on the verge of tears. "Can she get down? I'd get her myself, but he's got me pinned."

"I mean it, those meetings give me the creeps," my first friend continued as Abby was guided three feet down to safety. "It's like they're all replicants. I don't want to hear about some recall on a Winnie the Pooh musical mobile."

"That's because you don't have a Winnie the Pooh musical mobile," the diplomat pointed out. "You don't even have a crib, do you?"

"You're right. I'm a bitch. You know what I mean, though, right? We already spend every freaking minute with the children. Can't we talk about something else? Didn't anybody watch something on television last night? I'd rather hear about a rerun of *Friends* than another tip for getting a one-year-old to eat with a spoon."

"I'd rather hear about a Winnie the Pooh musical mobile recall than a rerun of *Friends*," I said, seizing the opening. "And I went to college with one of the stars of *Friends*.

A squawk went up at this delectable morsel of pre-motherhood existence. The conversation quickly devolved into a discussion of where everybody had gone to school, other brushes with greatness, which hit television series deserved its success and at what age a child could be expected to relinquish her fear of the baby slide. I was lucky to have tumbled into this glad company. I would encounter at least one of them on any unannounced visit to the playground. Around the time we were celebrating everybody's first birthdays, I bumped into my friend from the NICU. Jeremiah looked great. His mother told me that he was a bit behind the rest developmentally, but here he was in the playground, dressed like the hunky lead singer of an eco-conscious grunge band. "Look at you guys with your babies, talking about diaper rash and breast-feeding and all that stuff," she sighed as her older son dragged her

toward the big-kid swings. "That used to be me. I guess it's different when you have two. I never get to luxuriate in just being a
mom, you know?" She left us to our own little world.

What would have become of me if I did live in a suburb, or even a
city like Los Angeles, where it's normal for new parents to have cars
and backyards with their own swing sets? I would have gone mad
from the isolation! I would have had to join a mothers' group! I
would have crawled there on my knees if I didn't have a sports
utility vehicle. But I don't like to make appointments. I need to be
out moving freely among my people, laughing at how we never go
anywhere anymore, how our walls are covered in baby food, and
how we hate talking about our children all the time. I like to know
the buffet is open all night, just in case I need a snack. In the same
way that people who choose to live in areas of great natural beauty
would go crazy without easy access to the ocean or mountains, my
mental health hinges on my proximity to colorful characters, like
the transsexual who dresses in a tutu and a bedraggled cat suit to
ride an oversized bicycle with a harp strapped to the back, playing
accordion for tips. Having a child didn't change that, though Milo's
unflagging determination to stick every cigarette butt he finds on
the ground into his mouth leads me to think how nice it would be
to let him crawl out the back door onto a lush patch of green. Right
now we don't even have a back door, but we do have round-the-
clock access to green-tea ice cream, curried goat, bulk fava beans,
sashimi, one-dollar empanadas, vegan specials, fresh mozzarella,
the world's best bagels and a man who makes snow cones with fla-
vored syrups and shavings from the large block of ice he loads on

his wooden cart every day. My proximity to that kind of culinary and cultural diaspora keeps me from coming out like a biting sow even if I dine on the children's leftover macaroni and cheese six nights out of seven. I'd fish a thousand butts out of Milo's mouth for the privilege. For me, New York is a wonderful place to raise children. I hope it will prove a wonderful city in which to be raised. As long as Mama isn't miserable, kids have a fighting chance.

I grew up in a wonderful place to raise children, just not my children. My father won't let me forget a remark I made around age seven, when I told a playmate that I was "a city dude." It's still true. I enjoyed growing hose-like cucumbers in my small garden plot and riding my bike all over the neighborhood, but I was just biding my time. I always wanted to be in a big crowd. I dreamed of living in a "part-pent" before I could pronounce "apartment." I went apeshit for outdoor craft fairs, community theater, and vegetarian neighbors, anything that smacked of big-city glamour. Now I get peevish when Greg's mother interrupts my anecdote about a school friend's bar mitzvah to ask, "You had Jews where you grew up?" Of course there are Jews in Indianapolis! They just wear overalls and have straw in their hair. These New Yorkers assume I was raised in a corncrib, when in fact there were museums, a symphony with children's matinees, X-rated movie theaters and even a record store that sold bongs. Not only were there Jews, there were Democrats and homosexuals. There are probably Jamaicans there by now. For all I know, you can get jerk chicken from a restaurant in the shadow of the Hoosier Dome—I just require twenty places to get jerk chicken. The stimulus I need as a stay-at-home mother is not provided by clean yards, affordable housing, excellent public schools or natural beauty.

When I was a child, my mother stayed at home to take care of me, as did most of my friends' mothers. Their work outside the home consisted of volunteer activities on behalf of local charities and cultural organizations. I knew what a docent was from an early age and regaled my friends with an anecdote about a Chinese monk who tore his eyelids off, part of the patter from my mother's stint leading tour groups through the Asian collection at the Indianapolis Museum of Art. As a little child, I was hooked on the self-important buzz I got when I was entrusted with a simple yet essential task, like stuffing envelopes when my mother couldn't get a baby-sitter during her Junior League meeting. I chose the full-day kindergarten program over the half-day option.

When Inky started preschool, my mother laughed, telling me how I used to come home from all-day kindergarten so jacked up that I would do laps around the dining room table for an hour. I couldn't believe it. In my memory, I was a quiet little thing in spectacles no bigger than a credit card, patiently kneeling over the heat register in my nurse costume, waiting for the marshmallow I'd put there to toast. That long-ago time seems unrelated to my current situation, in which great monolithic slabs of time are spent reasoning with, picking up after and riding roughshod on small children. Young humans' anarchist bent is less heartwarming in practice than in theory, a real hoot when described in someone else's zine, particularly if the little whippersnapper has three thumbs and a smart-mouthed mother. Did I mention that Inky has three thumbs? It's not a metaphor, she really does.

Shortly after I entered third grade, my mother asked my blessing for her to return to work part-time. She had been the fashion editor of *The Indianapolis Star* before I was born, an impressive post for a twenty-four-year-old. (In the section of my baby book reserved for a photograph of the Baby's Mother, she had pasted in a clipping that announced her appointment to this position. In the glamorous, unsmiling portrait above the blurb, her hairdo is as stiff and sculpted as one of the Supremes'.) After eight years as a stay-at-home mother, she had been offered a position writing features for what was still referred to as the "women's pages." Her old boss offered a lot of flexibility: She could do some work from home and still pick me up from school. In fact, she could continue as the leader of my Brownie troop. Nonetheless, she offered to turn down the position if I was against it. Was she crazy? Except for my role understudying the star of the school Christmas pageant and the dollhouse my father bribed me with if I could pass a certain swimming test, this was the most exciting thing in my life! I imagined the exalted status I would attain as a result of my working mother. I would be given a key to the house. Even if it was purely ceremonial, I would be allowed to carry the key in case of an emergency. When my class took field trips to *The Indianapolis Star,* everyone would know my name. I would be seen as more mature, more responsible for having this mother. Only babies needed their mothers to stay home with them all the time. Perhaps if my mother had suggested going to work as an accountant or a laundress, I wouldn't have been so enthusiastic, though the Laundromat was a pretty exciting place to me. I'd been there once, when the washing machine in our basement broke down. I was eager for a return visit.

Eventually, my mother's job evolved into a full-time position and I spent my after-school hours at my grandparents' house, a few blocks from home. My maternal grandmother was raised on a small farm in Hopewell, Indiana, the third of seven siblings. Although my grandfather's job as a radio engineer took them to Chicago, Cincinnati and Indianapolis, Gran never managed to leave the farm, if you know what I mean. Sometimes, as I am wearily pulling together a meal of leftover rice and elderly stir-fried vegetables at an hour when many of Inky's cronies are in bed, I reflect upon my grandmother's prodigious output as a cook and a housekeeper. A normal lunch at her house included fried chicken, corn on the cob, mashed potatoes, canned pears suspended in lime Jell-O, iced tea and as many homemade chocolate chip cookies as you wanted with your peppermint ice cream. She washed her apple-pattern dishes herself while my mother chided me to help clear the table. I preferred to sprawl on the floor with a book and a few more cookies. My grandmother spoiled me as best as she knew how, by waiting on me. When I arrived after school, she had a little snack plate of summer sausage, Ritz crackers, carrots, celery and cheddar cheese ready. I ate it reading. When I spent the night, her knees creaked as she stooped to serve me seconds on a home-made chocolate milk shake. I lolled on the rug, complaining about *The Lawrence Welk Show,* a program that she loved, needless to say. For my sixteenth birthday, my grandparents bought me a beige Chevette. Periodically my grandmother tied a plaid wool scarf around her head and went out to wash my car with a bucket and a sponge, while I sat inside with my knees hooked over the arm of her rocking chair, gossiping on the phone with school friends.

I didn't appreciate these services, barely glanced up to say thank-you. My grandmother embarrassed me. I felt she cramped my style.

I didn't get a handle on her until a few weeks after her death. I was twenty-four years old, living in a seedy studio apartment in Chicago, in love with a guitar player who waited tables at the same restaurant I did. One night, when Drew was at the restaurant and the video I'd rented turned out to be a turkey, I huddled on the obligatory mattress on the floor, scribbling a poem in my journal.

Gran

After the funeral, Grampy gave me the extra linens.
I still smell Gran-Gran on my sheets and cry.
Elva Brockway was not a great beauty.
Elva Brockway was not a patron of the arts.
Elva Brockway was not a notorious freethinker.
She was not tied up in knots, but in nots.
This was a woman who baked with Crisco,
Dried cotton sheets on a clothesline
And ended telephone conversations with "Twill see."
Several years ago she lost a breast.
Elva Brockway was a big old woman with a lipstick frown,
Faded blue eyes, and the softest, sweetest-smelling skin.
I never knew the black-and-white photograph,
Prettiest one of four farm girl sisters,
Swept off her feet by Big City Bob in a red-wheeled jalopy.
Elva Brockway wrote weekly letters in a scrawly hand.
"Weather fine here, you take care, we love you."

Her boy never amounted to anything,
Her girl amounted to too much,
And she could not for the life of her understand
Why little Ayun went to Africa instead of coming home
for Christmas.
Elva Brockway did not care for movies or music,
Though she once read a book about Eleanor Roosevelt.
She sent care packages right up 'til the end,
Banana bread, applesauce and paper towels.

Poor Gran. I expect that she would have been horrified by my East
Village apartment, the multiracial, out-of-wedlock relationships
that produced so many of Inky's friends and most of the drawings
in my zine. She died years before I met Greg. I wonder what Gran
would have made of Greg's maternal grandmother, a Russian Jew
who lost relatives in the concentration camps of World War II and
worked long hours in the photo-retouching shop she owned with
her husband. Greg and I try to tell each other about them. I doubt
they would have found much common ground outside of the baf-
flingly modern, arty grandchildren who united their bloodlines. I
wish that my grandmother had lived to hold my smudged, naked
children. I wish that I could send her one of Inky's strange homemade greeting cards and take her out for a meal that she wouldn't
like. It's funny to think that I'm a housewife, raising a little girl and
boy, exactly the way my grandmother did in the '40s. Well, we both
liked garage sales, but Gran never made a zine and I never make
pot roast.

Despite my early pride in my mother's accomplishments, I developed a big chip on my shoulder about working moms. It's a pitfall, particularly when your baby is a mere two months old, your various careers never have amounted to a hill of beans and a lively media-fueled campaign is afoot to pit stay-at-home mothers against their counterparts who work outside the home and vice versa. When I was a childfree adult, the only mothers I knew were old enough to be my own. I had no models. On television, mothers with small children use fabric softener, pack lunch and mix up Kool-Aid by the buttload. In movies, they die young and struggle fiercely to protect their offspring from their unfaithful husbands' psychotic knife-wielding lovers. Judging by the child-rearing manuals that I hated because of their condescending tone, these mamas couldn't make a move without consulting the experts. According to the hippie-dippy birthing books I loved, they nursed forever, carried their young in slings and made their own baby food from organic produce. When I found out firsthand what mothers do, it was like noticing a cloud of locusts swarming toward my wheat. If you're a mother, you know what I mean. You know exactly what I mean unless you've got a team of nannies, personal trainers and chefs working round the clock because you're a celebrity with a top-ten album, a hit TV show, or a mainstream movie that I wouldn't go see even if I wasn't stuck at home taking care of little kids. Those of us whose photo only gets in *People* magazine when our kid falls down a well are bent over, picking that wheat as fast as we can. Our babies hang off our breasts. The older children are underfoot, fooling with burlap bags they were told not to touch. Some of us hurry home to shrug off business suits and cafeteria uniforms before we start swatting locusts. Others have been in the fields all day. If you're a mother, you do time in the fields.

Thank god I met other mothers in the playground before I'd had much of a chance to run off at the mouth about the superior quality of children whose mothers don't work outside the home. It was there I realized everybody scrambles to keep her family going. One mother persists in her administrative duties at the investment bank because Daddy's training qualifies him for modern dance but little else. Another working mother hoes her row alone. She decided to go ahead and have that baby, even though the romance fell apart long before she recognized that first fluttering kick inside her belly. Many mothers work and their partners work too. Between them, there's barely enough left over to pay for the part-time baby-sitters who work according to mystifying schedules always in threat of collapse. Some baby-sitters are mothers too, leaving their children with their mothers or sisters so that they can work.

The only easy thing is leaping to conclusions. You know that awful kid in the playground, the one who pushes without provocation, snatches toys away from babies and throws horrible gale-force tantrums while his nanny sits imperviously on the bench, praying that she'll get a nice, quiet little girl on her next assignment? It's pretty easy to assume that his working mother isn't out curing cancer, isn't it? Then is it such a stretch to suspect the second income she brings to her family is all going toward sailboat payments and the upkeep on a Bermuda time-share? She probably tells everybody her nanny is a gem. She thinks the nanny is devoted to her unappealing little boy. You've never seen her, but you know. It's easy. Too easy.

Greg got into a situation at the Union Square playground. Inky was building one of her hills in the sandpit. A boy who looked about five kicked it over. She protested, and Greg, sitting a short distance away with Milo on his lap, told her to build another one. She did. The boy ran over and kicked it down again. "Joshua," his mother protested weakly from the bench. "Play nice."

Every hill Inky built Joshua kicked to smithereens. It wasn't a personal vendetta. He was bugging everybody. He attacked a smaller boy, whose teenage mother came out screaming. As she dragged her child away, Greg used his high-school Spanish to decode her message: "Stay away from that bad boy! He's crazy!"

"What would you have done?" Greg asked me later. I didn't need to know the specific kid he was talking about. I pictured him with a bowl haircut, a little polo shirt and a fistful of sand. "The kid wouldn't listen to me. I couldn't believe that his mother just sat there. She looked totally fried."

I know the feeling: Mommy's a little tired now so she needs you to play quietly by yourself for five hours, okay? Thank god our kid's not a killer. But some days it seems like the world is conspiring against me. I had similar periods when I was waiting tables, but I could exorcise my evil mood in a movie theater, a bar or a steaming hot bath in which I soaked until the water grew cold. Watch out for me on those days, because any mild, implied criticism of my parenting skills may come under fire, and that's fire as in flamethrower. Parenting skills. What a toothless, wishy-washy phrase. It makes me nostalgic for a time before I was born, when a phalanx of housewives in shapeless dresses and headscarves made no bones about airing their opinions from the alpha female's front stoop. "That woman won't raise a finger to control that brat of hers. Have you seen the slovenly way she keeps her house? She's a whore!"

The Stacks

My dirty little secret is books on tape. I used to wonder about the market for these odd items. Why wouldn't you just buy the book and read it? If they're aimed at blind people, how come there's no Braille on the box? Is that what all the business-class travelers are listening to on their headsets as we bang past on our way to deep coach? Then Inky stumbled on to the kiddie version in our down-at-the-heels local library where they keep the books and tapes together in plastic pouches on a circular rack. With her love of sleazy fashion, Inky was drawn to them as if by a high-powered magnet. I think she thought they were some-thing to wear.

She was a few months shy of three, and I was bigger than the prize-winning hog at the Indiana State Fair. It is a fairly normal sight in our neighborhood, a pregnant woman whose two-year-old is threatening to run amok at an hour the librarians darkly refer to as "naptime." Which was worse? Dealing several low shelves of pic-ture books to the floor like a bad poker hand or rifling through the hanging books-on-tape pouches, shouting that you're shopping for a new bikini? I recognized one cover as it flashed by in its pouch. *Corduroy!* My old friend, the lonely stuffed bear who lived in a department store, waiting for someone who'd love him despite the minor flaw of his missing trouser button. I never owned it, but Cap-tain Kangaroo used to read it out loud to us on the television. I used to vow that given the opportunity, I would save Corduroy. One of my earliest memories is of my mother's great fondness of an illus-tration in which only the fuzzy brown disks of Corduroy's ears are

Maybe if I felt really fired up about supply-side economics or the Democratic Party or some occupation that might earn a living wage, I too would work outside the home. But I'm very well suited to staying home with the children. I've had years of relevant experience. I don't have a degree in early childhood education, but I'm pretty good at flopping on my side to fiddle my hind legs together. I'm almost always satisfied that the sounds I produce are music. The kids' needs can wreak havoc on my schedule, it's true. I barely have time to squeeze in the most basic of grasshopperly activities, let alone to learn to play the accordion, make batik T-shirts or keep the baby books up-to-date. Still, I get clapped on the back from time to time by people who think I'm doing the right thing. They talk about me on TV without mentioning my name. We stay-at-home mothers should keep up the good work! We're doing a far better job than the mother who has to leave the office in the middle of the day because the school nurse called. Don't even get them started on those welfare mothers! Those women can't even hold down a lousy minimum wage shift flipping burgers, so how can *they* expect to raise responsible youngsters? Some of my supporters would be horrified to learn that I breastfed Inky until she was two and a half, still sleep in the same bed as Milo and regard the highly popular Ferber technique of getting children to sleep through the night by leaving them to cry as close to sanctioned child abuse. Not that I judge anybody who Ferber-izes her child! Oh no no no no no! We all do what we have to in order to make it work.

I figured out how to jerry-rig this stay-at-home mother game when

I started reporting on our daily wanderings in the *East Village Inky*. We're like retirees, the kids and I. We get out, keep busy. We know the UPS man, the mailman and every cashier on both sides of the block. We get special attention at the butcher shop because we show up midafternoon when there's no line. The butcher is an old man with fingers as stubby as his ever-present cigar. He gives Inky lollipops, but Milo is his special honey baby. "Give me this guy," he demands, coming around the counter to help me with the heavy glass door. "I'm in love with this guy." As a very lapsed vegetarian, I frequently feel guilty about eating meat, especially when earnest young punks who read my zine send me gory vegan propaganda pamphlets that I rush to recycle before Inky gets a gander of conditions in the abattoir. Those poor animals. Inky's bookshelf is crowded with friendly cows and insecure pigs. I wonder if she'll make the connection between Wilbur and the suspiciously pig-shaped carcass hanging in Milo's boyfriend's window. I feel bad about the meat, but good about the butcher. Housewives are supposed to know the men who sell them meat. It's reassuring. My grandmother used to take me with her to buy meat. The butcher always gave me a rolled-up piece of bologna for a treat. Once, I wolfed down my bologna, barfed all over my dress and announced, "I fwoed up." I was pissed but not ashamed, oblivious to the self-evidence of my statement. Participating in these time-honored traditions connects my children to my childhood and me to my community.

I wish I could take the butcher home with me. I wish he'd call me up and say, "Miss, seeing as how we always have such a good time together, I thought I'd offer to take the kids off your hands for an hour or two. I'm not up to any funny business. I'm a grandfather:

I know how it is. I'll just close the shop for an hour or two and take your babies to the playground so you can get your hair done or start some chops. Work on your zine. Whatever it is you need to do, sweetheart."

Until he calls, I have to remind myself to relish the constant, exhaustive demands little children make on my body and my time. I'm preparing myself to miss Inky's frequent bleating—I'll miss it when she can't wait to ditch me. Sweet memory will soften the edges of their razor-sharp fingernails, those sticky paws and all the little elbows and heels that have found their way to my eye sockets. I'll long for the old burdens when Inky and Milo are sneaking out the window to swap bodily fluids with their friends. Right now they just lick each other's spill-proof cups and prevent me from writing the Great American Novel. I'm already nostalgic for Milo's habit of steadying my face with both plump hands so he could suck my lips with undisguised ardor. A shocked, childless friend shrieked, "Ooh! Ayun's frenching the baby!" I didn't care. I was in love. I still am, but Milo's moved on to hair pulling. He also takes a clinical interest in pinching, inflicting purple bruises the size of capers. It helps him pass the time since I won't let him fool around on the computer.

The day is coming when I'll be free to fly the coop. What will I do with myself when the kids are at school? Go back to waiting tables or the wicked stage? Forget about practicing massage. If anybody needs a massage, it's me! Medical school doesn't sound like such a bad option after a few years in the trenches as a stay-at-home mother, a noble profession but the pay just sucks.

• • •

visible above a bedspread. "Hey Inky," I said, dangling the hanger-shaped pouch invitingly. "Want to take this one home?"

Eureka. We took it home, popped it in the tape player and presto! I had ten minutes all to myself. No simpering television characters sliming my child with a simpleton's message about sharing. This was Corduroy! Not Corduroy re-imagined as a smart-mouthed hipster in wraparound shades and red high-top sneakers, but the genuine, old-fangled Corduroy of my childhood. It was marginally higher tech, but even so. It was as wholesome as a Waldorf rag doll with a wooden bead for a head. "I wanna hear dis again," Inky said decisively.

Anything, my angel. I floated over toward the rewind button, as gentle and patient as Mama Walton or Laura Ingalls' Ma. "You know to turn the pages when you hear a beep, right?" I asked. She nodded with the heightened awareness of someone being cranked up the side of a roller coaster. I jabbed the button marked "play." Whee!

I like the idea of taking my child to the library regularly, which is a good thing because those books on tape rack up stiff fines when they're overdue. As a girl, I spent hours in the Nora Branch Library. They had yellow plastic bubble chairs and wicker stools topped with shag carpet to resemble mushrooms. I was always among the first to be awarded the premium for the Summer Reading Club. The medals I received for reading and reporting on eight books every summer hung on my bulletin board. They're the closest I've gotten to athletic trophies. From third grade on, I lurked in the young adult section, dazzled by its intimations of boyfriends, street gangs and the illegal substances that ruined teenage lives. I loved the library the way that Fern loved visiting Wilbur and Charlotte in Zuckerman's barn. It is important to me that Inky be initiated into the joys of the library, especially in this increasingly electronic age. If only it weren't such a schlep. I like our new neighborhood in Brooklyn, but good lord, getting to the bank, the post office or the library is like crossing the Great Divide. When we lived in the East Village, the library was right there at the top of Tompkins Square. Every time it rained, we shot over from the playground to whoop it up in the overheated kids' section on the third floor. The library's lobby acquired a reputation as an excellent place to get your stroller stolen on a rainy day. Those poor librarians. Any kind of precipitation, and their blood pressure skyrocketed. On sunny days, they could make a concerted effort to keep the junior high school boys off the Internet porn sites. When the weather turned inclement, pandemonium reigned. Toddlers screamed with glee as they danced atop slippery piles of board books, diapers were changed between the stacks and the usual suspects bookmarked MistyBeaversAnalFantasies.com for next time.

These days, a trip to the library is complicated by Milo. He's no longer the sleepy sling-dweller. He can't walk, but he can climb, made from the same genetic material as his sister. He likes to unshelve books with much fervor and little ceremony. Inky's moved on, preferring to lie primly on a child-sized chaise lounge, pretending to read a couple of the innumerable volumes concerning the continuing adventures of Curious George. Is it just me, or is the original Curious George story kind of creepy? The man in the yellow hat snares him in an African jungle and George is transported to America in the cargo hold of a seafaring vessel, inside a bag. It's very pre-Revisionist. I can't read it without categorizing

Maybe if I felt really fired up about supply-side economics or the Democratic Party or some occupation that might earn a living wage, I too would work outside the home. But I'm very well suited to staying home with the children. I've had years of relevant experience. I don't have a degree in early childhood education, but I'm pretty good at flopping on my side to fiddle my hind legs together. I'm almost always satisfied that the sounds I produce are music. The kids' needs can wreak havoc on my schedule, it's true. I barely have time to squeeze in the most basic of grasshopperly activities, let alone to learn to play the accordion, make batik T-shirts or keep the baby books up-to-date. Still, I get clapped on the back from time to time by people who think I'm doing the right thing. They talk about me on TV without mentioning my name. We stay-at-home mothers should keep up the good work! We're doing a far better job than the mother who has to leave the office in the middle of the day because the school nurse called. Don't even get them started on those welfare mothers! Those women can't even hold down a lousy minimum wage shift flipping burgers, so how can *they* expect to raise responsible youngsters? Some of my supporters would be horrified to learn that I breastfed Inky until she was two and a half, still sleep in the same bed as Milo and regard the highly popular Ferber technique of getting children to sleep through the night by leaving them to cry as close to sanctioned child abuse. Not that I judge anybody who Ferber-izes her child! Oh no no no no no! We all do what we have to in order to make it work.

I figured out how to jerry-rig this stay-at-home mother game when

I started reporting on our daily wanderings in the *East Village Inky*. We're like retirees, the kids and I. We get out, keep busy. We know the UPS man, the mailman and every cashier on both sides of the block. We get special attention at the butcher shop because we show up midafternoon when there's no line. The butcher is an old man with fingers as stubby as his ever-present cigar. He gives Inky lollipops, but Milo is his special honey baby. "Give me this guy," he demands, coming around the counter to help me with the heavy glass door. "I'm in love with this guy." As a very lapsed vegetarian, I frequently feel guilty about eating meat, especially when earnest young punks who read my zine send me gory vegan propaganda pamphlets that I rush to recycle before Inky gets a gander of conditions in the abattoir. Those poor animals. Inky's bookshelf is crowded with friendly cows and insecure pigs. I wonder if she'll make the connection between Wilbur and the suspiciously pig-shaped carcass hanging in Milo's boyfriend's window. I feel bad about the meat, but good about the butcher. Housewives are supposed to know the men who sell them meat. It's reassuring. My grandmother used to take me with her to buy meat. The butcher always gave me a rolled-up piece of bologna for a treat. Once, I wolfed down my bologna, barfed all over my dress and announced, "I fwoed up." I was pissed but not ashamed, oblivious to the self-evidence of my statement. Participating in these time-honored traditions connects my children to my childhood and me to my community.

I wish I could take the butcher home with me. I wish he'd call me up and say, "Miss, seeing as how we always have such a good time together, I thought I'd offer to take the kids off your hands for an hour or two. I'm not up to any funny business. I'm a grandfather:

I know how it is. I'll just close the shop for an hour or two and take your babies to the playground so you can get your hair done or start some chops. Work on your zine. Whatever it is you need to do, sweetheart."

Until he calls, I have to remind myself to relish the constant, exhaustive demands little children make on my body and my time. I'm preparing myself to miss Inky's frequent bleating—I'll miss it when she can't wait to ditch me. Sweet memory will soften the edges of their razor-sharp fingernails, those sticky paws and all the little elbows and heels that have found their way to my eye sockets. I'll long for the old burdens when Inky and Milo are sneaking out the window to swap bodily fluids with their friends. Right now they just lick each other's spill-proof cups and prevent me from writing the Great American Novel. I'm already nostalgic for Milo's habit of steadying my face with both plump hands so he could suck my lips with undisguised ardor. A shocked, childless friend shrieked, "Ooh! Ayun's frenching the baby!" I didn't care. I was in love. I still am, but Milo's moved on to hair pulling. He also takes a clinical interest in pinching, inflicting purple bruises the size of capers. It helps him pass the time since I won't let him fool around on the computer.

The day is coming when I'll be free to fly the coop. What will I do with myself when the kids are at school? Go back to waiting tables or the wicked stage? Forget about practicing massage. If anybody needs a massage, it's me! Medical school doesn't sound like such a bad option after a few years in the trenches as a stay-at-home mother, a noble profession but the pay just sucks.

● ● ●

The Stacks

My dirty little secret is books on tape. I used to wonder about the market for these odd items. Why wouldn't you just buy the book and read it? If they're aimed at blind people, how come there's no Braille on the box? Is that what all the business-class travelers are listening to on their headsets as we bang past on our way to deep coach? Then Inky stumbled on to the kiddie version in our down-at-the-heels local library where they keep the books and tapes together in plastic pouches on a circular rack. With her love of sleazy fashion, Inky was drawn to them as if by a high-powered magnet. I think she thought they were something to wear.

She was a few months shy of three, and I was bigger than the prize-winning hog at the Indiana State Fair. It is a fairly normal sight in our neighborhood, a pregnant woman whose two-year-old is threatening to run amok at an hour the librarians darkly refer to as "naptime." Which was worse? Dealing several low shelves of picture books to the floor like a bad poker hand or rifling through the hanging books-on-tape pouches, shouting that you're shopping for a new bikini? I recognized one cover as it flashed by in its pouch. *Corduroy!* My old friend, the lonely stuffed bear who lived in a department store, waiting for someone who'd love him despite the minor flaw of his missing trouser button. I never owned it, but Captain Kangaroo used to read it out loud to us on the television. I used to vow that given the opportunity, I would save Corduroy. One of my earliest memories is of my mother's great fondness of an illustration in which only the fuzzy brown disks of Corduroy's ears are visible above a bedspread. "Hey Inky," I said, dangling the hanger-shaped pouch invitingly. "Want to take this one home?"

Eureka. We took it home, popped it in the tape player and presto! I had ten minutes all to myself. No simpering television characters sliming my child with a simpleton's message about sharing. This was Corduroy! Not Corduroy re-imagined as a smart-mouthed hipster in wraparound shades and red high-top sneakers, but the genuine, old-fangled Corduroy of my childhood. It was marginally higher tech, but even so. It was as wholesome as a Waldorf rag doll with a wooden bead for a head. "I wanna hear dis again," Inky said decisively.

Anything, my angel. I floated over toward the rewind button, as gentle and patient as Mama Walton or Laura Ingalls' Ma. "You know to turn the pages when you hear a beep, right?" I asked. She nodded with the heightened awareness of someone being cranked up the side of a roller coaster. I jabbed the button marked "play." Whee!

I like the idea of taking my child to the library regularly, which is a good thing because those books on tape rack up stiff fines when they're overdue. As a girl, I spent hours in the Nora Branch Library. They had yellow plastic bubble chairs and wicker stools topped with shag carpet to resemble mushrooms. I was always among the first to be awarded the premium for the Summer Reading Club. The medals I received for reading and reporting on eight books every summer hung on my bulletin board. They're the closest I've gotten to athletic trophies. From third grade on, I lurked in the young adult section, dazzled by its intimations of boyfriends, street gangs and the illegal substances that ruined teenage lives. I loved the library the way that Fern loved visiting Wilbur and Charlotte in Zuckerman's barn. It is important to me that Inky be initiated into the joys of the library, especially in this increasingly electronic age. If only it weren't such a schlep. I like our new neighborhood in Brooklyn, but good lord, getting to the bank, the post office or the library is like crossing the Great Divide. When we lived in the East Village, the library was right there at the top of Tompkins Square. Every time it rained, we shot over from the playground to whoop it up in the overheated kids' section on the third floor. The library's lobby acquired a reputation as an excellent place to get your stroller stolen on a rainy day. Those poor librarians. Any kind of precipitation, and their blood pressure skyrocketed. On sunny days, they could make a concerted effort to keep the junior high school boys off the Internet porn sites. When the weather turned inclement, pandemonium reigned. Toddlers screamed with glee as they danced atop slippery piles of board books, diapers were changed between the stacks and the usual suspects bookmarked MistyBeaversAnalFantasies.com for next time.

These days, a trip to the library is complicated by Milo. He's no longer the sleepy sling-dweller. He can't walk, but he can climb, made from the same genetic material as his sister. He likes to unshelve books with much fervor and little ceremony. Inky's moved on, preferring to lie primly on a child-sized chaise lounge, pretending to read a couple of the innumerable volumes concerning the continuing adventures of Curious George. Is it just me, or is the original Curious George story kind of creepy? The man in the yellow hat snares him in an African jungle and George is transported to America in the cargo hold of a seafaring vessel, inside a bag. It's very pre-Revisionist. I can't read it without categorizing

George as the mythically happy slave who makes lemonade out of every lemon in his new country. Babar's weird that way too. Perhaps the uncomfortable noble savagery of the classic tales led publishers to commission all these tepid modern adventures with the classic characters. The original creators aren't around to object, and there's gold in them thar hills! These books read like some hack dashed them off in line at the post office: Curious George Makes Pizza. Curious George and the Cell Phone. Curious George Rents a Video. One of these days, Curious George is going to hook up with Barbie and spawn a whole new imprint. I hear Barbie's very into literacy these days.

Inky heads straight for this dreck, but it's important for the child to discover the library on her own terms—the pleasure is in the bushwhacking. The problem is Milo. Anything Inky touches is platinum as far as he is concerned. He wants to see it, hold it, rip it and savor it with his mouth. At home, we work it out. She protests. I tell her that he's too little to know what he's doing, she used to do the exact same thing, he does it because he loves her, isn't she lucky to have a brother who looks up to her so? Her tiny chest puffs up with sororal pride. She allows that perhaps she has room in her heart for this little baby after all. I know it's a thin line. I'm an only child, inexperienced in having my stuff mauled by a sibling. When something is boiling over on the stove, I take the low road. "Inky, I know that Au Jus and Joe and Joe-Joe are sleeping on the couch and you've got them set up just the way you like them, but Milo wants to play too. It would be a great favor to me if you would let him in on the action, even if he keeps pulling their blanket off. Before you start whining because you look like you're about to start whining just let me say that that blanket you're using isn't even a blanket in the first place, it's my good scarf that Daddy and I bought in India and I wore to our wedding, so if you want to keep using it for your dolls, I suggest you let your little brother play with you. Please, honey, or you're never going to get any macaroni and cheese."

That good little Inky, she almost always lets him play, even when he goes after her carefully constructed reality like Godzilla in oven mitts. I am much obliged. My stay-at-home-motherly heart over-flows with joy. The macaroni and cheese makes it to the table before the blood sugar dips below the point of no return. Inky hops off her chair after a few mouthfuls, taking it upon herself to appease Milo. He hates the restraints of his el cheapo plastic high chair only slightly less than he abhors his car seat. Irritation prickles from my scalp to my spine. I want her to sit and eat her expensive organic junk food. I'd like to staple her to the chair. Instead, she's swinging from Milo's tray, singing his special song as loud as she can. She tries to poke a pea between his lips, knowing that all he likes is bread, twenty-four hours a day, bread bread bread. The sun breaks through the clouds and he laughs. He thinks he's getting the joke. After a couple of tries, he manages to lift a pea between his thumb and forefinger and pop it into his sister's open mouth. Between them, they dislodge the plastic tray from its runner, sending a shower of fresh peas down to join their dehydrated brothers. I did not sweep last night and chances are good that I will not sweep tonight either. I am exhausted, crabby and burdened, but seeing my two little goats gently butting their heads together, one dark, one light, I laugh too. I laugh at my good fortune, while the parents of teenagers everywhere wait for my bubble to burst. May these two good friends remain united, hopefully not in opposition to their mother.

Milo gets away with a lot, but still, some things are sacred. He shouldn't be permitted to horn in on his sister's library time. I grin apologetically at the older Caribbean nannies scattered around the children's section, wishing that one of them had been hired to keep Milo away from Inky's book. He's like a windup toy: I move him several feet away, and he crawls right back, his hands smacking the floor purposefully, cheerfully. He thinks it's another one of my crazy games. I crawl after him, dragging my albatross of a purse. I hate taking my purse. I don't want the nannies to think I'm keeping it with me because I think that they are thieves. Their ladylike pocketbooks are small enough to be slung securely across their chests without discomfort. I'd love to leave my huge honker unsupervised on the table, as disposition inclines me to do. The problem is that if some ten-year-old boy raised in the lap of plenty helps himself to my wallet I won't be able to check out any books on tape. I *need* those books on tape. After half an hour, the desire to abandon my purse and my children is so strong that I give Inky a five-minute warning. On the way out, she spies an unoccupied computer. "Mama, we didn't do my turn on the computer like you said!" she gasps. Fuck me. She's right. I did say. I could tell her that the computer is broken, but it isn't. I could pretend that someone else is signed up to use it, but that would be a lie too. Fooling around with that Paul Bunyan CD-ROM is a library trip highlight. As a toddler, Inky innocently destroyed our hard drive by poking the power button every time our backs were turned. In response, Greg and I instigated a no-children-on-the-computer rule. To us, a computer is like a white sofa that nobody's allowed to climb on. Next year, when we win the lottery, we're going to have to invest in a second computer for Inky and, while we're at it, a set of shackles for Milo. Until then, she gets to blunder around on the computer at the library.

This is why, when we're out and about, I dust off the bagels that Milo drops from the backpack. Yeah, I know, dogs and worse pee on the sidewalk, but bagels roll. Something has got to keep that baby's hands off the keyboard for half an hour. I would hate to have abandoned our only bagel in a gutter when, on our way out of the library, Inky suddenly remembers that I promised to let her use the computer. I would nurse him if that would get him to back off. The preadolescent boys are too busy surfing porn to be interested in the semi-exposed dugs of a woman old enough to be their mother. They've seen it before anyway. This neighborhood is crawling with women who hoist their shirts at the first squall. Sadly, Milo is not the little sucker he once was, even though he still rouses me a dozen times a night to set him up with a shot. At two in the afternoon, he may eschew the pleasures of the breast to bang on a nearby keyboard, especially if his sister appears to be doing the same thing. I can whip 'em out all I want but I know there are times when he's thinking, "Lady, get that thing out of my face!" or at least he would be if he were one of those babies from *Look Who's Talking Too*.

I look forward to the day when the children and I can nestle under an afghan, reading about Stuart Little, Pippi Longstocking and those weirdies from Oz. The hardback copies from my childhood have been preserved under my mother's eaves, but I don't want to send for them until Milo is cured of his tendency to yank the most exciting pages free of their binding. Fortunately, the New

York Public Library has yet to take issue with my Scotch tape repair jobs. They just want me to return the book that's been checked out in my name for ages. I know exactly which one they're referring to: the one that's not under the couch or the bed, not mixed in with the laundry or the dress-up clothes, not in Inky's bookshelf or behind the refrigerator. I have no idea where it could be. We returned the cassette tape in its plastic pouch months ago.

Nitpicking

Stalking lice is not so far removed from my childhood hobby of spilling a vial of tiny beads onto my green shag rug for the pleasure of picking them out with tweezers. The big ones were easy enough to spot, scurrying purposefully about Inky's scalp like extras in A Bug's Life. The little ones required magnification. I peered into her hair with Greg's photographer's loupe. Little did the youthful actor I married suspect that his loupe would prove far handier for plucking head lice off his child than for picking a winning headshot off a contact sheet.

My family had no history of head lice. My school didn't employ a uniformed nurse to inspect the children's heads for telltale nits. When my mother volunteered to work in the Junior League thrift store, she was shown a film about living conditions in the inner city. "They put the baby to bed with peanut butter on his face," my mother reported to my father and me after her orientation, "and a rat snuck into his crib and chewed his face off!" My childhood was rat-free. Lice-free. A possum did get stuck in our fireplace once.

The over-the-counter remedy for head lice contains pyrethrum. When I was in Africa, I saw women in bright headscarves tending fields of pyrethrum in the early morning mist. For a powerful insecticide, it sure looks a lot like daisies. It smells pleasantly like something I smoked in college. I don't doubt that it does a number on head lice: I just question what it might do to a two-year-old. After all, the scalp is not that far from the brain. Luckily, the health food store closest to our East Village apartment stocked a nontoxic treatment. Our favorite cashier, the one who slipped Inky carob candies that looked like tinfoil ladybugs, recoiled as she rang up our purchase. I guess if I had organically shampooed strawberry-blond hair down to my ass, I'd shrink from vermin carriers too. Reading the ingredients, I realized that I had just paid seventeen dollars for four ounces of olive oil scented with a few drops of rosemary and tea tree.

None of the other kids on the playground were scratching like apes, so where did my kid pick up lice? I remember my family's south-of-the-border trip to Nogales. My grandmother paid for a souvenir Polaroid of the family seated in a colorful little burro cart, but she refused to don one of the photographer's velvet sombreros. "You don't know whose head's been in there," she whispered. "Their hair might not be clean." I, of course, wore the velvet sombrero, but suffered no ill effects. In fact, I never have turned down an opportunity to try on a velvet sombrero. The fact that my kid came down with head lice the first time she played with dress-up clothes at that nifty children's museum in SoHo seems about as fair as getting pregnant the first time you have sex.

I called the parents of everybody my daughter had played with since our visit to the museum. "Oh my god," they said when I gave

them the news. I wonder if they were thinking that it figured. I'd always felt Inky's jaunty, scruffy look reflected well on her mother's anti–Baby Gap platform. Maybe this was my comeuppance for bragging about the price of her thrift store clothes, the little leather aviator helmet I got for a dollar. Knowing that this kind of confession would have killed my grandmother, I decided to be loud and proud. I gave them all the juicy details. I told them I had lice too. My acting teacher once said the world can be divided into people who drop their lunch tray and curl up, wishing that the earth would swallow them, and people who shout, "Oh my god, I just dropped my lunch tray!" Oh my god, I just dropped my lunch tray.

Greg was disgusted. He feared for his own hair. There was nowhere else for him to sleep in our apartment so he hugged the edge of the mattress, nervously eyeing our pillows. He worried that the washing machines at Cosmo's Launderama were not hot enough to kill the lice. He was in favor of throwing all of Inky's hats and toys away. He wanted to give himself the oil treatment too, just in case, but I wouldn't let him because there wouldn't be enough left over in case the lice came back.

The lice came back. The health food lice remedy was packaged with a wimpy little plastic comb. Its teeth fell out the first time we tried it. We had enough oil for a second treatment, but nothing to rake out the suffocated bugs. I carried Inky to a pharmacy on Second Avenue that sells all sorts of beautiful boar's bristle wooden-handled hairbrushes and asked for a lice comb. What I had in mind was the sort of close-teethed metal job my mother had when I was a child. I took that comb with me when I went to spend the night in Anna Garcia's tent, and her dog Prince chewed it up. When I got mad, Anna said, "My mother says that's a lice comb anyway." I was so offended. Now that my head was a hatchery, I wanted one just like it. The pharmacist didn't stock vintage delousing tools, but his assistant was sweet on Inky. "Just take it," he whispered, cracking open a box of pyrethrum-based lice remedy and pressing the heavy-duty black comb that came with it into my hand. On the way out, I fretted that the door alarm would go off and I'd be busted for shoplifting a lice comb, and on the street, I worried about the next poor lice-ridden sucker to cross the threshold, seeking relief. Boy, would she be pissed when she got home only to discover that the package was missing a comb.

I was captivated by the strange things coming off our heads. I pulled the comb through our oiled locks and then quickly held it up to Greg's loupe. I am still not sure I know what a nit is. The instructions described them as whitish specks, eggs glued to the hair shaft. I poked at the white specks on my comb with a needle before transferring them to a paper towel for a more scientific viewing environment. I saw a lot of dandruff, blown up like cornflakes under the loupe. One louse was perfect, reddish-brown, uncrumpled by his encounter with the comb. I wanted to pin him on a velvet-covered board like a butterfly. It was gross, but I can't help myself. It was like picking a scab or pouring beads on a shag carpet.

More than a year later, Inky has yet to forget. On a routine burrowing mission, she came across the loupe in a drawer and shouted, "This is for bugs in hair!" Western Union trucks remind her, because she has a yellow bandana printed with the Western Union logo that she received as a souvenir from a West Indian Parade float and I used it to tie up her oily head when her father refused to lend any of his hankies for the "let sit for two hours" portion of the lice treatment. "I had this when I have bugs in hair, you 'member that?"

I remember.

Head lice were outed on the PBS children's program *Arthur* this year. In an effort to destigmatize the problem, the writers had Muffy, the rich girl, start an epidemic at school. I guess I'm glad that lice have hit the mainstream, though it does take the gutter thrill out of my story. What's next for Arthur and his pals? Heroin addiction?

When the nursery-school teacher who lives downstairs came up to borrow my vacuum cleaner, she dragged me into the hall so Greg wouldn't hear the personal question she wanted to ask me. "This isn't going to be one of those 'how can you tell if you're pregnant' questions, is it?" I asked. No, a kid in her class came to school with bugs crawling all over her head. She needed my advice on how to treat her own head even though the school nurse assured her she was nit-free. She'd already spent thirty dollars taking her linens to the dry cleaner. She had bought a box of pyrethrum-based remedy. "I hope you're not offended that I'm borrowing your vacuum cleaner to suck up...lice." Old pro that I am, I doubted there were any lice to be sucked off her hardwood floor, but I assured her that I didn't mind. I counseled tea tree oil and a sense of humor. I told her that if it comes to it, there's a photographer's loupe we weren't using.

• • •

Holy Flurking Snit

I never said "goddamnit" in front of my grandmother, but midway through the third grade I started telling classmates that I had. "It happened long ago," I boasted. "When I was five." I claimed that shocked relatives had called me on the carpet to reveal where I had picked up such a bad word. My giggling audience was thrilled to learn that I had blamed my father right in front of his mother, a blunder we eight-year-olds thought typical of a kinder-gartner. I was strictly bush-league compared to other third-grade tale spinners, notably the pornographically inventive David Sykes. I wanted my peers to respect and envy me as someone worldly. To my young eyes, my father, with his timeworn penny loafers and gin and tonics, represented adult sophistication. I wanted to be like he was. My father said "goddamnit," so, goddamnit, I would too, though never if I might be overheard by an adult. In theory, my parents adored the idea of a smutty little kid operating outside the laws of propriety. If it appeared as a cartoon in *The New Yorker*—"I say it's spinach and I say to hell with it"—it was hilarious. If their only child blurted it over Grandmother's relish plate, it was not.

Inky started cussing in earnest at three. It wasn't the same thing as rush hour at Grand Central Station when, barely two years old, she had chanted, "Oh fuck! Oh fuck! Oh fuck!" over my shoulder all the way from the Great Hall to the subway turn-stiles. In those days, she got the Shirley Temple treatment every time she mimicked an adult. We said "cantaloupe," she said "can-coke," and the place went up for grabs. We sang "Happy Birthday," she called presents "happy to yous" and was showered in them. So when Daddy realized he forgot to set the VCR and Inky echoed him phonetically, we couldn't help but find it adorable, even in a terminal full of commuters. She didn't know what she was saying, and, I hope, neither did the hordes racing past us. A year later, Inky was hip to the idea of context. Having spent the better part of an hour absorbed in her doll-sized tea set, she glanced at the setting sun and muttered, "Oh shit. I forgot to watch *Arthur.*"

"Oh shit," I thought. "The chickens have come home to roost."

Greg grew up in a home where the foul language flew fast and free and midwestern squares like the ones who raised me were the avoided archetypes. He figures he turned out okay. He expresses himself articulately and nails me for the "ums", "likes" and "you knows" that litter my speech. He is, however, deaf to the "fucks," "shits" and "assholes" that riddle his. He knows other words. His sailor talk is as extraneous as the Valley Girl flourishes of which this educated Hoosier gal is guilty. Take away the profanity, and he still would make sense. He turns to them out of laziness and habit. Of course, to Inky any word she hears deserves immediate rotation in her ever-increasing vocabulary.

She couldn't get a puzzle piece to fit after two seconds of concerted effort. "Fuck," she sighed. I looked up from the laundry I was folding. Here I was at the crossroads. In the olden days she'd have been gagging on a bar of soap in the time it was taking me to weigh my options. Perhaps hoping to offer some assistance, Inky remarked, "I say 'fuck,' and daddy say 'no!'"

"Yeah, well, Daddy's right."

"Daddy say 'fuck.'"

"Mmm, that's true, but, you know, it's one of those words that adults—"

"You say 'fuck' too."

"Ha. Oh. Well, yes, that's true, but you know what? Every time I do, I think to myself. 'Gosh, I wish I had used a different word, like 'nuts' or 'heck' or 'dang it all to pieces.' The problem with 'fuck' is it isn't very articulate. There are much more descriptive—"

"What means 'rod tickle it'?"

Hey, I'd much rather define 'articulate' for a three-year-old than fuck. You know what I mean.

Greg and I worked to clean up our language around the little pitcher. Nursery school was fast approaching and Inky was at high-risk for declaring that a surreptitious sand flinger was being a real asshole. We didn't go as far as spelling out the forbidden words, as when we communicated important information about I-C-E-C-R-E-A-M, S-A-N-T-A and the horror of local news stories in which children D-I-E-D. Still, there were pitfalls. Our friends hauled it out to eat dinner at our home in Brooklyn to spare us the rigors of restaurants and late-night returns, schlepping sleeping children on the subway. We were grateful. Inky could play with her own toys when she got sick of sitting at the table and listening to the boring adult conversation we so craved. We didn't have to supervise her with the hawk eyes a restaurant requires. We were delighted to excuse her after a few mouthfuls so that she could ignore us. She seemed thoroughly engrossed in the tangle of tutus, stuffed animals, blocks and crayons she'd deposited at our feet. We pumped our childless friends for details about their unfettered lives, the bars they frequented and the plays they'd attended. "It's too bad you didn't get a chance to see it," one would say about a brilliant fugue of cheap theatrical invention that had come and gone before we'd even heard about it. "That was some fucked-up crazy shit! The director's out of his fucking mind! I've heard he's a bitch to work for, but who the fuck cares?" Finally noticing the pained smiles on our faces, the speaker would rein himself in. "Oh, shit, the kids, sorry. Sorry Inky!" Had her ears been pricked up all along? It was hard to tell. Mine were.

To be fair, Mommy and Daddy and all their foul-mouthed friends aren't the only bad influence on our little spawn. Our street is a popular shortcut for drivers trying to avoid a main thoroughfare in Brooklyn. Traffic starts early in the morning and continues well past midnight. Because a school is across the street, the corner has a stoplight. We hear whatever the motorists listen to on their car stereos during the minute it takes for the light to change. When insomnia strikes at two in the morning, I enjoy my brief snatches of Arabic pop and Indian movie musical sound tracks. I pretend to be a world-music aficionado, imagining that the cabdrivers and I would find lots in common if my sleeping children didn't prevent me from venturing out into the night. It's the only time I can stomach contemporary soul. Hip-hop is the most popular with our four-wheeled disc jockeys, reflecting the language the junior high schoolers use on the subway. Maybe they're parroting the language in their favorite songs, but that's a political ballyhoo I'd prefer to avoid. Cop killing, bitch slapping, drug dealing: In my book as long as it's word and not deed it's valid under the First Amendment. I usually experience our domestic background rap as a bass-heavy beat, but every now and then a chart-topping lyric jumps out at me.

What the drivers were listening to the night I returned home with the newborn Milo went something like this: "Motherfucker, motherfucker, shut your motherfucking mouth, bitch shit, mother bitch, gonna fuck your shit up!" I wouldn't let Inky watch *Teletubbies* because I was afraid it would rot her brain. You've got to wonder how that much "motherfucker" is going to imprint on a mind less than eight hours old. Children love repetition. We get another heaping helping of the word I've learned to pronounce "melon-farmer" every time we open the window. When I was a child, the filthiest song we could find on our AM dial was the infamous ballad "Having My Baby." We couldn't believe something so X-rated was permitted on the airwaves. When the singer demanded of his ladylove, "That seed inside you, lady, can't you feel it growing?" we screamed. I prayed it wouldn't come over the radio in the station wagon, my parents in earshot. How will Inky and Milo ever learn they're supposed to protect me from that kind of language when our street has such bad potty mouth?

I remember my great-aunt Frances praising her son-in-law at a luncheon for female relatives. It was undeniable proof of his great character that she'd never hear him utter anything stronger than "oh fudge." No one suggested that he might talk differently when his mother-in-law wasn't around, like when in bed with his wife, for example. It wasn't really a "fudge me, honey, fudge me harder" kind of crowd. They liked the kind of funnies *Reader's Digest* prints. These ladies all concurred with Aunt Frances' evaluation. It made a strong impression on me, the youngest guest. I concluded that her son-in-law was a big simp and that "fudge" was a pretty lame substitute for "goddamnit."

I have revised my opinion as Inky persists in using the word "fudge" was intended to replace. The moment I swear needlessly over some petty grievance Aunt Frances pops into my head, her expression brimming with pride at her son-in-law's restraint. I think she was right. We can and should express ourselves in language suitable for all ears, little pitchers' and little old ladies' alike. The only trouble is, I've taken to exclaiming "oh fucky fudge" every time I push through the turnstile in time to see the F train pulling away. What if Inky repeats it at school? When her teacher asks her where she picked up this unsavory expression, the finger will point straight to me.

Because I'm the Mother, That's Why

Poor Inky. The day Milo was born, the curtain lifted, and I could see her as she really was: corrupt. Barely turned three, she seemed more akin to her craven, attention-seeking mother than to her newborn brother. I barely remember her as an infant. I remember having another infant. I just can't reconcile myself to the fact that that infant was Inky. Was she not always as she is now, smudged, napless, agitating to use sharp scissors and blow out other people's birthday candles? Was her obstinate, protruding belly ever topped off by the alien tassel of an umbilical stump? Of course it was. I know exactly where we were when it dropped off! We had been discharged from the frying pan of the Neonatal Intensive Care Unit into the hellfire of a New York City heat wave. Some well-heeled acquaintances took pity on us as they decamped for their summer home, letting us swap our dinky un-air-conditioned East Village slum for their palatial Tribeca loft. In return we kept an eye on their dog, a gentle, self-reliant Rhodesian ridgeback. I remember sitting on their huge couch in glorious climate-controlled comfort, listening to Tom Waits and sobbing because my little baby and I had escaped that hospital at last. Clear of beeping monitors, nurses' schedules and diagnoses that beget other diagnoses, we were free to enter what one of my midwives had referred to as "that timeless state" where a newborn and mother lollygag in each other's miraculous presence. While the rest of New York broiled, I pulled on a light sweater and changed my baby's outfit every hour. I pretended that the loft and everything in it was my bonus prize for making it through NICU. Boy, life would be easier from here on out. My fancy new stereo sure was nice.

Suddenly, I noticed that the little raisin that had tethered her body to mine had disengaged from her belly button. It was lying on the couch cushion. I got to it just barely ahead of the hungry dog. It's secured in a tiny envelope in her baby book, along with several hundred photos of the solemn dark-eyed baby we loved so absolutely unconditionally. The baby who, short of darting in front of a bus on Second Avenue, was never going to hear the word "no." The baby who would only know the gentlest of loving touches. The wonderful, holy baby who bestowed absolution on everyone, parents, strangers, our suddenly personable neighbors. You know, Milo— except he was Inky then.

It boggles the mind that before Inky started to speak her reputation was of sobriety. The other Tompkins Square playground denizens thought she was hilarious because she was so deadpan.

Lord knows she had some wild getups, which only enhanced the effect. We interpreted her serious expression as mild disapproval and were flattered that she might consider us too freewheeling to be responsible parents. Toddling around in a leopard-print pilot's cap and a prim blue wool coat from the Salvation Army, she was pleasantly evocative of the Puritans who denounced their neighbors during the Salem witch trials. Now Inky tattles until I want to tie a knot in her tongue. I never expected that she would be so wrapped up in who's hoarding Barbies and who won't cede the tire swing, with nary a word about who's dancing with the devil. Back before she could talk, we were exhilarated by the idea of an austere baby with diamond-hard morals in our midst. We couldn't get enough of it, of her.

Inky started talking late. If memory serves, she was about one and a half. I had given up checking her developmental progress when I traded the loathsome childrearing manual for a groovy secondhand outfit at Jane's Exchange, an East Village consignment shop for the sub-6X set. By then, she had amassed a playground triumvirate of little blond friends, all of whom spoke in complete sentences, none sharing Inky's remarkable prowess on the monkey bars. Her verbal skills rivaled an orangutan's but she could dart up the ladder and down the tallest spiral slide in less time than she now takes to put on one shoe. I liked that my kid was the fearless one, especially since I once inconvenienced a great line of fellow seven-year-olds when I chickened out at the top of a big slide. I liked that her lack of spoken words implied the possibility of profound thought. At least she never outed herself by announcing, "Me want juice now!" Inky is a great character; it's just that when she was really little I presided over her image like James Carville. Now she's in control.

I should have learned my lesson with "yes." When she finally started to speak, she said "yes" to everything. For many years now, I've rankled at a certain kind of authority. What a sweet "chuck you, Farlie" it was to those griping know-it-alls with their inevitable predictions of terrible twos and exasperating "no no nos." Oh yeah? My baby says "yes!" My baby was as affirmative and embracing as the tiny word Yoko Ono wrote on the ceiling of a London gallery, the word that caused John Lennon to fall madly in love with her when he climbed a ladder to peer at it through a magnifying glass. Yes! Yes! Yes! Yes! My baby was the last page of *Ulysses,* not that I've ever read *Ulysses.* Oh, was I proud.

Two weeks after she'd gained sufficient mastery over "yes" she cast it aside in favor of "no." Her unilaterally negative response to every question was far less annoying to me than my crowing about her prior preference must have been to everyone else. I still loved every little thing she did, and when I didn't I blamed myself. I never accepted the terrible twos. Instead, I claimed that she was reacting to my terrible thirty-fours. What can I say? She was a baby and I was an infatuated only child, short on experience.

You want to know a wonderful thing about babies? Their shit doesn't stink. Not until you start feeding them baby food. I remember a friend whose daughter was then two peeking over my shoulder as I changed the newly hatched Inky's diaper. "Oh, look at the baby mustard," he sighed wistfully. "Wendy and I used to call that butterscotch."

Milo eats from those little jars, though he wouldn't plug a hole with the homemade organic baby food I so laboriously prepared for his sister in our filthy and sunless East Village kitchenette. He washes his dinner down by licking the rims of his parents' beer bottles. I can testify that his shit now stinks. He can produce a stench that rivals anything emanating from the bulging diaper of a blubbering snot-nosed toddler belonging to someone else. I miss the Milo mustard, but I've got to laugh when, covered in the foul orange slime that's burst from his diaper to stain his T-shirt up to the shoulder blades, he flips on his belly, trying to wriggle free of all who would restrain him. "Help! Help!" Greg and I scream to each other, giggling helplessly as the baby prevails, rubberstamping his terrible heiner all over our king-sized quilt. (One of these days we should break down and get a changing table.) In our family, Milo is the only person allowed to crawl around the bed, naked, covered in shit. Why? Because as parents have admonished older siblings since time began, he's a baby! He doesn't know any better! We have learned from experience that babyhood is brief. It is over in a heartbeat. Enjoy it while it lasts, Milo.

May I rhapsodize about my baby's breath? It is as sweet as if he spent his days chewing clover and meditating for peace. So sweet. Milo, clamp your toothless jaws around my nose and breathe into my nostrils some more. Inky's breath can rival a dog's, largely because I forget to tell her to brush her teeth and she doesn't remind me until we are halfway down the stairs with three minutes to make it to the nursery school a ten-minute walk from home. I always feel bad that her teachers will get a load of that dragon breath.

Inky was potty-trained early, largely because I had a lax definition of what qualifies as potty-trained. My progeny has strained a lot of my DNA on the spongy asphalt of Tompkins Square playground, not to mention the carpets and polished hardwood floors of friends who have sensibly elected to keep their children in diapers until they hold their water for real. Inky tries hard to make it to the bathroom, but, as she herself has observed, sometimes pee happens fast. I don't want her to get the idea that her body's natural functions are shameful or disgusting, as she might if I rubbed her nose in the latest puddle, shouting, "No! Yucky! Bad! Dirty! No! No! Bad!" Still it's a drag to interrupt whatever I'm doing to halfheartedly swab a pool of urine around our gummy floors with a paper towel. In my light-as-a-feather favorite teacher's voice, I console, "Hey, it's okay, accidents happen to everybody. Just try to give yourself a little extra time to get to the potty the next time you need to pee-pee, okay? Okay? Can I hear you say 'okay'? 'Okay, Mommy'?" Stooping to pick up the reeking size two Curious George underpants abandoned at the scene of the crime, I think about adults who lead the gorgeous life. Their spotless Swedish-catalog homes. Their massaged backs, supple and uncompromised by stepping and fetching for messy little kids. They're breaking for a light repast of Chardonnay and goat cheese on toast points as I'm on my hands and knees mopping up pee. That's the reality of life with small children. Put that on the cover of *Parents* magazine and watch those issues fly off the news-stand! If I'm lucky, I'll have just enough time to swig a couple mouthfuls of juice from the carton before Jambo vomits in a corner. Just as I'm lumbering to my feet with a wad of soggy paper towels, I hear a little voice in the next room mutter, "Okay."

I know that twenty years after the fact, little kids pissing all over the floor will be funny, the way the idea of Greg and I ever having enough money to foot the bills for college is funny now. All the sassy remarks, the imperious demands, the outrages of which a three-year-old is capable, will seem nothing but funny when I'm old and unbothered, stretched out in a lawn chair, savoring my book and my iced tea. Actually, strike that tea. I'll have a gin and tonic. It'll seem funny if the kid doesn't turn into a drug addict or a murder victim or a prostitute on the West Side Highway, in which case every recollection of that long-gone childhood will seem bittersweet. Listen Inky, don't grow up to be a drug-addicted, murdered prostitute on the West Side Highway, or I'll never forgive myself for the times when I snapped at you for whining because you wanted to serve the salad at dinnertime. Your absolutely untrue assertions that you are capable of operating salad forks without making a mess are maddening only because you are three and I am momentarily wishing I could be left in peace to read *The New Yorker* or play Lady Macbeth opposite the late Sir John Gielgud. It might strengthen your case if you would eat a leaf or two of the salad you dump all over the place mats and your father's lap. Don't let your brother grow up to be a drug-addicted, murdered prostitute either, although it's impossible to believe he'll ever be anything other than a chubby, blameless baby, ingratiatingly unaware that he has carte blanche in every situation. Any irritating behavior is attributed to teething.

How does Inky drive me crazy? Great leaping Jesus, how doesn't she drive me crazy? It's rooted in desire. Her constantly voiced desire to purchase a "beauuuutiful dress" like the one she saw in the catalog at her grandmother's house. My desire for my children to look like something other than the hemophiliac off-spring of English royalty. Her desire, unwisely indulged by me in a staggering lapse of maternal judgment, to consume great quantities of sugar at three o'clock in the afternoon. My desire to prevent the little sugar-freak from applying lipstick, jumping on the couch, carrying her heavy yet defenseless baby brother unassisted, listening to *Songs for Wiggleworms* on endless replay, inserting an R-rated rental videotape into the VCR upside down, answering the telephone every time it rings, standing on a rolling desk chair to turn the lights on and off and evading a shampoo for the fourth night in a row. My desire for her to occupy herself quietly with a coloring book until it's time to go to bed early. Her desire for me to color with her. My desire not to do that. She drives me crazy.

I drive her crazy too. Within the last year, she has learned to express her frustration verbally. I think they teach that in nursery school along with the colors of autumn leaves and the importance of hand washing. Clad in a turquoise tutu, a winter cap and a pair of my shoes purloined from the forbidden closet, she plants herself in front of me, arms akimbo, a dark cloud settling on her brow. "Why do you not ever let me do the stuff I want to do?!" she demands in a tone decidedly different from the one we've dubbed her "restaurant voice."

I have to stop myself from shouting, "Because I'm the mother, that's why!" I don't feel like explaining that razors are sharp, that permanent markers leave permanent stains and that although that anthology of underground comix may look like something for kids, it's really for adults, so please put it back where you got it. I don't feel like manufacturing a reasonable, patient tone of voice. I don't feel like going through the motions of carefully weighing her dare-

devil impulses against common sense, historical precedent and the
weather, even though I know that this is exactly what will help her
to become a healthy, secure individual. There are times, usually
around four in the afternoon, when I just want to get from point A
to point B as efficiently as possible, with no screaming, no detours
and no discussion about equity. I imagine how smoothly things
would run if I were a career military man, brush cut, rapping out
orders. I'd hate to spend any time in my company, and I shudder to
think of my reading material, but just think how quickly my wife
would get dinner on the table! "Because I'm the mother, that's why"
was probably invented by guys like Oliver North, or at least some
enterprising drill sergeant. Even if it does come the closest to artic-
ulating my feelings after a long day with my children, I no more
could utter it in good conscience than I could have enlisted to serve
in the Gulf War. A friend gave me this slogan as a refrigerator
magnet. I slapped it up alongside the giant alphabet letters and the
diaper coupons that expired months earlier.

"What does that say?" Inky says, pointing to the magnet as I try
to retrieve an overlooked ingredient before the garlic turns to charcoal in the pan.

"Inky, move!" I use my foot to block Milo from joining us at the
refrigerator. If it were ten o'clock in the morning, I might be a little
more creative, but it's been a long day and I didn't sleep well last
night. Milo might be devoid of all sin, but he woke up every fifteen
minutes, jonesing for a snack. "Move, it's burning!"

She pirouettes reluctantly to one side. "But what does it say?" she
asks, grabbing hold of the hem of my skimpy T-shirt and giving it
a pull. Hooray! Now the people in the building across the way have

a nice, unobstructed view of my naked breast. I'm sure they're accustomed to this free show, given the way I run around unhusking whenever Milo calls.

"Stop that!" I bark, snatching at her hand as I turn back to the stove. Have I mentioned that the kitchen is the size of two or three bathmats stitched together? "You don't grab at people's clothes that way!"

"Why?" she pipes. "Why, Mommy? Why not do you grab at people's clothes that way?"

"Because!" I reply in exasperation, immediately realizing that I'll have to do better. "Because when you pull on people's clothes like that, their clothes can come off and it's one thing for the neighbors to see a little girl running around naked, but Daddy and I don't want them to look at us without our clothes on. It's not that there's anything wrong with being naked, it's just that grown-ups might like to keep that private, not for the neighbors to see."

Milo, miscalculating the distance to the bag of recycling he's reaching for, loses his balance and tumbles backward, smacking his head on the linoleum. Turning the flame off, I scoop him up and dance cheek to cheek, frantically singing his favorite song. I wonder if that just makes it worse. Imagine if every time you cracked your skull on a hard surface someone started bellowing your nickname into your ear to the tune of "O Mein Papa." At least he's used to the drill. He pipes down quickly, smiling at us through his tears. I put him down. He screws up his face and wails.

"Inky," I suggest. "Why don't you go sit in your little red chair and read a story to your brother? I know he would love that. I heard you reading that book we got from the library to yourself ear-

lier, and I thought it sounded really good. That book about manners? Could you please read it out loud to your brother in the other
room? Because that would really help me. You said you wanted to
help me with dinner, and right now that would be the best possible
way for you to help so he'll stop crying and I can cook and then
Daddy will come home, won't that be great?"

She pauses on tiptoe, her head cocked to one side, considering.
"Wellllllll," she decides. "I really just want you to tell me what that
says." She points at the refrigerator magnet again. Fine. I put Milo
on one hip and stand sideways, hoping that my body will protect
him from the sesame oil spitting on the stove. Damn, I just cleaned
that stovetop last week.

"Mommy, will you ever not tell me what that thing says?"

"Oh, it just says something silly, that grown-ups think is funny.
Carol gave it to me, for a joke."

"Why did Karen give it to you for a joke?"

"Carol, not Karen. Carol. Ol. Ol. Carollll. Kar-en lives in
Chicago. Car-ol gave you that book about—"

"But, Mawwwwww-meeeeeeeeee," she bleats. Oh my god,
Greg's right. She's developing a New York accent. Now she's really
going to drive me crazy. "Why did Karen, I mean Carol, give you
that thing?"

"I told you, for a joke. Because she thought it was funny."

"But why did she think it was funny?"

"I guess because she thought it was funny that I would ever be
the kind of mother who might say something like that or that I now
find myself in the situation I find myself in. I don't know what's
taking your father so long."

"Yes, but what does it say?" she cries, flinging her arms wide.

I stop what I'm doing and pry the little square off the refrigerator. It has a picture of a smiling housewife on it, a bit of *Leave It to Beaver*–era clip art. It's the kind of appealing doodad displayed near the cash register in those fun little stores that I'd never dare enter with an overstimulated three-year-old shopaholic. The place where we used to take our East Village Inky photos sold that kind of stuff, until the owner threw in the towel because he was so sick of watching his customers' kids handle his merchandise like Play-Doh. Maybe that's where Carol got it. I hold it up like a police detective's badge, so Inky can get a good look. "It says, 'Because I'm the mother, that's why!'"

"You said you'd let me cook dinner!" she parries. She drives me crazy.

I hear Greg's key in the lock and for the thousandth time this year think about single mothers. At least I've got relief troops. How the hell can they stand it? They're playing the game with no Get Out of Jail Free card. "I've already read that book five times today, go ask your father" is not possible for a single mother when it's an hour past bedtime and the child shows no signs of going to sleep. It's not a viable option when she is so tired that she feels embalmed, when she can't even sit on the toilet without interruption, or when she would prefer to remain facedown on the couch, thinking about a movie she saw when she was twelve. No one will break down and bring her a glass of water when she doesn't want to get up. She might get royally pissed about child support or custody battles, but she doesn't have another adult on whom to pin the small stuff. Of course, it must be nice not to find rank sockballs on the living room floor. The only paper towels that have been used for Kleenex and tossed on the table in a single mother's house are the ones upon which she has blown her own personal nose, unless she has a teenage son. This kind of slovenliness always rankles me, despite my pronounced tendency to litter every available surface with paper, cast-off shoes and buttons that I intend to sew on my coat. I shudder to think what my apartment would look like if I were a single mother. Greg is not the only thing standing between me and a pristine room, minimally decorated with a cushion, a low table and a bell. Inky and Milo generate many more dirty clothes than Greg and I ever have. Even when it feels like me against him, it's them against us. They are winning. I see evidence of Greg's mad scramble to beat back the chaos. He races to save the stove, the desk and, with a look of revulsion, the floors. I make the bed and tackle the toilet. When it seems like we are balanced on the brink of domestic disaster, division of labor kicks in, wordlessly. The little ones are driving the big ones crazy, so crazy we can't fight about it. There's safety in numbers. Recently, Greg looked up from a puddle of unknown origin and groaned, "I'll be so glad when they're old enough to go out on their own." This is the man who as a new father vowed he would go ballistic if a sneering boy in leather pants ever showed up to bear Inky away on a motorcycle. "I know what you mean," I commiserated. "Go out, children, and stay out until two A.M."

Somewhere out there, the mother of teenagers is laughing, licking her chops, thinking, "Oh honey, just you wait! Just wait until they give you something to complain about." Even the women who reassure me that teenagers get bad press, the ones whose teenagers are outspoken, affectionate humanists have knowing smiles on their faces. It strikes me as quite possible that by the time my children hit the teen years—I mean when Inky is a teenager and Milo is the same good-natured, blameless baby that he is today—I'll be the one driving them crazy with my idiosyncratic behavior, my infuriating desires and my interminable stories about the cute things that they did when they were little. At long last I will get my turn and use it to drive them right up the fucking wall.

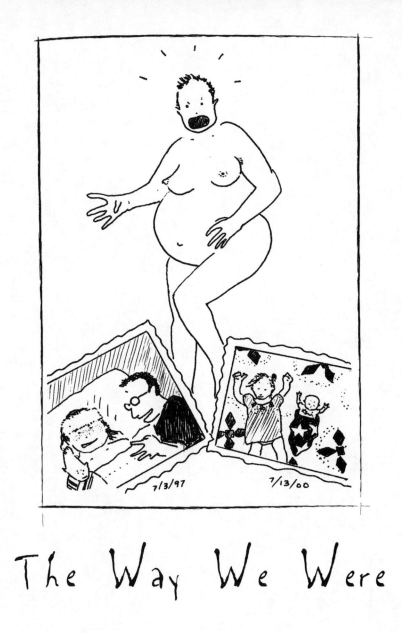

The Way We Were

NeoNatalSweetPotato: Dispatches from the New World

My water broke on July 2, 1997, while I was eating coconut shrimp with Little MoMo and Greg. We took a taxicab to the Elizabeth Seton Childbearing Center, where we examined my amniotic fluid under a microscope: It looked like snowflakes. I was given a bottle of peppermint-flavored castor oil to hasten my labor. The center had a rule that women have to deliver their babies within eighteen hours of their water breaking or they transferred them to the hospital. Once a mother's water breaks, an unborn baby is subject to all kinds of infections. I didn't know that at the time. I think the instructor may have brought it up in our birthing class, but I was preoccupied with imagining the Indonesian-print baby sling in which I would cradle my baby at all times. By the midwife's estimate, I wouldn't hit full labor until about six A.M., so she sent us home to get some sleep, or at least to try to rest. The midwife was the only one among us with direct child-birthing experience. We had no idea what we were in for.

It was a beautiful night. Little MoMo, Greg and I walked from the West Village to the East Village, telling each other that in a few hours we were going to see the baby. Greg wanted to call his mother so that she could be in the lobby of the birthing center when the baby was born. Little MoMo and I fought with him over this. We finally prevailed by telling him that on the very off chance something went wrong with the delivery and I had to be transferred to the hospital, the last thing any of us would need was a worried grandmother going berserk in the lobby of the birthing center.

I went into full labor on the corner of First Avenue and 9th Street. Then I rampaged through our apartment for four hours, yelling my head off (while Greg slept intermittently on the mid-wife's instructions), though our gallant neighbors insisted they never heard a thing through the thin tenement walls. I writhed on our unmopped kitchen floor, sandwiched between the refrigerator and the sink, watching a cockroach marching along the baseboard. That was the first omen that my labor was not going to be the beautiful experience I had anticipated.

What did it feel like? It felt like climbing alone into a canoe on a river, and starting to paddle, and the waters getting rougher and rougher and suddenly you hit the rapids and you realize that this river is way beyond your summer camp skill level and you're bouncing along over giant jagged boulders and they're battering the bottom of your canoe and your face is getting scraped from the branches of the trees on the shore and suddenly, the paddle is wrenched from your hands and all you can do is hang on and hope you don't tip over, just hang on, hang on, hang on. At four in the

morning, Greg pried my fingers off the kitchen sink and we took
another taxi back to the birthing center. It was now July 3.

According to Greg, the driver was really scared that I would
have the baby in his cab. He need not have worried. For about
eight hours, I tried out all the center's amenities as I struggled to
have the baby. I tried in a tub of hot water. I tried on the king-
sized bed. I tried in the shower. I tried squatting on a little stool
and leaning up against a wall and hanging on to Greg's shoulders.
I tried while sitting on the toilet. I was assisted by Little MoMo
and Greg, three midwives, two nurses and a student nurse. I
remember watching the clock on the wall. At first it seemed like
the baby would come quickly because the opening of the birth
canal was dilating so rapidly. By sunrise the baby's head was visible a few inches up inside my body but the baby couldn't make it
down. That little head just stayed where it was, corkscrewing
around in vain as it looked for a way out. The midwife in charge
gently informed me that she would give me another hour to
deliver. If I went past the deadline, we would have to go to the
hospital. I was no longer consumed with thoughts of Indonesian
baby slings. My labor was slowing down, I was exhausted and
every time I pushed, I did so with less resolve, less confidence in
my ability to paddle the canoe to the shore, where my baby was
waiting. The midwife even gave me two stays of execution but I
still couldn't deliver. Little MoMo retrieved my clothes—a red
paisley minidress and a pair of thong bikini panties embossed with
a glow-in-the-dark space girl. My new sandals were soaked with
amniotic fluid.

We took another taxi to the hospital. Little MoMo reported that the cabdriver disrupted his lunch to drive us the two blocks to St. Vincent's. When he saw the midwife spreading a blue paper pad over his backseat, he intimated that it would be an honor if the auspicious event occurred in his car. I don't remember him at all, just a faint impression of curry. I do remember getting out of the cab at high noon and having a whopping, wild contraction right there on Seventh Avenue in front of all of the sandwich carts and the peanut vendors. The elevator to the maternity ward took a very long time. When we arrived, the doctor was angry with the midwife for having taken so long to get me to the hospital—she didn't tell him about the second and third chances I'd been given. I lay down on a bed with white sheets in a cramped and grim delivery room. I refused to wear a hospital gown. A monitor was strapped across my enormous abdomen and I was given oxytocin, a drug that speeds up contractions, and oxygen. The oxygen mask kept slipping down my face. I had never been a patient in a hospital before. A St. Vincent's nurse with a tough New York accent joined Little MoMo and Greg and the midwife from the center. She kept telling me I had to try harder. She called me "Annie:" "C'mon Annie, you gotta do better than that. Push!" At some point the doctor appeared in the doorway to see how things were going. He never called me by name or looked into my eyes. I hear he's famous. I'm not 100-percent clear on what he's famous for, but I'd be surprised if it's his bedside manner. He was minutes away from giving me a Cesarean, when all of the sudden something changed, and I pushed until my eyes bugged out of my head like a Balinese mask and I felt a burning sensation and I knew that the baby's head was coming out and the baby's head came out and the baby's shoulders came out and the baby came out and Greg and Little MoMo were crying and at 2:37 P.M., they handed me a wet little alien with an enormous sloping cone head. It was a long time before anyone looked to see if it was a boy or a girl. It was a girl. To my great surprise, it was a girl, a girl with three thumbs. Little MoMo discovered the extra digit as I made a joke about counting toes. I didn't care. I was so glad that I was off the rack and that the baby was every bit as weird as a newborn is supposed to be. I found it difficult to wrap my head around the fact that our baby wasn't male. We didn't really have a girl's name picked out.

Little MoMo took a picture of us. Greg looks like he's having an allergic reaction, the baby's head looks like a Smurf hat and I look like an elderly male Samoan. I'd pushed for more than seven hours and it showed. My swollen face was sprinkled with red specks.

I spend the first night in the hospital. The baby sleeps with me. She doesn't wake up to feed. I don't roll over and squash her in my sleep. She has big sexy lips. She has a heart monitor, which I assume is standard hospital procedure. Her score on the Apgar test, performed a few minutes after birth to assess a newborn's health, was a nine out of a possible ten. The resident who performed the test told Greg that nobody gets a ten. The heart monitor's alarm beeps periodically during the night. One of the nurses had warned me that this would happen. It's an old machine that the hospital keeps around. She showed me how to jiggle the wires to silence the alarm.

At seven in the morning, the baby is wheeled away to the nursery in the maternity ward for tests. I start to feel uneasy when nobody brings my baby back and she doesn't come back and she doesn't come back. Two hours later, Greg discovers her still in the nursery, alone, untested and crying. A nurse tells me that the Fourth of July weekend is a bad time to be a patient in a hospital because all the doctors go on vacation and the new residents are left in charge. We ask that the baby be brought back to my room. My mother-in-law, brother-in-law and Little MoMo visit. A college buddy of Greg's arrives with his best friend in tow. They bring bouquets, take photographs and pass the baby around. Greg's friend's best friend has never held an infant before, but I am not unnerved. Nothing can flap this hippie mama now that the unforeseeable torture of delivery is over.

A pediatrician in a Hawaiian shirt examines the baby and orders tests. He tells us that they might want the neonatologist to check her out but hastens to add, "Don't worry Mom, it's no big deal. Boy, she's a beautiful one, isn't she? Here's my card. Call me if you have any questions."

Two residents arrive to draw blood from the baby's heels. I don't like this, but I give them permission to proceed, the way I sheepishly hand the dry cleaner forty dollars for a down comforter I expected would cost no more than five. The blood clots before they get around to testing it, so they come back for a fresh sample. We can tell something is wrong because her cries are so weak. Even when the sharp point of the heel stick bites into her flesh, she sounds like a tiny mewing kitten. Finally, at around ten P.M., she is taken away for good. I cannot walk, so Greg accompanies her to the NICU, where he keeps a vigil beside her tiny body. Outside the window, fireworks explode.

• • •

Salad Bin

My baby's bassinet in the Neonatal Intensive Care Unit looks like
one of the large plastic bins we used to store lettuce back when I was
waiting tables at Dave's Italian Kitchen. It is lined with half a dozen
hospital-issue baby blankets, expertly folded to perform a variety of
functions. They anchor the crib sheets, warm the tiny occupant and
form a protective horseshoe around the eggshell head. The bur-
gundy and turquoise stripes that edge the white flannel make me
think of Mother Teresa's order, nuns in homespun saris. I steal one
of the blankets to cuddle and cling to on the nights when I am in
bed on the maternity ward and baby is in her salad bin one flight
below. When I'm not crying into it, I hide the blanket in my fake-
wood nightstand. I don't relish the idea of being busted, but I have
reason to think I'll be treated with clemency if my theft is discovered. All the other new mothers here get to keep their babies. Who
would begrudge me a soft little blankie that smells like the dryer? I
have since come to the conclusion that blanket stealing is not limited to the parents of intensive care neonates. Not a week goes by
that I don't notice some other woman trundling down the sidewalk
with one of Mother Teresa's baby novices. There are so many of
them. They can't all have passed through the NICU but just in case,
I search the parent's face, veteran to veteran, to see if they've seen
combat too.

Due Date

Everybody who heard about our troubles leapt to the conclusion that the baby was premature but she came right on schedule. At my first prenatal appointment, I couldn't pinpoint the date of my last period. I couldn't even hone in on a general vicinity. The midwife did not think this was funny. I had expected her to be charmed by my nonchalance. I thought she'd throw up her hands and laugh, "Oh my, you have no idea how refreshing it is to hear that! Most women are so anal retentive about their menstrual cycles!"

"You have to try to remember," she said instead, tapping a pen against a chart with my name on it.

I had to concoct a date of conception. I was at least three months pregnant and knew that whatever sham date I came up with would be set in stone in my chart. The birthing center could only admit laboring mothers between their alleged 37th and 42nd weeks of pregnancy.

If I botched the date, there was a chance I wouldn't be able to deliver at the center. I couldn't go in forty-three weeks gone according to my chart, claiming that I'd made a mistake in my calculations. There were no do-overs. They'd refer my ass to the hospital. I didn't want that to happen, so I racked my brains. They felt about as sharp as wet cotton. I was clueless.

Finally, I had no choice but to resort to a fake-o numerology of my own invention. It involved postmarks and a bartender friend's birthday. I presented this random moment of fertilization at my next appointment and with a flick of the midwife's cardboard calculation wheel, my baby was scheduled to be born on July 4. My baby would be born on July 4!

I could name him Independence. He'd be born easily on an Independence morning, slipping quietly from my body into a tub of warm water, a bath his first task on the planet. We would doze for six hours on the big birthing center bed with the wrought-iron frame and then we would walk slowly home together. Sleepy as we'd be, we'd climb the six flights to the roof so that the last thing to happen on his first day on earth would be fireworks. My baby would have to come quickly so that the fireworks over Manhattan could proceed on schedule.

Brains

Nobody seems to know what is wrong with this child. She'd been started on an antibiotic cocktail the moment she was admitted to NICU, but the origin of her illness remains a mystery while the cultures are analyzed by the lab, which is operating on a holiday schedule. Meanwhile, I am informed that unnamed Baby Girl Halliday is to be taken for an MRI of her brain. I am told by a pleasantly grave young neurology resident that he needs my consent to give unnamed Baby Girl Halliday a high-contrast MRI. I don't know what that is so he explains it to me and he explains the possible side effects, the things that could go wrong. I forget the pros and cons faster than they can leave his mouth. I can only afford him the smallest fraction of my own brain. The lion's share is wrestling with an insoluble puzzle: Why is this happening to me? Why am I standing on industrial carpeting in a drafty corridor, wearing a hospital gown and no underpants, attached intravenously to a hat rack that has accompanied me for seven flights and two wings? I hobbled here behind the maternity ward's receptionist. She clip-clopped cheerfully through the hospital's labyrinth, making bright conversation about nothing. She was very chirpy. I chuckled automatically in all the appropriate places as I struggled to stay with her. We passed a chapel, which was empty, and signs outside the MRI room warning us about exposure to radiation and god knows what else requiring lead aprons and signatures of consent, which I will give.

Before I can bring myself to sign my name in ink though, I ask if I can use a phone to call my husband. I ask nicely, as if I don't want to impose. It is a tremendous effort to ask at all. I ask because if Greg were here, he would ask. Apologizing as if I know I'm fucking things up for the waiter by sending my steak back, I ask if I can use a phone. Actually, I ask if I can use a pay phone.

The young resident fetches a phone with a long extension from a private office. He ducks back in and returns with a stool for me to perch gingerly on, the vinyl cold on my exposed and pummeled "bottom" to use the term the nurses favor. I place the call. Greg is home. I say, "They want to do an MRI on the baby."

He says, "What is that?" I hear his hand raking through his hair.

I say . . . something, god knows I don't say magnetic resonance imaging. I cobble together some explanation in a measured and medical tone of voice.

"Well, if that's what they think they need to do . . . "

"There are possible side effects".

"Oh?"

"Yes—this, this and this," whatever the doctor just told me, my brain a million miles away on Mars, except for one tiny wrinkle, which is jabbering, *Oh man, if you forget to say a side effect and she gets that side effect, he's gonna be really pissed and if you forget to mention just one of these side effects, that's for sure the one side effect she'll get.*

"Excuse me," I say, apologetically extending the receiver to the young resident, "but would you mind going over what you just told me with my husband?"

Husband, my husband, when did I ever get a husband? I don't feel big enough to be married. Not today. I am way too young for any of this. I'm not thirty-two, I'm what? Four? Five? I'm five years old! I want to go outside and climb a tree. Just as the doctor hangs up, Baby Girl Halliday wakes screaming from her anesthetic slumber in the room just off the corridor. What, is she strapped to a cart, alone, screaming, a shadow on her brain? The doctor rushes in where I am not allowed. I sit shivering in the drafty corridor while the screams of Baby Girl Halliday seep out from under the door. They puddle around my ankles, making me far colder than any vinyl stool left to chill in the hospital's round-the-clock climate control.

The doctor comes out. He's rattled. He's new. He's a brand-new resident. It's the Sunday of the Fourth of July weekend and everyone else is out playing golf. They left him in charge of the store. Now something's gone wrong. I feel for him. I hope he doesn't get in trouble.

"Uh, they need to give her a new IV and they're having a little trouble getting it in," he tells me humbly. It's his turn to be apologetic. We have a great deal of sympathy for each other, the nice new resident and me. " I don't want to be there when they do that," he continues. "I think she's associating me with that. I think she sees me and she starts to freak out. They know, you know. They know. We'll try again later. Later this afternoon."

Okay. Later this afternoon, they call me to go down to the MRI lab. Greg arrives a few minutes later and reads aloud from a tattered copy of *Entertainment Weekly*. When he puts it down, I pick it up and look at the pictures, who wore what to last years Academy Awards. After a few pages, I have to stop because if my child is to be irreparably brain damaged, I don't want to be caught reading about Winona Ryder's evening gown, her creamy, flawless skin. I can't fill my brain up with trash at a time like this.

The receptionist places personal calls from the company phone, recklessly bitching about doctors and patients alike. Her eyes crackle with irritation. Her red business suit looks cheap and itchy. "Take your feet off the furniture," she snaps at Greg, who immediately removes his running shoes from the crappy, stained upholstery of the chair he's dragged over for this purpose. He's compliant but his eyes smolder like he hasn't slept in weeks. The receptionist demands to know what he's doing here. She thinks he's some young whippersnapper resident acting like he owns the place.

I feel like vaulting across the counter and shaking her 'til those earrings of hers clank back and forth. "This is the father of the baby who's in there getting an MRI!" I snarl, enjoying the power my rage affords me.

My nasty tone does the trick. Maybe I should try it out the next time I go to get my driver's license renewed. After that she's the very picture of bedside manners. "You put your feet up on the furniture, honey!" she commands Greg with great warmth.

The door to the lab swings open as employees come and go. Snippets of conversation between the MRI technicians float into the waiting room. "I hate this stupid fucking machine!" one roars.

We sit for a very long time, over an hour, I think. After a while, the technicians begin to wander out on a coffee break. They're all holding white plastic spoons. I overhear some mention of yogurt but leaning close to Greg's ear, I whisper, "You know what they do during an MRI, don't you? They shear the top of the skull off with a laser. Then they scoop out a tiny bit of the brain and eat it. That's what the spoons are for."

We about kill ourselves over that one. "Mmm, brains," Greg drools like the one-eyed aliens Kang and Kodo on *The Simpsons,* the ones who are scared off by an earthling brandishing a board with a nail sticking out of one end. We howl 'til the receptionist gives us the fish eye.

A marvelous organ, the human brain. It's no less delicious for having a shadow on it. No, that doesn't affect the taste at all.

Grandparents

I am sitting beside my baby's salad bin, watching her sleep, when Baby Wickline's grandparents arrive. Baby Wickline is not looking so good, he's been put in an incubator, the same kind that houses the tiny shaved-monkey preemies. Somehow, this looks more grim, Baby Wickline's strapping ten-pound form encased in this plastic box. He is asleep when his grandparents arrive unescorted from upstate New York. His grandparents look healthy, cultured. I guess they look like my parents, who don't look like grandparents to me. Not the way grandparents looked when I was a little kid.

The new grandparents stand shoulder to shoulder, gazing at

Baby Wickline through the plastic walls of his box. They look like the couple who doesn't know anyone else at the party. They stand awkwardly by the punch bowl, trying to think of things to say to each other.

"Well, there he is," his grandfather announces in a bluff, uncertain voice.

They can't touch him. There are twin portholes in the sides of the box that allow the nurses to reach in and do their business, but this is a hospital and Baby Wickline's grandparents don't want to touch anything without permission. They're unsure of how to proceed. They look but there's no one to congratulate, no mommy who's looking wonderful, no daddy to tease, no baby to hold, give him to me, come here you, hello, hello, I'm your grandma, that's who I am, yes, I am, yes I am.

They just look at him. Finally, without speaking Baby Wickline's grandfather pulls a tiny camera out of his windbreaker, bending his knees so that the incubator won't obstruct the view. You can tell he's the kind of man who embarrassed the hell out of his kids, making them pose in front of the Grand Canyon and Cinderella's castle at Disneyland while he tried to figure out the workings of his pocket Instamatic. He works his way around the salad bin, shooting from every conceivable angle.

His wife has been looking around the NICU, hoping that no one is watching. A dozen or so frames and she can't take it anymore. "That's enough!" she hisses. "Put that camera away! Put it away!"

Her husband is confused. "What?" he asks, blinking as he pulls the little camera away from his eye.

"I don't want Sherry to see him like this!" Baby Wickline's

grandmother glares at him. She gestures angrily at the baby in the salad bin. "Put it away! You've got enough! Put it away!"

Her husband straightens back up to his full height and says with great dignity, "I'm not taking them for Sherry. I want them for myself."

A few days later I witnessed the triumphant departure of Baby Wickline, who exited the NICU in six-month-sized shorts. Bless you, Grandfather of Baby Wickline. Bless you and your shameless Instamatic. Bless you for reaching into your wallet and fishing out a picture with your big bearlike paws, a picture of a large baby looking pale and out of it in a covered plastic salad bin. Bless you and bless your wife and give her strength when soufflés fall and hems come unstitched and the mail gets returned and the pictures don't come out right and something is wrong with the baby.

It's ok. It's ok. Everything's going to be ok.

What I Hate

What I hate: The constant interruptions. Miss Holiday? The complete lack of privacy. Good morning, Mrs. Holiday. Always someone barging in to hook up my IV or bring me another meal of starchy hospital food or see if I'm finished with my untouched tray. They come to take my blood pressure, get my signature on consent forms and remind me that it's once again time to pump my breasts. Just when I get a chance to go see my baby, who eats from an IV, I have to tether my breasts to a horrible machine that looks like it might grind them into hamburger at any second!

Miss Holiday? Good morning, Mrs. Holiday. How are you feeling today, Miss Holiday?

I hate the constant phone calls, repeating each development to my mother, my father, Greg's mother, Greg's brother, telling them about the upcoming test, CAT scan, spinal tap, MRI, telling them not to worry, forcing myself to sound positive, putting it in layman's terms as if I am a doctor myself, wishing I could just yank the goddamn phone out of the wall and go see my goddamn baby. If I can't, then at least let me go somewhere to cry in peace, maybe that chapel by the MRI lab. They wouldn't pursue a crying woman to the chapel, would they? I don't like anyone to hear me cry, so I draw the curtain around my half of the room, bury my face in my pillow and twist the little hospital blanket that looks like Mother Teresa's sari.

Miss Holiday?

I hate being called "Mommy" by nurses who can't remember my name. I know they're busy, but can't insurance cover this too? It's fairly critical. I just became a mommy a couple of days ago. I didn't expect it to be this way, but my baby's sick and my own name would go a long way right now. Instead, it's Mommy,

Hello Mommy. Good morning, Mommy. How are you today, Mommy Holiday?

They get my last name off the chart by my bed. This makes my husband, Greg Kotis, "Daddy Holiday," or "Mr. Holiday," which he tolerates with far more grace than I exhibit when a hapless telemarketer asks for "Mrs. Kotis." Greg is worried that I am on the verge of freaking out. I tell him that I hate the lack of privacy. I need a place to go where I can go cry where no one can get me. I can't stand it anymore! The phone's always ringing and I and I and I and I . . . I am losing it. Greg asks a nurse if the hospital has some sort of roof garden where I could sit. He wants to know if there's a chance they'd let me go outside for a short walk around the block. The nurse is amused by his request. "Daddy, she ain't even supposed to leave this floor!"

Like Rapunzel, I must stay inside. Still, I hold fast to an image of myself banging through the hospital doors and humping along Greenwich Avenue in my flapping hospital gown and paper slippers, trying to make it to the closest coffeehouse before security can wrestle me to the pavement. I hold this image in my mouth all day, suck on it like a sourball and feel much better.

Jung

At night, the fluorescent overheads are switched off and each baby's bin is spotlit. A few parents camp in scattered rocking chairs, Baby Wickline's father reads aloud from *How Proust Can Change Your Life*. The luckiest mothers get to rock their babies in their arms, their faces ecstatic, drunk from contact.

The nurses pad between the bins on their gum-soled white nurse feet, bending to the babies like seraphim, spotlit. The banks of monitors click and whir. The babies lie still, their eyes closed, even the crack babies, breathing together, in and out, their tiny hearts pattering like the hearts of mice. Sleeping. Or maybe they're born knowing everything and this is the time when they're busy erasing the tapes.

● ● ●

Ayun Halliday

Jeremiah

I recognize one of the other intensive-care mothers from the East Village. She is a tall, striking woman, about my age, her red hair wrapped in an enormous turban. She appears in the afternoons, holding the hand of a wild corkscrew-haired two-year-old, Jared. I've seen her before, definitely, doing her groovy-mother thing up and down First Avenue. I introduce myself and we become friendly right off the bat, jawing away like bunkmates at summer camp. She tells me how she planted her son Jared's placenta in her patch of the community garden at 6th and B. She tells me how with this second birth, she'd been looking forward to delivering the placenta because it had felt so good coming out the first time. Mmm-hmm! I remember the cool flop of the placenta, like a cartoon T-bone over a black eye. My friend didn't get to keep the placenta with this birth. They needed it in pathology.

"Do you know how much money hospitals make selling placentas?" my friend demands, not caring if the nurses hear.

Wow! I am thrilled to be a part of her club, this experienced, groovy single mother. Like me, she was transferred from the birthing center to the hospital when her labor slowed way down. Unlike me, who obediently dressed and climbed into a taxicab for the two-block ride, my friend was taken shouting, "Fuck you! Get away from me! I'm going home! I'll have this baby at home!"

Well, of course, that wasn't an option, and her birthing story ends with a doctor, that famous one who wanted to give me a C-section charging into the delivery room, shouting, "Hold on!" He flipped her over like a pancake, reached up inside her with what my friend refers to with a shudder as *"these hands"* and yanked the baby out. When she reached for the baby the nurses all shouted, "No! Don't touch him!" The baby was whisked away and now the baby is here, in intensive care and my friend comes every day sometimes with Jared, sometimes with her mother or father, who live on Long Island.

Her mother makes a big fuss over my baby, who lived for six days as Baby Girl Halliday before receiving a name. We had been so certain we were having a boy. After they took her to NICU, we worried about what might happen if we gave this sick baby the wrong name. "Oh India! What a lovely name! What a beautiful baby!" my friend's mother cries. I am flattered and blush with pleasure. "I could tell she was a girl, even before you told me. She's very feminine, you see. Oh, let me hold her!"

My friend's mother holds India for almost an hour, very glad, I think, to be holding a baby, any baby. Her baby, my friend's baby, her grandson, lies on his back in his salad bin and I think there are rules against picking him up. His head is carpeted with lush black fur, and he has big legs and big arms and a big wide nose. Strong cheekbones. He looks like he should be out cutting wood.

"Jeremiah," my friend's mother hums, approaching his salad bin with my baby in her arms, "This is India." She turns to me. "Do you think they might grow up and marry each other? I had friends who did just that. 'How did you two meet?' I said to them and they said, 'We met on the day we were born.' Well, not really, you know, but they were born at the same hospital and they were in the nursery at the same time, you see. So perhaps Jeremiah and India . . . "

Jeremiah, big Jeremiah, lies helpless on his back, his limbs swollen from antibiotics, his eyelids puffed shut. India is on antibiotics too, but she remains delicate, feminine, solemnly regarding Jeremiah's grandmother from her nest of hospital blankets. Jeremiah is nude. The nurses will not let my friend diaper him. Instead, he wears a washcloth folded over his penis and every few hours, the washcloth is removed and weighed to determine his urine output, a homespun test in this high-tech world. Every so often he twitches as if he is having a seizure. He looks like he is being electrocuted. His mother and I don't talk about this. We talk about Eastern-medicine healing therapies and restaurants we both like in the East Village.

One morning when my friend isn't there, I hear Jeremiah crying as a nurse tends to him. I am shocked. He is so big and hairy lying there without a diaper, his swollen limbs so dense with muscle that I had forgotten he is a baby.

My friend tells me that she dreamed of Jeremiah before he was born. She dreamed of a big, strong baby with dark hair. She decided that if she had that baby she would name him Jeremiah. If she had another baby, she would name him something else.

I guess she had that baby.

Dawn of the Dead

Those of us on the maternity ward with babies in the NICU are awakened several times a night to go feed them. Ten o'clock. Two o'clock. Six in the morning. I don't complain. For the first few days, I wasn't allowed to feed her. Instead, they woke me up three times a night to pump the milk out of my breasts with that hulking metal contraption. It looked like a ticker-tape machine from 1929. Sometimes, pumping in the middle of the night, I would drift off and the hand holding the suctioning device against my body would slip and I'd wake up to find a big red hickey on one of my boobs. So now when they come for me, I bounce right up. I am in *The Sound of Music,* the nuns gently shaking me into wakefulness so I can escape the Nazis.

At this time of night, there's not too much going on. Sometimes I catch sight of a maintenance man swabbing the halls with a dirty-looking mop. Once when I am waiting for the elevator at three A.M., I hear the piteous groans of a woman in labor and burst into tears.

Other mothers glide into the intensive care unit rubbing their eyes. Daytime visitors are made to wear yellow paper robes, but we get to wear our hospital gowns or the nighties we've brought from home. You can tell who's just given birth because they've got blood-stains soaking through the back. We don't speak. We sit in rockers, the shyer ones of us behind screens. We smile blissed-out zombie smiles when the nurses deposit the swaddled packages in our arms. We make up nicknames for our babies, murmur encouragements in the hopes that they will eat up, that things will improve and we can go home. It hurts at first, but it's good, those little gums clamping onto our defenseless nipples.

The Magical Fruit

Before I am free to move in to the intensive care unit's isolation room, I run through three roommates in a semi-private room in the maternity ward. My second roommate in the maternity ward is

Peggy. We have a lot in common. We're both white, American and educated. We're roughly the same age, but most importantly, Peggy's son Bertram has landed in NICU too.

"It's so unfair!" she complains as we sprawl on our messy beds like college freshmen. "It's because I had a fever in labor, one little fever that lasted no more that five minutes! That shouldn't count!"

Unfortunately for Peggy, them's the rules. If a mother runs a fever during labor for any amount of time, the baby goes directly to NICU, does not pass go, does not collect 200 dollars. So Bertram's stuck in NICU, though according to his mother, he's as right as rain. The catch is that they won't release Peggy from the maternity ward. She had Bertram by Cesarean section and they won't let her go until she farts. I forget why this is exactly, something to do with her incision. Maybe they need to know that she can pass gas without splitting herself open.

She spends huge amounts of time in our bathroom, trying to make herself fart. The nurses keep returning to check if Peggy has managed to fart yet. "Oh well, keep trying," they boom heartily as Peggy, ashen, reports yet another failure. "Don't worry, you will, sooner or later! We can't let you out until you do."

In a rush of co-housing generosity, I notify Peggy every time I plan to take a shower. I tell her she can barge on in if she needs to use the toilet, as if she needs indoor plumbing to fart! I am really enjoying the seeming normality of my relationship with Peggy, my comrade-in-arms. I like hearing about her Cesarean section, her husband and the various names they'd considered before settling on Bertram. When Peggy's around, my nightmare is confined to the NICU one floor below. Her nightmare is a pleasant diversion for me. Like the nurses, I'm convinced that sooner or later, she's going to fart.

Peggy's family arrives, mother, father, younger sister, roses, balloons. She's told me that they're very repressed. "Pass gas?" I wonder. Is that the term she's using with her family? "Demonstrate the ability to be flatulent?" Embarrassed as they may be, they're rooting for her, but . . . nothing. She can't fart. She cries when they leave without her.

I want to encourage her to eat beets, tofu, raw cauliflower and broccoli, but I stop myself because, really, what do I know? I'm not a doctor. I'm merely an actor with a diploma from massage school who likes to throw around medical jargon. What if after several bowls of vegetarian chili, the gas builds and builds in Peggy's body until it blows her incision wide open. I don't want to be held responsible for that.

Friends who've visited me in the maternity ward call to check on Peggy's progress. "Has your roommate farted yet?" they giggle, hoping for a funny anecdote. Everybody thinks it's hilarious except for Peggy, who sobs bitterly in her husband's arms.

"I'm trying," she wails, "but I can't!"

I wonder if it's enough to just fart or does she have to fart in a nurse's presence in order for it to be official. I tell her that I am prepared to act as a witness if and when she farts. I reiterate my offer several times.

One day I return from a visit to the NICU to find Peggy dressed in a brand-new outfit, one of those prim jumpers with vertical slits for discreet breast-feeding. She's triumphantly shoving roses and toiletries into the plastic bags the hospital provides departing mothers.

"You did it?" I cry as Peggy smoothes Bertram's Baby Gap homecoming outfit on her bed.

"Yeah," she acknowledges modestly. I'm losing my roommate. Her mind is already back on her real life.

Oh, man, I am so jealous. Not because—hey, look, I can fart anytime I want to.

Spacemonkey

She is getting better, I can tell. The nurses leave us alone and say things like "I'll bet you'll be glad to get out of here." We have to stay for the whole ten-day course of prescribed antibiotics but then we can go home. I was discharged from the maternity ward the day we named her. I raced to the East Village, flipped through the mail, burrowed around in the clean laundry and called my friend Karen in Scotland. She hadn't heard anything since I emailed her to tell her I was in labor. She'd been too afraid to call, terrified that something had gone horribly wrong. Like dead kind of wrong. I gabbled a four-minute version of the birth while across the Atlantic Ocean, she stood clutching a bath towel around her. "I have to go!" I shouted happily, delirious with humidity and smells. I grabbed Jambo and buried my face in his fur while he writhed in indignation. As soon as I could, I bolted, shouting instructions to Greg over my shoulder. I took a cab back to the hospital, scrubbed at the sink outside the NICU, and moved into my new home, an isolation room for contagious infants. Sometimes, if they know the end is near, the nurses move a salad bin into the little room to give the family some privacy. I'd been told that I could stay there as long as they don't need the room. I cross my fingers, hoping that my selfish wish will inadvertently spare someone else's infant from contagion and death. A nurse shows me how to convert the vinyl easy chair into a bed. She brings me sheets and a blanket. It's so much better than the maternity ward. I'm just steps away from the baby. The only thing lacking is a bathroom, which is a bit of a problem, given the tender condition of my no-longer-private parts. Peeing is agony. Sometimes I slip out to buy a sandwich or shower at the home of some friends in the West Village, but I can never stay away for long. Greg comes every night in his temping clothes.

The nurses keep telling us to take a break. "We've got everything under control here. Go on, have dinner, enjoy!" They ham it up like relatives who can't wait to be pressed into service as unpaid baby-sitters. "Don't worry about us! We'll be fine," they chuckle, patting our arms.

So Greg and I go on a date. It feels sort of irresponsible, eating in what is to us a nice restaurant while our baby lies in intensive care, but the nurses were adamant in a jocular way. To not go would seem disrespectful of their hospitality. They don't have to let me crash on their isolation room Hide-A-Bed, after all. We go to a pasta place around the corner. I hate pasta, but that's okay. I can barely eat, I'm so hyper. I'm like Jambo on those rare occasions when he's set foot on grass. We order wine. I need some. It's bizarre, the waiter doesn't know we have a new baby. Nobody would know unless we tell them. It's like we have this secret baby. I want to get back and see her. "Let's go see the baby!" we tell each other halfway through the meal. I twitch in my seat, pleating and unpleating my dinner napkin while Greg tries to expedite the bill.

When we return from dinner, we are told that India has to get a new IV. The baby-sitting-grandma game is over. A tough-as-nails Israeli nurse shows us how our baby's skin has become discolored and rotten where it is punctured by the current IV. When we unwrap the Velcro cast that keeps the IV tube from tangling with the heart and pulse monitors, it looks like her whole arm is eaten up with gangrene. I think about junkies shooting up in the soles of their feet when the veins in their arms collapse.

The nurse shoos us into the isolation room so she can insert a fresh IV. Feeling powerless, we allow ourselves to be shooed. I feel like we're waiting out an execution. A baby's scream splits the air. Not to be dramatic, but a baby's screams split the air. It is nighttime. All of the babies are sleeping except for one baby, my baby, who screams like she is being cut in half.

I am not chained to the wall. No one is restraining me at gun-point. I could rush to her bedside and try somehow to save her from what she surely experiences as hopeless excruciating pain, torture. But I don't. I huddle in the isolation room, staring miserably at Greg, crying. All I do is cry these days. What a shit situation this is. What a shit situation for us and our poor, poor baby, our little baby girl. My god, what are they doing to her? It sounds unspeakable, like something from Bosnia or Kigali.

The screaming stops and baby is wheeled in, calm and swaddled.

The IV is coming out of her head. Her head. An anthill of flesh-colored tape is stuck like a tumor to the top of her skull. Spouting out of that is the tube of an IV. There is a wad of tape in my baby's fragile, wispy hair. She has a tube growing out of her head. I can't believe this is happening to me, happy, pregnant me, who painted a mandala on her big exposed belly to prance along the boardwalk in the Coney Island mermaid parade just two short weeks ago. I'm the one whose baby who needs a tube in her head to keep her alive.

"Okay," the Israeli nurse tells me with a naughty smile on her face, "I didn't tell you where we were going to put it, because I knew you'd freak out."

Ha-ha. Stupid parents. I don't laugh. I'm usually good for a laugh, out of courtesy if not genuine amusement. There is a tube in my baby's head. I don't find that funny at all. I'm a bad sport. They're putting tubes in her head. Now they'll never let us out of here. God, it looks so bad.

Things appear brighter in the morning. I take to calling the tube the antenna. The Israeli nurse loves this. She tells me if we ever come back to visit, and she's forgotten who we are, just say "antenna" and she'll remember. Spacemonkey needs her antenna to receive transmissions from outer space. She is Spacemonkey. She comes from Space! Oh, you foolish earthlings, I am here to tell you that you can get used to anything. Anything. Especially when you wind up baptized by fire.

Perspective

People are always asking me if any of the babies died. Everybody wants to know if any of the babies died. And the answer is no. Not while I was there. The babies lived and were kept alive by some of the most sophisticated medical technology money can buy. The tiny preemies would die without it. India would've died without antibiotics.

"Do you know how sick your baby was when she was brought in

here?" one of the graveyard-shift nurses asks curiously as we stand shoulder to shoulder over India's salad bin late one night.

The answer again is no. I didn't know. I guess if we'd have had her in a cabin in Vermont the way we do in my hippie fantasy, she would've died. Greg likes to remind me that I would've died too. A hundred years ago, I would've died. But not now. The babies didn't die. I can't imagine what it would be like in there the day a baby dies. The isolation room where I lived had wall switches labeled "oxygen" and "vacuum" and an observation window just like an operating theater in a movie. I slept like a baby in there away from the phones and the visitors and the trays of hospital food and none of the babies died, no.

Four babies died that August in a neonatal intensive care unit in Boston. They were contaminated by a virus from outside and they died. The unit was closed down when the staff saw, too late, what was happening. I can't imagine, but I do.

A couple of months before India was born, a family friend gave birth to a baby with three holes in her heart. She's still alive today. They let her parents take her home after teaching them how to hook her up to a portable oxygen kit and how to insert a feeding tube down her throat. She's amazed the doctors. Everybody thinks she's lived as long as she has because she's got such loving parents, but you know, even with that, she won't grow up. She's brought her family a lot of joy with the heartbreak. "It's a hard road," my mother says sadly when I ask how they're doing. Very few people can speak of this child without shaking their heads, even as they describe how much her older brother loves her, how patient and strong her mother is. I can't imagine but I do.

Some nights I leaned my forehead against India's salad bin and wept. Looking up, I'd see a mother crying across from me. Another was crying a few salad bins down the aisle. "It isn't fair! It isn't fair!" one sobbed to a sympathetic nurse. Not only did she get a backrub, she got to go home with her baby two days later. Suspecting that I might get points for being a good sport as well as a good parent, I remarked to the same nurse, "I can't complain. I know there are other people here whose situations are much grimmer than mine. I have a friend whose baby has three holes in her heart."

"Well," the nurse replied, "it's a place of broken dreams. No matter what the situation is, it boils down to somebody's dream being shattered."

After she said that, I felt like I could relax. Yeah, my dream was shattered but my baby is alive. I used to dream about living in a huge loft in Manhattan. It was in Manhattan, but it had a Brooklyn Heights view of the Manhattan skyline. God only knows what that would cost. I'd be a long-haired actress with framed posters of my Broadway plays lining the walls. I'd live there with the pretty boy on whom I had a crush but we wouldn't get married because I never wanted there to be a shadow of a doubt that I was wilder than my preppy high-school friends. What are dreams? They're plates you can afford to hurl against the wall as long as the important things escape unharmed.

But Enough About the Baby

So, you're probably wondering what happened to me. All these veiled references to not being able to walk and pain upon urination? Just let me say that if anyone ever tries to pour hydrogen peroxide into your vagina, if they tell you that your stitches have disappeared and your seven hours of pushing resulted in a hematoma that went unnoticed for days, if they tell you that hydrogen peroxide is good for that, if they ask you to put your feet in the stirrups and scoot your butt down to the end of the table so they can apply hydrogen peroxide, if they give you a little squeeze bottle of hydrogen peroxide and instructions on how to use it yourself, you just tell them no. It's nothing like taking care of your freshly pierced ears.

The Fourth of July

My baby has never seen weather, has never smelled rain. Her sunrises have all been fluorescent.

It is our last night in NICU. July 14. My grandmother's birthday. Oh, how she would have loved to see this baby. Tomorrow morning we get to go home. Our friends Sarah and Jesse are coming for us in a car. They will pick up Little MoMo on the way. Greg won't be able to join us. He'll be temping at that bank in Long Island City, so we can continue to receive that wonderful, *wonderful* health insurance.

My friend the tough Israeli nurse throws India's last dose of antibiotics into the trash because the Spacemonkey's IV insertion site looks grungy. There's no good place left to stick a needle. If she were a junkie, she'd have to spread her toes or worse. The nurse tells me that India doesn't need the medicine anyway. I have a healthy baby. We still have to spend the night though, one last night on the NICU's couch.

I think about all the babies who have passed through this place. Thousands. We leave on July 15, the day after Bastille Day, the day that was my grandmother's birthday, one month shy of the 50th anniversary of India's independence from the British Empire. The tough nurse hugs me and plants a kiss on the baby whose name she has not yet forgotten. "Good-bye, India," she says, shaking her sensible, authoritarian head. "You're going home to sleep with your parents in the family bed, oh my god."

My friends have gained permission to enter the Neonatal Intensive Care Unit to help carry away my belongings and the many pink and white vinyl diaper bags the nurses have boosted for us from the supply room shelves. They've loaded them up with complimentary formula and diaper coupons. They present me with a stash of frozen breast milk, little bottles labeled with my name and the date they were pumped, relics from my days on the maternity ward.

My friends act like they're entering the convent of a cloistered order, which in a sense, they are. Only parents, grandparents and siblings of the neonates are guaranteed passage beyond those double doors. Once my friend Handsome Dick made it past the lobby security only to be apprehended near the scrub sink. He pressed his face to the glass but all he could see were a few unoccupied salad bins and a hamper of dirty linen. I teach my friends how to scrub their hands with the disposable pumice stones stacked outside the unit, how to attack their fingernails with the white plastic brush. We all agree that it seems like a waste to chuck these nifty wash-up kits in the trash after just one use, even if there is an undeniable surgical

thrill to the procedure. I usher my guests into my mysterious quarters, pointing out the various amenities. Like a retirement home
director intent on reassuring the adult children of a potential
inmate, I demonstrate how the easy chair in the isolation room con-
verts to a cot in one easy motion. I am trying not to cry.

Little MoMo treads around the ward on tiptoe, whispering,
taking note of Jeremiah and the crack babies. She has not seen
India since the day after she was born, several eternities ago. In the
interim, a satellite has landed on Mars and beamed photographs of
its surface back to earth. I have not seen a single one of these
images. "You aren't missing much," a nurse told me. "It looks like
Arizona."

Who cares about Mars? At last I get to hear a friend run through
the litany. "She's so beautiful," which she is, and "God, she's so big,"
which she isn't. "She's so alert!" MoMo whispers. "She's looking
right at me! Did you see that? Did you see what she did?" Nothing
can describe the joy of having someone, not a nurse, not my husband, not me, admire my almost-newborn baby. Later, MoMo tells
me about a dream she had while I was in the hospital. In the dream
India was sitting on her lap, muttering "It was so much farther than
you think. It was so much farther than you think."

My favorite nurse rides the elevator to the lobby with us. She's
excited too. She tells us that she loves to be around for happy end-
ings. It's weird, for a moment there, I almost don't want to get out
of the elevator. I want to go back down to the isolation room and eat
a pear and look at India in a salad bin. Sarah is waiting in the car on
the corner of 11th and Greenwich. She's been ready to drive this
baby home from the hospital since Little MoMo called on July 3 to

tell her that I was in labor. We have a car seat and everything. Without looking backward, we step over the hospital's threshold into the first sunlight India Reed Kotis has ever seen. The heat wave hasn't broken. It feels almost like the Fourth of July.

Waiting for Milo

On the eve of Inky's third birthday, I got up at two in the morning to stuff goodie bags with rubber aliens, colored markers and paper cocktail umbrellas. The temperature had dropped to the low 80s, but it felt more like a toasty 425 degrees since I was a week shy of my due date and as big as a sauna. My insomnia usually doesn't result in productivity; instead, I let my mind race, tabulating past misdeeds and singing the same verse of "Hello, Dolly!" over and over until sleep comes. This time, though, I had to get up. I knew if I lay awake fretting about going into labor the night before Inky's party, I would go into labor before Inky's party and one of the guest's mothers would find herself stuck in the role of hostess with a bunch of unstuffed goodie bags. It was too big of a risk. Half of the children who'd be attending had younger siblings in the pipeline. What if Nancy took over the helm, only to go into labor herself? I started stuffing faster. Once the bags were done, I stuck candles in the cake. I took the cellophane wrappers off pointy hats and paper plates decorated with suitably noncorporate smiley faces. Mission accomplished, I returned to bed and stared at the stripes of light the Venetian blinds cast on the ceiling. I still couldn't sleep.

What if I went into labor before our friend Karen arrived from Chicago to witness the miracle of birth, video camera in hand? What if I didn't go into labor until after Karen had returned to Chicago on her nonrefundable ticket? What if I wound up in the hospital again instead of in the birthing center? What if the baby came out on the Brooklyn Bridge, with Inky jabbering beside me in her car seat? What if none of the friends who'd volunteered to take Inky were home and the contractions were coming at two-minute intervals? Hellooooooo Dolly.

I made it through the party. The other pregnant women fetched me cake and lemonade, insisting that I remain seated, that I was nuts to throw a birthday party when I looked ready to drop that sucker any minute. I acted like it was no big deal, although as anyone who has ever thrown a birthday party for a dozen small children in a comparatively small un-air-conditioned New York apartment over the July fourth holiday can tell you, it's almost as stressful as planning a wedding. The prospect of my water breaking midway through the festivities only added to the high-tension fun. Only later did it occur to me how wonderful and strange it would have been for my babies to arrive on the exact same date. That's the only-child's perspective. "Are you kidding?" Greg said. "That would suck!" He should know. Not only is he a younger brother, his birthday comes just a few days after Christmas.

I made it through the Fourth of July. You have to go early to get the million-dollar view of the fireworks showering the East River with the Statue of Liberty in the background and the windows of Wall Street reflecting the colorful dandelion bursts. Citing the heat, Greg suggested that we stay at home in front of the fan. If Inky went to sleep early, we could rent a movie. "You reached your goal with the birthday party," he said in an attempt to persuade me. "Why not take it easy?" I glared at him like a great motherly battleship. You don't move to Brooklyn from the East Village to spend the Fourth of July nodding out on a video! The spirit of family fun possessed me. We were going to see those fireworks. "At least let me carry your bag," Greg said as we set off toward the river. It wasn't even dusk and already a great throng had gathered on the public basketball courts on the other side of the expressway. Inky was showing signs of wear and tear, having been too jacked up on presents and leftover goodie bags to retire much before midnight on the third. We stood with the rest of the herd, Greg refraining from saying "I told you so," me frequently asking, "Isn't this fun?" Eventually, a young couple gave up their valuable curbside seats to the wilting little girl and the enormous woman with the swollen ankles. Our neighbors shot us nervous, sidelong glances. "Lucky there's a hospital up the street," several jokers remarked, each well pleased with the originality of their comment. I smiled and nodded, worried that a preternaturally loud boom might be all it would take to push me over the brink. If I suddenly found myself screaming towards one of those speedy second labors while watching the fireworks on the Brooklyn side of the East River, that's exactly where I'd end up: the hospital two blocks away. I had just gotten out of that place, having spent twelve days in June hospitalized for listeria, a food-borne bacterial infection that targets women in their third trimester of pregnancy. I was told that I was lucky, that many pregnant women with listeria go into pre-term labor, often delivering stillborn babies. Ultrasounds confirmed that Milo was just fine and as a "bonus" I had to spent twelve days in air-conditioned comfort while the rest of the city sweltered through a heat wave the likes of which hadn't been seen since Inky was in St. Vincent's. Hopefully, my luck would hold. I wanted to have my baby at the birth center in Manhattan, the one where I'd labored so hard precisely three years and one day earlier. I wanted this baby to come out underwater: no IVs, no oxygen masks, nobody calling me "Mommy Holiday" because they didn't know my name. I didn't want to wind up in any hospital, even if the windows of the maternity ward up the street offered the best possible view of the fireworks that would hopefully refrain from sending a pregnant lady into labor. That first supersonic *kaboom* did nothing to me, but it scared the bejesus out of Inky. Greg and I pointed at the sky, gabbling, "Pretty! Pretty!" while she screamed in sustained terror and clawed at my jutting belly like a cat climbing out of the toilet.

I looked at Greg. An unusually blissful expression animated his face as he met each explosion with an appreciative "ooh" or "ahh!" He was having a New York moment. "Greg, I think we have to leave," I whispered.

When we got home, I stripped naked and forced Greg to apply wet plaster to my breasts and belly so that Milo and I would have a lasting record of our shared humongousness. Little MoMo and I had planned to make a belly cast right after dinner the night I ended up going into labor with Inky. I'd always regretted that we'd cut it too close to the bone with that one. Greg could see that I had my heart set on this embarrassing monument, so he spread some newspaper on the floor and told me to get comfortable. Even with the fan aimed at me, I was sweating bullets. I imagined that it would be a leisurely affair, almost like getting a massage or being worshipped as a graven fertility image. Instead, the strips of plaster-saturated webbing felt as clammy as eels going over my belly. Little rivulets ran down into my pubic hair, which we had inexpertly sealed off with masking tape and Saran Wrap. I started panting through my nostrils. "You gonna make it?" Greg asked. "Try to hold still. We're almost done." I tossed my head and gurgled.

"You're not going to throw up, are you?" Greg stepped back, his plaster-coated hands held high, like a surgeon's.

"Just hurry," I hissed through gritted teeth. Oh, man, I didn't feel so good. It was like that time in college, when I collapsed during a costume fitting for *Antigone*. I'd come to in a heap, trapped under the folds of my heavy robes, that hideous mask still attached to my face. This felt worse. The skin prickled on my exposed back and the room started to spin. I was suddenly afraid I might lose control of my bowels. Like a panicky crab, I dropped to my knees and scuttled free of the white dome that was calcifying around my vulnerable flesh. Lurching off the newspaper, I collapsed on my side, hugging my knees and moaning.

"Okay. Okay." Greg held my abandoned plaster torso gingerly. "Uh, okay."

"Get me a beer," I whimpered once the danger of shitting myself had past. I stood under the shower, scratching at stubborn flecks of white with my fingernails. The baby shifted just under my hands, my abdomen temporarily asymmetrical as his little heinie bulged from its new location. It was a relief to feel him move. I was worried I might have suffocated him, like that Bond girl who gets dipped in gold paint in *Goldfinger*.

Cleaned off and calmer, I lay beside Greg, admiring the sculpture we had just made. It was a good thing I'd bought fast-drying plaster. Bailing out early hadn't affected it too adversely—it was a little caved in, maybe. Greg was dissatisfied that it wasn't perfect. He suggested that the next morning one of us make a trip to the little West Village pharmacy where I'd bought the plaster rolls so we could try again. I decided that I could live with a slightly inaccurate record of this pregnancy. It was big enough, that was what counted.

Milo was due on July 10th. Five more days to go. With the birthday party and the fireworks out of the way, all I had to worry about was making it until Karen's flight arrived at 11:59 P.M. on July 8. I was keen on pretending that other people's babies might arrive days ahead of their due date, but not mine. On the other hand, nature laughs at the puny calendar to which we women affix so much importance: It has rained cats and dogs for almost every outdoor wedding I've attended. I figured I'd better make a plan. Inky used her final days as an only child to pester me into playing with all the toys she had received for her birthday. I prefer to do my thinking sprawled flat on the couch, but toiling in the Play-Doh factory doesn't tax my mental capacities too heavily. As I pressed round after round of inedible pasta shapes for my three-year-old boss, I compulsively ran through the elaborate system I'd worked out in case I went into labor while Greg was on his way to meet Karen's plane. As soon as my water broke, I would call my old roommate Carol, who lived around the corner with her husband, Brian. She swore on a stack of figurative Bibles that they would be home between the hours of 10:30 and 1:30 and not out tossing back margaritas at some hot new dance club, the way childless couples do, and even promised she wouldn't screen the calls. I felt guilty in advance about the possibility of interrupting a video or a matrimonial clinch. Carol told me to stop being such a queerball. If I went into labor, I could call them and they would come. With Carol and Brian rushing the two blocks to our apartment, I would call Greg's cell phone to redirect him to the birthing center. Hopefully, he would have Karen in the car with him by this point. I wasn't worrying for nothing; Karen's not known for her plane luck—she travels frequently and has a history of missed connections. Once her diabetic meal poisoned her over the Atlantic Ocean. I had fixated on a couple of hours past 11:59 P.M., July 8 as my all clear to go ahead and have the baby. In all likelihood, that magical moment might find Karen on the tarmac at O'Hare while a summer storm lit up the corporate complexes in the cornfields surrounding the airport. "Don't think that way," I chastised myself. "She'll get here. This is just an exercise, a just-in-case."

And I *did* have a plan. I had worked it out with Carol to escort me to the birthing center. Brian would get into bed beside Inky. Chances were she'd sleep through the night if she were butted up against a big, warm mammal. Brian seemed a little embarrassed by his job assignment, but I figured he'd rather do that than accompany a bucking, screeching woman to the birthing center. Let him do that when it's his own wife. Until then, he'd just have to put up with Inky's feet in his ribs. "She's a thrasher," I'd warned him over the phone. "Hopefully, my water won't break in bed, but even if it does, it's a king size, so you won't have to lie in the wet spot. I'll try to remember to put Inky in a diaper so there's no accident. Don't worry, Brian, it'll be fine."

"Uh, okay," he'd said. "I'd better hand the phone back to Carol now."

In the end, Karen's plane landed with Karen aboard five minutes before 11:59, July 8. I was still pregnant. Carol and Brian were let go.

The morning before my due date, I took Karen and Inky to Atlantic Avenue to stock up on middle-eastern groceries. Imagining my labor as a Lebanese buffet was a pleasant antidote to imagining my labor on the Brooklyn Bridge. The birthing center's food policy is particularly appealing. A laboring mother is not permitted to eat in the hospital, but at the Seton Center, the midwives encourage you to fuel the machine for the grueling task ahead. You can eat before, during and after. "Pack carbs," they had advised. What a kick that was for a miserable athlete like me. I haven't participated in a race since the potato fell off my spoon midway through Field Day twenty-six years ago. On the way to Sahadi's, I strutted like a 180-pound Wilma Rudolph. "I need to pack carbs," I announced with great self-importance. Karen, who's got six-pack abs and the endurance of a Grand Canyon mule, nodded. It was almost too hot to speak. I would probably go into labor while we walked the five blocks to the market. I wondered if there'd still be time to grab a couple of tubs of hummus if the pangs started right then.

We bought that hummus, and goat cheese, pita bread, tara-masalata, fancy crackers, pumpkin seeds and dried cherries. Watching our favorite bulk-bin guy slip Inky a handful of choco-late raisins, I realized that the next time I saw him, Milo would be on the outside. What a mind screw! I had felt the same way replacing the filter in our water pitcher a few days before Inky was due. Sure enough, the next time I changed the filter, there was a baby staring at me from the massage table we used as a couch.

Back at home, we immediately dug into our stash. Why not? Life's too short not to pack carbs whenever you feel like it. If we ate it all, we could go back and buy more. I'd gone to the cash machine earlier in the week and made a big withdrawal for emergency cab fare. Now that Karen was here we could buy middle-eastern food every day of the week! Why refrain from digging in until I was in labor? I might not go into a labor for a week! Oh my god, what if I didn't go into labor for a week and Karen had to fly back to Chicago and didn't get to be there for the birth?

Milo was hogging the real estate usually taken up by my stomach, so I couldn't eat much, but Karen and Greg had a good feed. The only thing I didn't get a taste of was the goat cheese. After the whole listeria episode, Greg forbade unpasteurized cheese and deli meats for the remainder of the pregnancy. "Obey me, woman!" he shouted, whisking the small plate out of reach. "Karen, please have some more. Inky, do you want to try this cheese? It comes from the goat."

"That's yuck," Inky said, sticking out her tongue. "I want more chock-lick raisins."

I detoured toward the hummus instead. Milo would be here any day. I could eat as much goat cheese as I wanted next week, nursing the baby on the couch while Greg did all the housework.

Milo didn't show up on his due date. Instead, we took the eighth issue of the *East Village Inky* to the printers. On the way back, we swung by the birthing center so that Karen could see where we would be having the baby. Elissa, the midwife on duty, examined me. "You look good," she said. "Anytime now."

I got my hair cut so that I would look tough in the first few photos of Milo's baby book. The woman shearing me like a sheep insisted that I was carrying a girl. Five billion sonograms to which I submitted in the hospital meant nothing to her. I told her that we had seen that little twig right from the start. We locked eyes in the mirror. "I am psychic. Is girl," she growled in a heavy Russian accent. Jesus. What if she was right? We had plenty of newborn diapers on hand, but nothing resembling a girl's name. Maybe a bad haircut wasn't the only thing she was saddling me with. She looked pissed that I had dared to question her authority. What if she really did have supernatural powers? She could put a hex on me like Baba Yaga!

The next day was E. B. White's 101st birthday, a good day to be born. If Milo had come out on July 10, when he was supposed to, he'd have had to share his birthday with David Brinkley. In my opinion, it was far more auspicious to have something in common with the man who wrote *Charlotte's Web, Stuart Little* and dozens of essays praising New York City, an unequivocating humanist with no patience for the politics of segregation. Plus, it was Karen's anniversary, which meant almost two years had gone by since I began work on the first *East Village Inky*. The heat had not broken. The soles of our feet were black with that awful New York grime that covers everything in the dog days, even if you don't go outside. Dispiritedly, we polished off the last of the middle-eastern food. I tried to make it through some of White's essays, hoping Milo would be inspired to come out, but it was so humid, I could barely concentrate. I stopped between sentences to see if the essays were having the desired effect. Inky whined, trying to get us to budge from the couch to play some long, nonsensical game of her own invention. "Why don't you get a good book out of your bookcase and read to yourself in your room?" I suggested, turning my sweaty face toward the fan.

"But I don't know to read by my ownself!" she wailed.

"Sure you do," I lied, hoping one of the other adults would be the first to cave in when she came around the next time, that execrable, oversized Busytown tucked under her small arm.

The next day, Karen and Greg woke up sicker than dogs with grass hangovers. Their misery was so extreme, I was sure it was a hoax. Greg curled shivering under our purple and white quilt, calling weakly for more blankets despite the waves of heat the morning sun sent through the window. Karen lay motionless on the couch, her arm flung across her eyes. Inky poked her tentatively in the ribs. Karen barely made a sound. They weren't kidding. I was hot, huge and irritable, but compared to them, I was a silver medal- list on the parallel bars. All fingers pointed to the goat cheese that my lord and master had forbidden me to eat. Before my own taste of lis- teria, I always thought food poisoning was something people cooked up to get out of gym class. It turns out that delicious things really can cause pounding headaches, killer diarrhea and high fever. Oh no, what if Karen and Greg were seriously ill? What if Greg missed the birth of his son because he was too sick to take his head out of the toilet? I paced around our tiny kitchen in ever-diminishing circles. "Daddy smells bad," Inky reported from the bedroom.

Somebody had to take charge of the situation. Slapping a big smile on my face, I offered to go around the corner for iced coffee and Tylenol. "Inky and I can use the fresh air!" I said, as chipper as a nurse in an old folks' home. Karen flexed her fingers once by way of goodbye.

Outside, it was humid and smoggy. The sidewalks along Smith Street were dotted with dog shit, escort service flyers and the damp acrylic sweaters disappointed trash pickers had discarded on top of the Hefty bags they'd torn open. I could barely open my eyes for the glare. Inky wanted pizza, so after we got the Tylenol, we walked a half a block farther to the place where the most hard-bitten of the local juvenile delinquents hang out, talking trash and dropping their crumpled napkins on the floor. What a disgusting day. Dismally, I predicted that the cloud of bad vibes enveloping Brooklyn would do for me what the fireworks had not.

When we got home, I went directly into the bathroom. I must warn you, the next sentence contains a phrase that will cause unease in most men and uncontrollable mirth in children aged eight to fifteen. As I suspected, I had lost my mucous plug. I never noticed this savory little item the first time around with Inky, but it's one of those things midwives tell you to be on the lookout for if you're worried that you won't be able to tell if you're in labor. This begs the question of how you'll be able to recognize a mucous plug. To that I can only say: You'll know. Unless you absentmindedly spilled half a bottle of rubber cement in your pants, it's the mucous plug. Its appearance means that the seal is broken. The cervix is ready for action. I poked my head out of the bathroom to give Karen the joyous news. "Oh, that's...great," she whispered, rolling herself into the fetal position.

I called the midwife on duty to report this development. I told her that I didn't feel like birth was imminent in the next hour or two, but I asked if maybe we could come to the center anyway. Normally the midwives won't admit you unless you're howling like a monkey. Given my recent illness, my Brooklyn Bridge phobia, and the tendency of second children to come more quickly than first, Catherine said she would be willing to make an exception in my case. Lest she think I was some nervous Nellie, I told her that my birth partners appeared to have food poisoning.

"God, what is it with your family?" she asked. "Okay. Come whenever you want."

I bounded around the apartment, filling a grocery bag with extra clothes and the tapes I'd made for Inky's birth, the ones we'd completely forgotten to play. The only food in the joint was a gnarly banana, but I figured Karen and Greg wouldn't be hungry and I could pick up something for myself when we dropped Inky off in the East Village. Inky's backpack had been hanging from a hook on the front door, ready to go for days. Just in case, I unpacked it to reassure myself that she hadn't been pulling stuff out of it on the sly. She never asks permission to replace her snack and extra panties with seven wooden blocks, one of my bras and the handset of the cordless phone. Satisfied that she had all the gear I thought she needed, including a crisp twenty-dollar bill and xeroxed contact sheets for everyone who had agreed to baby-sit her, we headed into the city. Traffic flowed like water from an artesian well. Greg's face was drained of all color, but somehow he managed to operate our vehicle, his mother's 1987 un-air-conditioned Dodge Shadow. I chattered gaily from the backseat, trying to keep up everybody's end of the conversation. Greg and Karen could do little more than grunt. Every time we hit a pothole, they moaned. I felt guilty, knowing that they were upright because of me. When I'm that sick, all I want is the bed at my grandmother's house, a cool breeze to lift the white curtains and a glass of water, sweaty with condensation, on the nightstand. When that's unavailable, as it has been for well over a decade, I like to lie very still and think about it. That's how sick they were. My heart sank behind my chipper front. I wanted them to be as excited as I was. I felt like the kid who's spent all semester talking about her Halloween costume, only to find out on the afternoon of the big party that no one else in the dorm feels like getting dressed up. I wondered if there was any chance of them making a miraculous recovery in time for Milo's arrival. Probably not. It was miracle enough that Greg hadn't steered us off the bridge into the East River.

We swung by the East Village to drop Inky off in front of her best friend Abby's building. She was so concerned with undoing the tricky clasp on the doctor's kit she'd insisted on bringing that she could barely be bothered to kiss me goodbye. "You're having a baby!" Abby's pregnant mother, Anna, laughed as she herded the girls into the building. "I can't believe it!" Finally, someone felt healthy enough to show the proper excitement. I knew what she meant too. Despite months comparing notes on morning sickness, ligament pain and our daughters' dimly recalled infant behavior, I too found it difficult to wrap my head around the notion that the moment was indeed at hand.

"I'll try not to take too long," I called out the passenger window.

"Don't worry about us!" she cried. "Take all the time you need!

Inky, wave to your mommy." Inky glanced over her shoulder briefly. Abby obediently turned and waved, a wide grin splitting her face. Strange. I didn't experience anything near the sense of discombobulation I'd felt saying goodbye to the bulk-bin guy at Sahadi's as I left my first child to give birth to my second. I was already busy figuring out where we would park the car on 14th Street, where the meters cost twenty-five cents for fifteen minutes.

"Is there a garage?" Karen asked. She told us a story about her first husband, how he was nutting out on the way to their wedding because he was uptight about finding a place to park near the courthouse. He was so thrifty that he'd rather drive around for an hour, hunting for a space on the street, than pay to park in a downtown Chicago garage. Finally, Karen and their two witnesses had convinced him that it was okay to cough up the expensive hourly rate in exchange for peace of mind on his own wedding day. I was convinced. I fingered all the money I'd gotten out of the cash machine, trying to act like I'd never for a second entertained the thought of sending Karen out to feed the meter at regular intervals throughout my labor.

With the car squirreled away indefinitely, we entered the center. Both receptionists turned out to greet us. "If you're here to deliver, just go on back!" they said. The women awaiting their prenatal appointments on the lobby couches peered at us, smiling. I was there once when a woman in labor arrived. She was pretty cranky, but still I felt lucky to witness the special moment. Like when a rumpled father emerges from the back, carrying a brand-new baby in its car seat like a basket of eggs. The whole waiting room coos and the man looks like he can't wait to get home.

I led the way to the inner sanctum, a comfortable common area surrounded by three birthing suites. They each have a king-sized bed, a deep oval Jacuzzi, a rocking chair with a removable seat, a bathroom, and cabinets stocked with disposable blue pads and stainless steel instruments. Their cleanliness is very Zen—you have to take off your shoes just to enter. The common area they open onto is equipped to accommodate extended family members' needs with a kitchenette, comfy couches, a TV, a VCR and an appealing wood and wire puzzle table. I could just imagine Inky jamming a tape into the VCR upside down as my mother listened to me screaming on the other side of the door. Prior to Inky's arrival, I had tried to convince Greg that we should invite the six friends who had stood up with us at our wedding to join us for the birth. When he'd objected on the grounds that he didn't want his brother and his best friend staring at my most internal parts, I lobbied to have them in the common room. In the end, Little MoMo was the only one of the six who attended. Now it was Karen's turn.

The common area also serves as the midwives' break room. Several of them were gathered around the circular table eating Chinese food from cardboard containers when I glided in, eager to be assigned a birthing suite.

"Oh, no, she's smiling!" Elissa remarked. Elissa was the caustic one. There's always a caustic one, a no-nonsense one, a sweetie pie, a hippie-dippy one, one you want to be best friends with and one you never manage to meet until you're in labor. Really. Ask anyone who's ever gone through prenatal care and delivery at a birthing center staffed by six or so midwives. The others laughed and nodded at Elissa's bon mot, their cheeks bulging with noodles.

Greg and Karen limped in behind me. "She looks like *she's* the one in labor," Catherine declared, aiming her chopsticks at Karen. "Make yourself at home on the couch. You're not having a baby anytime soon. We'll get to you in a while."

"Wow, she's really no-nonsense," Karen whispered as we settled into the family waiting area. Greg stretched out like a corpse on the couch. I went to the kitchenette to fetch us some water and put our humble banana in the fridge. I'd been told that lots of families like to bring a bottle of champagne. We had some Pepto-Bismol, but that didn't need to be refrigerated. I hoped that I would be a little more obviously in labor soon. Maybe this was going to be one of those super-easy births, where the baby all of a sudden pops out, with no real pain to speak of. Maybe that's why I felt so regular. Maybe when they examined me, they'd find out I was already dilated to nine centimeters. That would be a good surprise. I really didn't want to be guilty of sounding a false alarm. That glob of goo I'd seen earlier had been the mucous plug, right? I returned to the waiting room feeling as joyful as a traveler who's just learned her plane won't be boarding for hours due to mechanical problems.

"Here, maybe this will help you get in the right mood," Karen said, positioning the headphones of her minidisc recorder over my ears. She had brought it along to record the birth. We had asked her to pack her video camera too. I'm not much of a one for seeing myself on video. I'm always horrified by the overanimation of my eyebrows. They look like bagworms, the way they writhe around on that big old forehead of mine. Photographs I can handle, but not video. The bridal edict I had issued prohibiting all video cameras from our wedding did not stop my sister-in-law's well-intentioned father from smuggling his Handicam into the ceremony. "You'll be glad when you see this," he'd assured me, overriding my strong objections to screening the tape at a family gathering a few weeks into my marriage. He was right. I did feel glad when we discovered that his grandson had recorded over our vows with *The Mighty Ducks II* before any of us had had a chance to relive the moment. As much as I hate my squirmy-wormy eyebrows and the sound of my own voice, I did like the idea of my son having a document of his first moments on earth. Plus, Karen has a master's degree in film and her tastes run along a much sharper edge than mine. I harbored hopes that her record of Milo's birth might turn out sufficiently arty that even I could stand to watch it. At the very least, I could listen to myself kicking up a rumpus on the CD she'd promised to burn from the minidisc. That held forensic appeal.

She'd done a dry run at my last prenatal appointment to be sure everything was working properly. I felt awkward around the microphone's big clown's nose, but Inky was a complete natural. She spent the first few minutes of the appointment tugging on the blood pressure cuff, insisting that she would take the reading her ownself. Jumping on a rolling desk chair, she scribbled furiously on my belly with the little wand that detects the baby's heartbeat. She flicked the lights on and off, chortling maniacally. She darted out the door and down the corridor more times than I could count. Something about that birthing center got Inky all jacked up, like a stand-up comedian on a talk show. At the seven-month mark, the midwives began to encourage me to set up a baby-sitting plan well in advance of my due date. "You're not going to want to deal with this," one of them remarked, gesturing to my gibbering, spinning child, "when the contractions start coming two minutes apart."

When Inky was a placid newborn, I had read something about a four-year-old who attended the drug-free birth of his younger sister. The mother in the article stated that whenever the pain had threatened to overwhelm her, she had looked into her child's attentive, trusting face and kept it together. As a result of this intense bonding experience, her children experienced zero sibling rivalry. At the time it had sounded like the wisest thing in the world, though with the traumatic delivery of Inky still fresh in my mind, I wasn't completely confident in my ability to channel my impulse to scream into reassuring yogic deep breathing. A couple of years after the article was published, I couldn't tap enough potential baby-sitters. I had nine names on my list and would have felt better with ten. I was eternally grateful to Anna and Little MoMo and all the other volunteers. What a nightmare that would have been to have Inky here with us. Except Inky was here with us. Karen's minidisc had captured it all. With that last prenatal visit broadcasting the headphones, I couldn't believe how pervasive and invasive my child seemed. She was horrid! I took this child to restaurants? Drawers banged, wheels squeaked and a handful of tongue depressors hit the floor as she whirled around the small examining room. Every now and then my own loathsome voice floated tentatively above her persistent jabber. "Inky, honey, Elissa needs that. Don't touch, please. Honeydew, we need you to stay here with us for a couple more minutes, okay?" No wonder she was wild. Her mother was a textbook case of ineffectual management. It was humiliating. Did

Karen really think this would make me feel more inclined to give birth? What if Milo turned out to be a carbon copy of his sister? My battleship would be sunk for sure. At least the sound quality was excellent.

"I think I'm going to go for a stroll," I announced, ripping the headphones off my ears.

When I returned, the midwives had finished lunch. Greg had choked down half the banana and was sitting up, reading my E. B. White essays. "So, what's going on? Are you having a baby today?" Catherine asked.

"Definitely," I told her gamely as I hopped onto the examining room's table, eager for it to be true. She looked sort of dubious. I didn't know her very well. Maybe she always looked dubious.

She snapped a pair of disposable gloves over her wrists. "Hmm. You're about four centimeters dilated. Six to go. I could try to stretch you to five with my fingers to get the labor going. Or we could wait and see what happens. Up to you."

"Anything but castor oil," I told her.

She inserted several fingers and started Rolfing my delicate lady parts. "Had a bad experience with castor oil last time around?" she inquired politely.

"Yeah." I grimaced. I didn't want to go into detail. Wild explosive diarrhea had racked my poor tortured bod, splashing everywhere as I clung to the edge of the sink. I haven't been able to let go of the suspicion that that's why Inky got so sick. Maybe some fecal matter made its way into the birth canal and nailed the baby. It wasn't the most conscientious wiping of my life. When I ran my theory up the flagpole with a friend who'd done

time as an Army medic, he agreed. "Oh, yeah, if you've got anything resembling an open cut, you definitely don't want to get
any poo in there."

Catherine managed to stretch the opening of my cervix another
centimeter, though. I was glad when she pulled her fingers out.
"Why don't you guys go out to dinner or see a movie?" she suggested. "Once you take your mind off it, nine times out of ten, the
labor'll get going."

We took her advice as gospel. Filing up the aisle as the credits
rolled, I told Karen and Greg that the movie had worked. I was
feeling some little contractions, pretty close together. I started
goose-stepping. This was what I had wanted but it didn't feel so
good. I hung on to Karen's arm, an invalid supporting herself on
another invalid. "Walk faster," I snapped to Greg, who was
creeping along probing his abdomen with his fingertips.

The midwives were lounging around their round table,
snacking. Catherine looked up expectantly. "So?"

I nodded. "We saw *Blood Simple* like you said."

Her jaw dropped. The other midwives screamed in mirth. "You
guys actually went and saw a movie?"

"We saw a movie last night too."

Catherine gave me another examination. Nothing had changed
since the last time she'd examined me. According to birth center
policy, we should have gone home but Catherine offered to let us
sleep in the breastfeeding room. "We can make up the sofa bed for
you in just a minute. We've got to deliver a baby first. Don't worry.
It'll be any second now."

We sat on the couch, eyeing the door of the room where a mother of three was about to become the mother of four. The midwives padded in and out in cotton pajama bottoms, barefoot. "She's amazing," Elissa told us, jerking her chin toward the door. "I was with her for two of her other births. She doesn't make a sound. She never stops smiling."

"Wow," I commented, remembering how I had bellowed like a wounded water ox the last time I'd been in labor. I recalled a conversation between two doctors at a dinner party I'd attended soon after moving to New York. My barely discernable pregnancy had caused them to start bitching about deliveries they'd attended in medical school. Chinese women, they agreed, were the best. They kept quiet, bearing down without complaint or histrionics. Indian women made a racket and arrived with a great entourage of sisters, cousins and aunts who contributed exponentially to the cacophony. "Who are your least favorite?" I had asked.

"Oh, it's no contest!" the anesthesiologist cried. "The educated white women in their thirties who come in with their birth plans and all these ideas about how their labor is supposed to go. Don't get me started on their aromatherapy!"

"Or their Pachelbel's Canon!" the child psychiatrist agreed, seizing the salad tongs. "They're the worst! Hands down."

I was one of the worst. The only difference was the cassette tapes. I'd brought Bessie Smith, Tom Waits and the "Theme to Mission Impossible." The only reason I hadn't selected Pachelbel's Canon was that it reminded me of work, the nonthreatening background music of six massages in a row. I'd temporarily hated my doctor friends for their sweeping generalizations, but perhaps after a hundred or so births, they were entitled to some service-industry obser-

vations. Any waiter can tell you who's a good tipper and who will
run you ragged with salad dressing on the side and lemon for their
water for a measly seven percent. By these doctors' estimation, not
only was I the worst, I bellowed like an Indian. What if the midwives thought I was one of the worst too? What if they turned my
birth into a funny workplace story at their next dinner party?

"Elissa, you better come in here," the nurse beckoned, poking
her head out of the birthing suite. "A baby is about to be born."
Elissa disappeared into the suite. A few minutes later we heard the
sandpapery cries of a newborn infant. We looked at each other in
wonder. Nothing beats eavesdropping as another human being
enters the world. The midwives got to do this every day.

After a few minutes, Catherine emerged and led us around the
corner to the tiny room where lactation consultants coach mothers
who are experiencing trouble nursing. The bright pink walls pulsed
with positive sisters-helping-sisters energy. Elissa dragged a massage table in so that the three of us wouldn't have to share a double
sofa bed. When we turned off the lamp, the little womb was pitch
black. Within minutes, Greg and Karen were snoring softly. I
wished I had my flashlight so I could read some E. B. White, even
if it was a day past his birthday. It felt strange to have spent so much
time away from Inky. I imagined that she was having the time of
her life spending the night at Little MoMo's. They'd probably
gotten milk shakes. I drummed my fingers on my belly, trying to
coax some kick turns out of Milo, but apparently he was sleeping
too. My impotence was getting embarrassing. Was I scared of the
pain? Was that the problem? Maybe it was just performance anxiety. Maybe the knowledge that Karen's plane was heading back to

Chicago in two days was preventing me from delivering the baby in time. I should just forget about that fucking plane. At this moment, I desperately wanted some Supreme Midwife to give me explicit instructions on how to speed things up.

In the morning, we brushed our teeth in the bathroom where I customarily peed in Dixie cups. It felt strange, like putting on deodorant in a café. Catherine passed us in the hall. She didn't have to examine me to know where I stood. "Why don't you guys go get some breakfast? When you come back I'll be gone, but Esme will be here and you can talk to her about doing an enema or going home or whatever." Esme, which one was Esme? I couldn't remember. Oh yeah, the sweetie pie.

We stepped blinking into the early morning sunshine. I made Greg take a picture of the sky. Now Milo would not only have a plaster reproduction of his pregnant mother's breasts and swollen belly, he'd know what the sky looked like on the day he was born, or possibly the day before. Young people dressed like temporary secretaries jostled past, rushing to the subway. We wandered around indecisively before settling on a neighborhood place with a friendly waiter, horrible coffee, and a corner table by the window. "The light is perfect in here," Karen observed as she snapped a picture of me and Greg to add to Milo's rapidly growing collection of belongings. Karen and Greg ordered oatmeal, marveling to each other that they felt like eating. It was their first real meal since the goat cheese felled them. I picked at my food, a little apprehensive about my impending enema. Never having had one before, I didn't know what to expect. Better not to have a gut full of waffles, I imagined.

The new shift of midwives had bellied up to the round table by the time we returned. They were slurping coffee. Catherine had filled them in. "Ready to get this labor going?" they asked. "Want us to give you an enema?"

"I guess so. I've never had one before."

"Oh, it's no big deal," Pene asserted. I'd forgotten about her. She was the pregnant Australian one. "Basically we just put a hose up your bum, pour some warm water in and wait for nature to take its course. You don't have to wait long. We can put some herbs in there too, if you're into that."

"I used to get enemas all the time," Greg offered. This was news to me. "My dad gave them to me."

"Why?" Pene spluttered, choking on her coffee.

"I don't know. For everything, I guess. He was a big believer in enemas."

All the women screamed with glee at this revelation from the only man in the room. "Well, how often did he give them to you?" Karen asked.

"I don't know. A lot. Once a week, maybe."

"How old were you?" Esme asked, smiling behind her hand.

"Thirty-four," I interjected. We screamed again.

"I don't know," Greg said sheepishly, backing toward the door. "I was a kid. I don't remember the details. I just remember getting lots and lots of enemas."

"You were a child prodigy," Pene pronounced, raising her mug in a toast.

"Sign me up," I said, and everyone cheered. Labor was more fun now that Karen and Greg weren't dying, especially since I didn't have to deal with any painful contractions. Esme directed me to go wait in the large bathroom just outside the inner sanctum. Gazing down the corridor, I could see women in various stages of pregnancy checking in for their appointments. What if one of them needed to use the toilet while I was getting my enema? There were two other bathrooms in the waiting area, but that's not necessarily enough for a lobby full of pregnant women. A nurse in pink scrubs knocked and entered carrying a length of rubber tubing and a bladder of warm water. She invited me to find a comfortable position. I ended up draping myself over a plastic chair, tail in the air, my dress flipped up over my hips.

"I'm Yvon, by the way," the nurse said, feeding the tube into my heiner.

"Pleased to make your acquaintance," I said over my shoulder. The water sped down the tube at an alarming rate. I had thought it would be more like the slow drip of an IV bag.

"Okay. That does it. Now all you need to do is hold that water in your body as long as you can stand it. It'll be hard, but try."

"And then?"

"Then you release your bowels. Once you're on the toilet, I mean. I'm going to put a sign on the door so no one disturbs you." She excused herself, leaving me alone with my book in a spotless bathroom twice the size of my kitchen. I didn't feel like reading. I knelt backwards on the chair, gripping its arms like the handlebars of a motorcycle. I've succumbed to some powerful urges to purge in many a skanky, flyblown hole in India, Africa and Southeast Asia, but no toilet has ever mocked me like that sparkling porcelain bowl. After enduring a hundred or so seconds of sheer psychological and intestinal torture, I hurled myself onto the seat. I expected to be shitting for hours, but it was all over in a disappointing few minutes. What a waste. I had that big beautiful bathroom all to myself. If I were at home, Inky would be barging in shouting, "You need privacy?" Knowing that there were probably a dozen pregnant women with their legs crossed in the lobby, I felt too guilty to enjoy my solitude. In other circumstances, I would have idled on the throne much longer.

Greg and Karen were huddled on the couch in the pink breast-feeding room, sharing the morning paper. "Anything?" Greg asked.

"Other than a lot of shit? I don't know. We'll find out. Anything happening in the world?" I helped myself to the Arts section, but it was hard to concentrate. I kept waiting to be blindsided by a thunderous contraction. It never came. We sat there for twenty minutes.

"What are you thinking," Karen asked in the deliberate, reasonable tone of voice she used to use mediating aesthetic spats in our old theater company.

"I'm thinking that I wish someone could tell me exactly when I'm going to have this baby. I sort of feel like we're wasting their time. It also feels like I'm taking advantage of all the people who agreed to baby-sit Inky. Presumably, we're really going to need their help at some point. I don't want to use up all their goodwill before I really need it."

"I don't think you should worry about that," Greg said.

"Yeah, but I do. Maybe we should just call MoMo, get Inky and head back to Brooklyn. I don't think I'm really in labor. If I were, something would have happened by now. Of course, if we do that, we're right back where we started with the Brooklyn Bridge...." By babbling cyclically, I managed to avoid making a decision for another ten minutes.

Finally Karen interrupted. "It sounds to me like you want to hang out in the playground in Tompkins Square. So, why don't I call MoMo and tell her to head over there with Inky? Greg can consolidate our stuff while you go find Esme so she'll know what we're doing." I nodded, grateful to be friends with a responsible adult, particularly since she had guessed right. I did want to lounge on the playground's spongy surface. It was too beautiful a day to be cooped up inside.

We walked to the East Village, following the same route MoMo, Greg and I had taken home from the birthing center three years earlier (except then I actually was in labor). We stopped so Karen could get some tea and check her blood sugar in the window of Starbucks. I waved at the red double-decker tourist bus cruising up Second Avenue, hoping that the out-of-town visitors would consider us an appropriately seedy East Village composition: the junkie shooting up next to her crew cut, pregnant friend in broad daylight. MoMo and Inky had beaten us to the playground. Abby was there too, accompanied by two of her baby-sitters. The little girls ignored the adults. They only needed us for our fingernails, which they self-importantly glopped with many layers of cotton-candy-colored polish. Even Greg submitted to a manicure. I was pleased that he would meet his son with talons as glittery and gaudy as Barbie's. Several mothers stopped by to pay their respects.

"What are you doing here? Aren't you supposed to be off having that baby? Anna said you dropped Inky off because you were in labor yesterday."

"I'm AWOL from the birthing center," I snickered. Framed like that, my inability to get the labor going seemed subversive in a good way, like blowing off biology to smoke cigarettes in the bad girls' bathroom.

Helene sported her two-month-old daughter in a navy-blue carrier strapped across her chest. "Have a great time," she said as if I were bound for a tropical island from which she'd recently returned. "I had a ball the second time around. I thought I would die when I had to push Gussy out, but with Phoebe, pushing was so much fun! I was laughing my head off, that's how fun it was."

"She's out of her mind," muttered a woman standing nearby as Helene sailed off. Greg, MoMo, Karen and the baby-sitters nodded in agreement. They'd none of them experienced the miracle of childbirth, but they knew enough. Pushing was never fun.

Around noon we decided to escape the broiling overhead sun by relocating to the shady area in the middle of the park, where permanent sprinklers take the place of jimmied fire hydrants. Inky and Abby were thrilled, galloping hand in hand through the jets in tank suits the size of oven mitts. Karen was seeing another side of New York. Usually, she's booked solid with trips to alternative performance venues, the Museum of Modern Art and record stores specializing in obscure European noise. But under the tall trees of the park, the pace is unhurried, grasshopperly. It's a very pleasant place to fritter away the hot hours, particularly while playing hooky from a labor that won't get going. I took off my shoes and dive-bombed the children.

"I don't want to break up the party," Karen said, wading out to join me, "But if I don't get something to eat in the next fifteen minutes, I'm going to go into insulin shock and die. You could tell me where a restaurant is and I could go eat lunch by myself. You could come with me. I could get something for carryout and bring it back here. Any of these options are fine with me. However, I do need to eat something very soon, so tell me what you'd like to do."

"Ayun, don't worry about the baby-sitting," Little MoMo broke in. "Anna and I took care of it. We called some of the people on the contact sheet. People want to help you. Let them help you."

"Well...," I glanced at Inky. She was busy stuffing the leaves and twigs Abby brought her into the drain. Depending on my choice, she could either bask in the company of her friend or wreak havoc in a restaurant and later, the birthing center. "I guess that it might be a good idea to stick to the schedule you and Anna worked out. Thank you. Inky, come over here! I want to give you a goodbye hug!"

Squatting down to squeeze my little wet-bathing-suit gal, bam! I burst like one of those water balloons hurled by an eight-year-old big boy. Amniotic fluid ran down the insides of my thighs, as warm as tea. I barked in surprise, alerting the others. MoMo insisted that I hitch my dress up to let her see. There was no mistaking it. My water had absolutely, without question, broken. We womenfolk commenced to jump up and down, screaming. The little girls joined us, seizing our hands and twirling, without the slightest understanding of what this fuss could be about. Greg whipped out the camera and took a picture. A family who'd been sitting on the low cement wall, speaking quietly to one another in Spanish, beamed when they realized what had happened. "Wait'll I tell my professor!" one of the baby-sitters crowed.

"Should we jump in a cab?" Greg wondered.

"No, let's walk crosstown to get the labor going," I said, full of beans and decisions now that we were seeing some action. "Karen's got to eat. Let's call the birthing center to let Esme know that my water just broke and then we'll go to that weird little Japanese place I was telling you about, the one that just opened, the okinomiyaki stand. We can get some okinomiyaki and eat it on the way."

"What's okinomiyaki?" Karen asked as we passed through the gates of the sprinkler area.

"I don't know. I forget. I had it in Japan. It's really weird. You'll love it."

We hadn't gone a hundred yards, when I felt the need to revise my plan. I didn't know if we had much time to spare. Okinomiyaki could take a while. I knew Greg was suspicious of the salad bars in the corner delis, but maybe just this once it would be okay. I doubted food poisoning could strike us twice in one week. We crossed Avenue A onto my old block. "You guys?" I asked through gritted teeth. "I think maybe we should find a cab."

Our old super was sitting on a stoop halfway up the block. He's quite a character when he's coherent. He calls Inky "Indy," and favors weird wigs and no teeth. I usually have all the time in the world to chew the fat with him, but now the prospect of one of his rambling monologues filled me with blind panic. I dug my claws into Karen's forearm, explaining in a rush my urgent need to cross the street.

"Ayun, you don't have to talk to him. You have a pretty airtight excuse," she reassured me as I panted in pain.

"This is happening too fast," I whined.

"Just keep walking. We'll be able to grab a cab at the corner."

"Shit!" Greg shouted as we stumbled past our old building. "I forgot to charge my cell phone. The battery's dead. Esme said to call her if anything started happening. Does anyone have a quarter?"

"Where's the pay phone?" Karen cried, fumbling in her purse.

"Across street! On corner! By bakery!" I wailed, working hard to retain my command of the English language. Collapsing against the corner deli's Dumpster, I yelled, "Tell Esme! Fill tub! Fill Jacuzzi now! *Unnnnnnghhhhhhhwwwwhhhaaaa!*" Seizing the Dumpster, I sagged in agony as a bagful of bowling balls rumbled through my lower body. When I lived in the East Village, I saw hundreds of men decanting the contents of their bladders against that very Dumpster but right then, I didn't care. That baby was going to come out right there on the pissy, fetid sidewalk. Karen grabbed the back of my dress and muscled me across the street.

The cab Greg flagged down had a little Hindu shrine set up on the dashboard. The driver seemed to take his responsibilities seriously. He permitted Greg to take his picture for posterity. Greg also got off a couple of shots in the rearview mirror, where I was reflected groaning while Karen kept tabs with a tight smile. The driver overshot the birth center by a couple of buildings, letting us out on the wrong side of the street. He offered to go around the block so he could drop us off in front of the door, but we all screamed "*no!*" While Greg paid for the cab, Karen jaywalked-jay-dragged me across 14th Street and then hurried ahead to buzz the center's intercom. Unruddered, I attached myself to the nearest brick wall like ivy, howling as the contractions came rushing up almost without interval. There were plenty of passersby, but to my relief none of them stopped to help. Three cheers for New York

City, where a pregnant woman shopping for middle-eastern food on her due date is an Amazon and a pregnant woman giving birth on the sidewalk is invisible. Eventually, Karen realized that she'd abandoned her charge and doubled back to collect me. Greg buzzed the intercom again. They got me into the lobby, where several expectant women looked up in alarm. "Take her to the back!" the receptionist shouted. I wasn't smiling this time.

We staggered to the inner sanctum. I gaped at the crazy quilt of faces pinwheeling at me from the big round table in the common room. Esme and Yvon hustled us into a birthing suite, where the tub was almost full. I grabbed onto the sink, desperate to splash water on my sweaty face. Was I losing my mind? I couldn't find the faucets anywhere. How was I supposed to turn it on? Frantically, I waved my hands under the spigot. Maybe a motion-sensitive infrared light like in the ladies' room at the airport activated the water flow. Nothing. What the fuck kind of sink was this? Another contraction slammed into me, sending me crashing against the cabinet door below. The moment the contraction ended, I was up again, grappling with the basin. Karen and Greg seemed very far away, filling out forms and setting up the minidisc recorder. Why didn't they just order a round of cappuccinos while they were at it? Oh my god, another contraction and I still hadn't figured out how to make the water work! I shouted like my babies were trapped in a burning building. Greg came to my assistance, stepping on some discreet foot pedals that sent water gushing into my cupped hands. Hey, foot pedals. That's handy, unless you've spent thirty-five years controlling sinks with your hands. I dropped, writhing to the floor.

The polished oak planks were wonderfully clean, the way I

always imagined art galleries in SoHo to be until Inky spent a Saturday afternoon gallery-hopping in her stocking feet. It felt like a red-hot cannonball was plotting its escape via my anus, but the floor was a great comfort. I withstood the contractions on my hands and knees, roaring, unable to believe it had been this bad throughout Inky's eighteen-hour birth. Esme came in and smiled when she saw me on the floor.

"Do you want me to help you to the bed while we wait for the tub to fill?"

"No. Floor."

"Would you like to sit in the rocker?"

"Floor good."

Yvon placed a low stool in my line of vision. I closed my eyes and patted the floor. Another contraction clobbered me. Esme squatted alongside, rubbing my back. Her pajama bottoms had really cute contrasting trim. I was pretty sure I'd seen some like them at Old Navy. I wondered if they still had a pair in my size. Another contraction.

"Ayun, I'm going to have to examine you to see how far you're dilated. After the next contraction, you should try to get yourself to the bed."

This was awful. I pressed my forehead against my beloved oak planks. The bed was several hundred miles away, all uphill. That cannonball was going to come bursting out my back end, leaving a ragged cavity as pulpy and red as a watermelon. If only there was a way to call a time-out. Esme shared a little twinkle with Karen and Greg.

"Okay, let's just examine you here on the floor." I lay as docile as a farm animal, dumbly awaiting the next blast of torture. "Oh yeah.

You're ready. You're really really ready. You guys might want to help her into the shower. A lot of women find that helps."

Esme slipped back out. I wondered who was sitting around the round table, eating Chinese food and listening to me scream. The rooms couldn't be that soundproof. Karen and Greg encircled my biceps, gently urging me to get to my feet for the short trip to the shower. Their hands felt as authoritative as fish fillets. I'd get in that shower if they bridled me and dragged me every step of the way. Maybe if they cracked me on the ass with a cat-o'-nine-tails.

"C'mon now, little Ayunnie," Greg cajoled, humoring me as one might a sulky baby. "Don't you want to get clean? Think how good that water's going to feel." I fell for it, allowing him to haul me up and inch me along toward the bathroom. It took five contractions to get there. Stripped of my dusty dress, I felt eager to get under the spray. It would feel good to have something pounding against me from the outside for a change. Greg started the water and I stepped under it.

"Wahhh! Cold!" I screamed, drawing my arms up like little dinosaur hands. "Get it away! Get it away from me!" Greg reached in and fiddled with the knobs, doing his best to stay dry himself.

"Hot! Hot!" I shrieked, scuttling in a circle. I couldn't figure out how to get away from this pernicious boiling oil. Greg started laughing as he hopped in to adjust the temperature.

"Cold! Too cold!" I wailed, batting at the spray with my hands. "It's not funny!"

"I'm sorry. I'm not laughing at you," he chuckled unconvincingly as another contraction threw me against the tiled wall. Karen stuck her head around the rubber curtain. "Help me!" I sobbed. She twisted the knobs until the water temperature was just right. It felt good. For the twenty seconds or so between contractions, the water streaming down my face felt like a benediction.

"Tub's full," Esme called from the bedroom. Karen and Greg hooked my armpits over their necks, two soldiers dragging their wounded buddy to the safety of the choppers. Only the clothes were different. Instead of muddy, bloody olive drab, I wore a soaking-wet birthday suit. I kept my eyes on the Jacuzzi, a luxurious oval lit in soft-porn tones. I was pitched in in slow motion.

"Hot!" I cried in distress. "Too hot!" I love whirlpools. I adored the Korean bathhouse Karen and I used to visit in Chicago, soaking for hours with towels on our heads and ridiculous lurid masques smeared on our faces. The contractions were what skewed the experience. An immersion that feels like heaven on a day of beauty feels like a goddamned lobster pot in the middle of labor. "Greg, I'm not going to make it if it's this hot!" I panicked.

"She says it's too hot," Greg told Esme, biting his lip. This was quite a step for us. We're the kind of people who eat what the waiter brings us even if it's bright red and what we ordered was pale green.

"We can fix it," Esme said, opening the drain and twisting the cold water tap to full blast. A breathtaking mountain stream poured from the spout. I stuck my face under it, lapping like a slobbery golden retriever, happily snapping my big dumb jaws beneath the hose my humans had provided for me.

With the Jacuzzi refilled to my specification, Esme retreated to the edge of the bed to complete a clipboard's worth of paperwork. She tucked her legs up under her. She looked like a well-behaved fourteen-year-old doing homework in her bedroom. Greg perched near my right shoulder, his toes gripping the narrow lip of the tub as he leaned against the tiled wall. Karen knelt on the floor, aiming her minidisc microphone near my head. I arched my back and keened. I felt so mad that I was the only one experiencing these unbelievable grinding spasms. There was something unfair about it. They'd gotten to go through goat cheese poisoning together and now they were business as usual. I felt like a shark had gotten hold of my inflatable air mattress—I was a scene from *Jaws* that they were watching on TV. They looked a little bored. You'd think they'd at least have the courtesy to cover their eyes and scream.

"How much time do you get on one of those minidiscs?" Greg asked Karen.

"Forty-five minutes," Karen answered quietly.

"Can you buy them in different increments, like audiotape?"

"Yeah, you can."

"And the sound quality's good?"

"Excellent."

"How much do they cost?"

"This has to stop now," I ordered tersely. I felt like strangling Greg. His wife was on the rack, birthing his son, and he was comparison shopping for electronic accessories. He was supposed to be breathing with me, complimenting me, tenderly fitting a straw between my lips so I could drink some of the fruit smoothie he just happened to have on hand. "You cannot talk about this now," I reiterated. "Later."

Greg immediately shut up. I closed my eyes grumpily. Later, I hurt Greg's feelings by entertaining friends with the story of how I'd nailed him for discussing minidisc mileage while I was in labor. "I was worried that Karen was going to run out of recording time," he protested. "I was afraid there wouldn't be enough left for his first cries." I'm a heel.

I rolled onto my back like a capsized ocean liner. It was almost three o'clock, only an hour since we'd left the sprinklers. The others were probably still there, eating peanut butter sandwiches and grapes from Ziploc bags. The cannonball in my bowels announced its intentions again. I braced myself, but something had changed. It still hurt like the fires of hell, but I got the impression that it might actually pass through my body in a logical way. I no longer felt like the cartoon duck who's been tricked into eating a powder keg with the fuse lit. Something was happening.

"Esme, I think I'm pushing," I gasped from the tub.

She smiled modestly, making a note on her clipboard. "Yeah, I think you are too," she murmured.

I closed my eyes and saw Helene from the playground She looked at me cheerfully, the sunlight glinting off her glasses. *"Pushing is fun,"* she said. *"I was laughing that's how fun it is!"*

What the hell, I decided. The last hour had been torture, but perhaps I could pretend like I was having a good time. I have a degree in theater after all. Might as well put it to use, for once. I floated on my back. Greg lowered his legs into the tub and gripped my right hand. Karen squeezed my left. Esme squatted a couple of feet away. A round light was mounted directly overhead. It looked like a giant breast. I stared at it fiercely, the way I used to look at a crack in the gym's far wall to help me endure the stair-climbing machine. When a contraction came, I let my head dip back in the water, my mouth gaping in a silent-scream. I bore down as hard as I could. The water tickled the outermost edges of my eyes. It was kind of fun, in a horrible way. I was the heart of a very dangerous machine, the part without which the machine could not function.

"You're so strong. You're such a strong woman," Karen coached from the sidelines. I rolled my eyes toward her, wondering where she'd picked up a corny line like that. Not wanting to hurt her feelings, I bit my tongue. She got a little extra consideration since she'd flown in all the way from Chicago. I may have been Greg's short-tempered, bitching wife, but I was still Karen's hostess. Lucky for him, Greg said nothing, except when I accidentally pinned his legs against the side of the tub.

Stare at the light, dip head back, silent-scream, you're so strong, stare at the light, dip head back, silent-scream, you're so strong. It was a sustainable rhythm. As long as no one fucked up the groove, I felt capable of keeping it up for seven hours, maybe longer. I hoped the others were prepared to stick with this order. Stare at the light, dip head back, silent-scream, you're so strong. I had no way to tell them. If I opened my mouth to say "Don't fuck up the groove," it would fuck up the groove. Without my mouth, my eyes became very keen. I saw Catherine leaning on her elbows nearby, her expression one of attentive, sporting enjoyment. God, those midwives work hard. She'd barely gone home. I wanted to greet her, to show her that I knew the difference between the labor I thought I'd been in last night and the labor I knew I was in now. I couldn't speak though. Couldn't fuck up the groove. It was time to silent-scream. Esme crept to the side of the tub, put her hand between my legs, took it out. I could feel her smile on me as I stared at the light. Dip head back, silent-scream, Karen forgot to say "you're so strong," didn't matter. That part was expendable. Good.

"Yvon, can you, uh, get something?" Esme whispered, cocking her head toward the tub. I caught a flash of pink surgical scrubs heading toward the door. Our machine continued on, punching and pressing, doing what it was supposed to do. Stare at the light, dip head back, silent-scream. The pink scrubs reappeared. I turned my head to see Yvon twiddling a tiny net, the kind the pet store people use to scoop goldfish out of their aquariums. My helpers laughed at her tiny instrument. "It was all I could find," she giggled.

As if I hadn't yet been divested of every shred of modesty, I blushed, certain that I had dropped a Baby Ruth in the pool. Had the enema worn off that quickly? Poor Yvon. She wasn't even a regular employee. She was a mercenary temping nurse! What an assignment. You come to work and it's just shit, shit and more shit, compliments of me. If only we'd met under other circumstances. It's usually one of the few things I can control about myself. Gentle Esme guessed why I was worried. "It's just gore," she reassured me. "We've got to clean it out of here so we can see."

On the next push, a blistering stream of acid washed over my genitals. Good Lord, that felt good. I hadn't felt anything like it since 1997, when Inky's pointy head finally emerged after seven hours of pushing. How could Milo be coming out already? "Is that the head?" I gasped.

"Yes." Esme confirmed, her eyes pinned to my crotch. "Stop pushing. Wait until the next contraction."

Milo had made it as far as his forehead and stopped. Mother of
God, was this how the tunnel felt when the train ground to a halt
between stations? "This is very uncomfortable," I whimpered.
Everyone burst out laughing. I beamed, proud that my uninten-
tional understatement was the source of such mirth. I was feeling
more like my usual self, except naked, with a bit of a baby hanging
out my hinkie. The tracks started to vibrate. I looked at Esme.

"Okay!" she shouted. "Push!"

I didn't need to be told. Out came the head! Out came the body!
Out came Milo, oh plump little moon monkey covered in Crisco!
Oh Milo! Oh, here you are! This was him. This was the boy we'd
been waiting for!

"Mmm, look at that vernix," Catherine said, approaching the tub
as stealthily as a housecat smelling ham. "It's really good for your
skin."

"I know," I laughed, massaging it into the baby's baggy back.
His head was enormous and perfectly round. He had hair and a
snub nose and the big pouchy lips his sister was born with. His
feet were like brand-new erasers. How could he be on the outside? We'd just left the sprinkler park. "Oh, hello. Oh thank you.
Look at this baby, Greg! Oh thank you, Esme. Thank you,
Karen. Thank you all. This was great! Oh, this was so easy! Milo,
you came fast!" I was gabbling, and even though I hate my voice,
I have to say, I sounded just like normal. Unless you're listening
to the uninspired monologue, you'd never guess that I literally
just had a baby. It was all captured on minidisc. We have footage
of Milo's first minute on earth, though not his head emerging.
Karen reported that just as that fateful push was beginning,

Catherine caught her eye and mouthed, "Video camera." She'd run to get it, returning just in time to see his little body flopping out of mine. It's okay. I'm glad to have the tape, but I don't think I'll be forcing the relatives to watch it after Thanksgiving dinner anytime soon.

"May I?" Catherine asked, rubbing a dollop of vernix from Milo's face into the back of her hand. "You want some, Yvon?"

Yvon shook her head, laughing.

"He's beautiful," Esme told me, running one finger up his spine.

"Moon boy," Greg croaked. "Moon-faced boy." He peered into his son's face. It felt like when Inky was born but better, more everyday. That newborn weight slopping over my shoulder was like riding a bicycle. I hadn't forgotten how to hold one, my one, one minute old.

"You're incredible. You're so strong," Karen said when I turned the baby to face her. This time it didn't sound fake.

Yvon tucked a flannel baby blanket around Milo as he lay on my breasts. The hem trailed in the bright red water. The wonderment of birth had faded just enough that Greg discreetly pulled his legs from the bloody tub.

"I hate to ask," Esme said, "But do you think you're ready to try moving to the rocking chair? We don't want Milo to catch cold."

I delivered the placenta five minutes later, as my son nursed in the crotchless rocking chair. Shortly thereafter, Greg was given a small pair of scissors to sever the umbilical cord. It was thick and fibrous, like a white hose. Greg remarked upon its toughness. "Yeah, that's a really chewy one," Catherine commented.

"Do you want us to put it in the refrigerator so you can take it home?" Esme asked in the professionally sensitive tone I recognized from my days as a massage therapist.

If I'd really wanted to eat a placenta stir-fried with hot chiles, I should have married a different man. I wish we could have planted it under a tree, but the logistics of that for a yardless urban dweller like me are a nightmare. Maybe that's why they've taken to posting cops nightly at every entrance to Tompkins Square. It's to prevent women from sneaking in to bury their placentas under the cover of darkness. Even if I could get away with it, I wouldn't want it to be exhumed by a hungry rat, a diseased pigeon or a thrill-seeking gutterpunk. "We can let it go," I told Esme.

"Wait, let me take a look at that thing," Greg said. When I had Inky in the hospital, nobody asked us if we wanted to keep the placenta. Esme obligingly lifted it out of the silver basin she had caught it in, displaying the smooth side that looked like liver and the rough side that had fed Milo for more than nine months. It reminded me of poking at jellyfish on the beach.

She spread the thin amniotic membrane with her fingers, pointing out a tear several inches in length from when I'd squatted to hug Inky in the sprinkler park. It was a fairly gorgeous specimen, my placenta. It would have been good eating.

The midwives and Nurse Yvon cleared out, telling us to let them know if we needed anything. "I need something," Karen announced the second the door closed behind them. "Food! Right now! Or I'm going to die!" What a good soldier. She hadn't made a peep about her blood sugar since leaving Tompkins Square. I asked her what would have happened if it had turned out to be one of those marathon labors that go on for hours. "Well, I would have died," she said, grinning broadly. "Actually, I have some sugar pills in my purse that I could have popped. If it had gotten really bad, I would have slipped out for some okinomiyaki."

And then the moment we'd all been waiting for: Yvon knocked and asked if we were ready for our daughter to come in. Inky's head poked uncertainly around the door. Her face was framed in humidity curls. MoMo had dressed in her in a red Mexican dress that made her look even smaller than usual. "Is that my baby brother?" she asked timidly. The adults looked at each other with suspiciously moist eyes.

Minutes after this tender entrance, Inky was whooping around the room on the wheeled blood pressure apparatus and riding the rocking chair into a lather. She couldn't get enough of the bloody bathtub. She shrieked and bounced, destroying all hope for that big bed as some sort of luxury getaway. She yanked open the door and rocketed down the corridor as if her size-two Curious George panties hid jet-propulsion packs. If she did it once, she did it twenty times. It was a miracle she didn't barge into one of the other birthing suites to demand if a laboring woman needing privacy. "What a character," one of the midwives remarked delicately. Milo slept through it all, as alien and valuable as a freeze-dried Martian. God, his head was big. No wonder I needed stitches.

I hobbled around the room, as fresh as a daisy, shoving our belongings back into the grocery bag we'd brought from Brooklyn. Despite Milo's amazing resemblance to the full moon, the clothes we'd brought him were way too big. I did the best I could and wrapped him in a blue cotton blanket printed with stars. We filled out the forms required to issue his birth certificate and reviewed umbilical stump care with a nurse who'd come for the overnight shift. "Ask her about his penis!" Greg hissed.

"Yes?" she smirked.

"Greg wants to know if there's any special penis care involved." I forced myself to refrain from making blow-job jokes.

"Oh, no, soap and water," she smiled. "Tender loving care. You're talking about the baby, right?"

Less than eight hours after he was born, we were zipping west on the Brooklyn Bridge. For the first time, we had two children sleeping in car seats in the back. The skyscrapers were all lit up, as was the Statue of Liberty, eternally hoisting her torch to our right. I started singing "New York, New York" and waited for the credits to roll. It was a very New York moment. Milo slept through it, but I remember. When we rolled up to our brownstone, a shadowy figure was crouching on the stoop. It was Elissa, the midwife. She waved a tiny pair of sandals at us. "Forget something?" she called. We looked at Inky. She was barefoot.

"Damn, that's full service," Karen remarked.

"Yeah, you can't expect treatment like that if you have your baby in a hospital," I told her.

"Don't worry about it," Elissa said, bounding down the steps. "You're on my way home and I figured it'd be easier for me to drop them off than for you to have to haul it all the way into the city with a new baby."

We laid sister and brother side by side on the king-sized mattress, standing over them to take sixty virtually identical photographs, which were developed, in double prints. Jambo padded out from the closet, nosing the new baby's unwashed head disdainfully. "This monkey is Baby Brother!" Greg trumpeted, pinning Jambo to the bed for some uncatlike roughhousing. "He is the little prince! He is your brother! You must never ever bite the baby brother. You understand, little man? You must obey your father!" Jambo bounded away, yowling complaints.

Karen had made herself at home in the kitchen, whipping up quesadillas out of ingredients I didn't even know we had. I could have eaten a million of them. We cracked open a six-pack and settled in to rehash the events of a day. It reminded me of those hangover breakfasts when my housemates and I went over the details of the previous night's party, savoring the gossipy bits, except I wasn't hung over. I was drinking the best beer of my life. There was a dirty little girl crashed out in the next room and beside her, a moon-faced boy. He was entirely strange and exactly how I had imagined him. What a busy day it had been. My bottle was empty. The quesadillas were gone. It was no longer Milo's birthday. The last thing I saw before falling asleep was that little baby's head and when I woke up in the morning, he was still there.

Human Anatomy

Topless Lunch

I remember my first bra. It was about as sexy as a cotton ball. I was grateful for my school's dress code, which required every girl in seventh grade and above to wear a bra. I would have sooner died than ask my mother for such a racy piece of equipment. The snapping started on the first day of middle school, the fast girls shrieking in indignation to ensure that every boy in earshot knew that they had been singled out for sexy horseplay. The rest of us suffered in silence and watched our backs. I worried that people could see my white bra shining through my shirt. I worried that the strap would slide down my shoulder like my grandmother's—that everyone would see.

Now as I grapple to unhusk a breast to quiet my fretful baby I am absolutely certain that everyone sees. And I don't care! I nurse that baby everywhere. I'm so used to it that I wonder why our waiter gasps, "Oh sorry, I'll come back!" beating a hasty retreat.

Where the hell is he going? I'm hungry! My menu is closed. Who cares if my shirt is open?

I forget that not every lady is as nonchalant when it comes to opening the traveling titty bar. In between seventh grade and Inky's birth, I had nearly twenty years to get comfortable with the idea of letting it all hang out. Shortly after college, I joined the ranks of a decidedly off-off-Broadway theater company, where I gained recognition for squishing the fat around my navel to resemble a bagel. The approval our audiences lavished on me for this simple trick polished off the tattered remains of early modesty. As a girl, I never left the house without gym shorts on under my dress lest the boys should glimpse my underpants from the lower rungs of the monkey bars, but years later, spurred by the roar of the crowd, I routinely hoisted my hem to my clavicles to show off my jiggly tanned bagel.

That's the way I feel about whipping 'em out in public. Something wonderful is on exhibition. The bagel started as idle fooling around in front of the mirror. By the time I had to quit doing it because the skin over my pregnant belly was so taut there was nothing to squish, it had become liberating. At least that's what the women in the audience told me. I had come up with an irresistibly cute fuck-you to corporate advertisers and fashion magazine editors who had given us the choice of emaciated or ashamed. There wasn't a supermodel on earth who could make a bagel. They wouldn't dare. Maybe they could come up with some amusing party trick for their silicone breasts. It gets my goat that most people think breasts are at their most powerful covered up with a few scraps of tacky teal acetate in the Victoria's Secret catalog. Some folks think that looks really good. I say there is no sight so beautiful as a breastfeeding baby. I don't mind if people see. Look upon the milk of human kindness. It's like wildflowers on the highway median strips and colorful murals on the brick walls of inner-city schools. It's a life-affirming, nonviolent, free-to-the-public moment that makes the world a slightly better place. Nothing beats the plump little hand resting casually on the breast, asking for nothing more than what it's already getting. Man, that's sweet!

The mechanics can be awkward in the beginning. I don't begrudge a new recruit the urge to cover up while she gets used to this mind-boggling new function of glands that had seemed purely decorative. I reserve my animosity for the geniuses who market ridiculous, pricey nursing tents to inexperienced mothers-to-be and for the parenting magazines in which they advertise. Buy one of those rags if you want fifteen coupons for formula and a cover story on what you're doing wrong, backed up by ten expert opinions. Sleep-deprived new mothers don't need that kind of support. They need to hear things that will make their lives easier. Like get the hell out of the house. Take a book and go sit on a park bench. If the baby starts to cry, hike up your T-shirt and let her eat as long as she likes. If anyone shoots you a nasty look, fuck 'em. If they have the temerity to say anything damning about the activity in which you're engaged, double fuck 'em. Bop 'em over the head with your nursing pillow. Don't worry about giving your child the impression that it's okay to hit. Your newborn baby has the brain of a primrose and the vision of a bumblebee. She is too little to wish anyone ill. Of course, if your nursing child is an observant two and a half, you'll know better than to come to blows with a pantyhosed defender of public morals. A career warrior knows when to sheathe her arms, if not her breasts.

I have been lactating for more than four years. That's nothing! A woman I know from the playground has been servicing two breast-feeders at a time for eons. She lives in a one-bedroom apartment with her four children and her work-at-home husband. According to her, tandem nursing is the ideal antidote to sibling rivalry. She is brazen when it comes to feeding her young. The only time I've ever seen her accompanied by fewer than two children was in the Bargain Bazaar right after the birth of her youngest daughter. At the first whimper from her week-old infant, she dug down the front of her leotard and popped a milk-white breast into the baby's mouth without missing a beat in our conversation. Her indiscreet over-the-neckline approach is remarkable even within the iron bars of the East Village's loopiest playground, so imagine the stir it created among the housecoated grandmothers shopping for discount shower curtains and porcelain figurines of Jesus. I shifted uncomfortably under their laser beams of disapproval, but my acquaintance babbled blithely. She isn't a breastfeeding militant. There doesn't seem to be a "fuck you if you can't deal with it" bone in her milk-swollen body. Ignorance, even willful ignorance, is bliss.

Too much maternal energy is expended plotting logistics and trying to carry out top-secret nursing missions. Every nursing mother should receive a special dispensation to go around topless for the duration. Don't they do something like that in Sweden? I've never used one of those little tents designed to shield a working breast from the public eye. I was looking at one in catalog the other day. It looked like something only an experienced camper could put

up without help. I doubt I could even figure out how to fit it in my
purse. Odds are I'd succeed eventually in attaching it to my neck by
its elastic straps, but I wouldn't be able to get it off. It would get
caught on my earring, or I'd try to take it off backward. Milo would
be trapped screaming as I struggled to get free. The crescent of
breast I'd kept under wraps would bounce out, mooning the Good
Samaritans who'd leap to my aid. I'd rather use an old hippie scarf
or a hardback library book. They're handy and easy to operate.
They can keep the rice off the baby's head in the restaurant. Any
baby with the motor skills to pick up a Cheerio and the desire to
admire the view can push them away pretty easily, but at least they
don't attract attention. If people gape at a woman suckling her baby
in plain view, what do you reckon they'll do when they see her
strutting down the street wearing a teddy-bear-print pup tent?
Avert their eyes? Applaud?

I would have a fit if I knew someone was watching me try on
bathing suits through a hidden security camera, but I don't care if
people see my breasts in the line of duty. Even if I did mind, I doubt
I'd be able to pull the act off discreetly. I never have been able to eat
a salad without getting lettuce stuck in my teeth and a big gob of
garlic dressing down the front of my blouse. I can't even walk in
high heels! Amazingly enough, my klutzy body has no problem
producing a limitless quantity of perfectly blended, vitamin-rich
food. I'm a great cook, but a crappy waiter. Serve from the left, clear
from the right? Serve from the right, clear from the left? Oh hell,
the baby's crying. Let them look. Most choose not to. Many don't
like to watch me eat a salad either.

Rarely have I felt the impulse to shield this wholesome activity. I get a little jolt out of bucking social convention on my own turf. I unhusked a breast at a Northwestern University alumni affair at the Yale Club as coolly as if I were ordering a glass of Chardonnay. A Kappa Kappa Gamma who preceded me through Northwestern's hallowed halls by twenty years couldn't stop herself from clucking. She probably wondered where the baby-sitter was. The grinchy expression on her face might have winched her asshole a few notches tighter. It didn't do much of anything to mine. I think of her from time to time, my fellow alumna. When I'm feeling put upon, disenfranchised, sick to death of the fucking wheels on the bus going round and round, I daydream about her mashed-together lips. I rise up, one powerful arm cradling a baby to my breast, the other raised in triumph as I kick the evil naysayer right in the chops. Pow! Thank you, Motherwoman! Thanks to your courageously defiant behavior, Gotham City is safe for breastfeeding women again!

On airplanes, other passengers should let me have the armrest and thank their lucky stars that the baby sitting next to them won't scream for more than a few seconds the entire flight. They should let me put my drink on their tray tables because I can't open mine with this bundle on my lap.

On the beach, sunbathers should feast their eyes on flesh far firmer than mine. I know it looks a bit indecorous when I have to slap at the nipple to get the sand off, but I'd be doing the same thing with a bottle.

At the midday aquatic show, they should face front and watch the dolphins.

Usually, I don't talk so tough. One look at my reflection in the subway window is all it takes to remind me of that. I'm soft and squishy. I greet the homeless men like they're fathers from nursery school. Even the tourists can tell that I'm not a native New Yorker. Only in the fertile fields of fantasy am I capable of shouting "Yo buddy, you got a problem with feeding a hungry child? It's the best food on earth, you prick! Wipe that stupid sneer off your face or I'll shove this Barbie umbrella straight up your ass!" I think all sorts of nasty things, but unless I'm married to you chances are excellent that I won't come right out and say them. If you mutter a snide but inaudible observation to your seatmate, I'll think an earful at you. If the expression on your face equates public breastfeeding with over-flowing public toilets, I'll dig for the sarong. You'll be satisfied that your disapproval was so righteous, it sent the sinner scuttling to cover herself. As long as the milk is flowing free over the gums, the kid has no complaints. I get something too. I get to hate you and to see you as the root of all my problems, even if all you are is cranky after another long day at the Department of Motor Vehicles. Prob-ably you breastfed all seven of your homeschooled, home-birthed children until they started kindergarten and your only beef with me is the length of my kids' fingernails. Any mother with half a pin's investment in her children's welfare would keep those talons trimmed. We're all looking for whipping boys, even if all we do is think at them. You should hear the bile I mentally spew at the bearded Orthodox Jews I never have seen offering their seats on the F train to women with small children. It's enough to make me down-right culturally insensitive, particularly when the woman and chil-dren are me and mine.

When Inky was much younger than Milo is now, we took the subway to the Cloisters, an hour uptown. I was in denial about her need to hit the biological bottle before we reached our destination. Our closest neighbor was a bald man in his fifties, a working-class José who remained where he was despite my fervent wish for him to move. Inky's nickering was on the verge of becoming nutting out. With no choice, as discreetly as I could, I unsheathed myself, studying the ads for Dr. Jonathan Zizmor's Miraculous Chemical Peel in an attempt to render everything below my neck invisible. Inky clamped on, grunting in relief. I could feel my neighbor's eyes upon me. "Breastfeeding!" he shouted.

I returned Dr. Zizmor's gaze, offering only the faintest murmur of assent.

"Breastfeeding," my seatmate thundered again. "It's the best thing! My mother, she's in heaven now, god rest her soul, she breastfed all of us, and she had eleven kids."

I turned to face him. He was grinning from ear to ear. He pointed at the little gobbling head. His voice resounded like a gong. "Look at her. It's a girl, right? Oh god bless her. *Que linda.* Look at how much she loves it. I'm telling you, you can't do better than breastfeeding! Good for you, Mami! God bless you!"

"Thank you."

"It's the best thing, breastfeeding!"

"That's what they say."

"Yeah, and it's the best thing for the baby too. She knows it, right? It's better than the Gerbers even, for a baby. Good for you, Mami! God bless you!"

I thanked my advocate again. Never have I so yearned for a book so that I could resume reading. With not so much as a magazine, I returned my attention to Dr. Zizmor's shill.

"Look at this little baby breastfeeding," my neighbor called to a couple of women seated across the aisle. "Look at how much she loves it!"

The ladies nodded companionably. "Oh, que linda. God bless her."

"It's the best thing!" my friend trumpeted, as if any of our fellow riders might harbor doubts. He slapped his ample thighs, bringing a heavy work boot down for emphasis. "My mami breastfed me. I'm fifty-seven years old and strong as a bull! I'm telling you. Breastfeeding's where it's at."

I should've gotten this guy's phone number. He'd have made a great lactation consultant. He outed me, but who cares? He was on the righteous side. As long as he was riding shotgun, I could nurse with the impunity of the Virgin Mary. Sometimes you find champions in the least likely places.

When Inky got a little older, I tried to time it so I wouldn't have to nurse her in the subway. I rarely succeeded, but by then I had discovered the many uses of the heretofore useless sarongs I had collected while knocking around below the equator in my early twenties. I try to carry one at all times as a low-rent nursing tent. They also make jim-dandy diaper-changing pads and picnic blankets to lay over the cigarette butts and bottle caps in parks. Inky even wore one home after a double accident left her bottomless. In my heart of hearts, I'm hoping to run into an outpost of Indonesians who will accept my sarong as the password to join their never-ending backgammon game. Any culture that shucks off its restrictive, dirty work clothes to wrap itself loosely in a big piece of flower-printed cotton is A-OK in my book.

I can't remember if I saw women breastfeeding openly in

Indonesia. I saw plenty of children. I bicycled past several naked women bathing in a river. As the guidebook had instructed, I behaved as if they were invisible. Sneaking a peek, I saw them soaping up their armpits and heinies. Apparently this arrangement afforded them adequate privacy. I feel the same way, breastfeeding Milo in the front window of our favorite restaurant. As long as no passerby stops to gape, we might as well be in our living room. It's easy. Milo's little and looks younger than he is.

The humorists in the enemy camp assert that any child old enough to ask to nurse is too old to nurse. These same wits ask if you intend to accompany your nursing daughter to the prom and follow it up with cracks about kids, big enough to open the refrigerator by themselves. A woman who finds these jokes funny told me that she could think of nothing so embarrassing as having a child announce in the grocery, "Mommy, I want booby!" I have a feeling that if this woman had kids she could imagine far more distressing things for a piping voice to observe in public. Like "Mommy, why didn't you give the man money for that steak you put down your pants?"

Inky's word for nursing was "num-num." All our baby friends had special nursing words. "Num-num." "Yum-yum." "Su-su." "Boo-boo." My personal favorite was the idiosyncratic "nak-nak," invented by a champion suckling who was too young to pronounce "snack." Usually I went for my buttons the second she said "num-num," but sometimes I tried to get away with playing dumb. When Inky was two years old, we took the subway to Queens to see if we could see ourselves living there. Nothing against cheap rents and big apartments, but I got gun-shy when I saw all the plastic deer on the AstroTurf lawns, not all planted out of irony. I equated lawn ornaments with decent people, as in "You can take your dirty business elsewhere, ma'am. We're decent people here." I couldn't wait to get back to my overpriced little East Village hovel. On the subway ride home, Inky none too quietly demanded, "Num-num." I smiled at my fellow passengers. They were a veritable United Nations. The only group that seemed to go unrepresented was the white American lawn-ornament owner as imagined by me. Odds were good that at least half of my fellow riders hailed from warm countries where extended breastfeeding was the norm. I looked around for the man who had made our trip to the Cloisters such a pleasure.

"Num-num," Inky insisted. "Num-num num-num num-num num-num!"

I clapped my hands over my eyes. "Inky! Where did I go? Where did I go?" I let my hands go, hoping for a big response. She looked at me like I was a moron. What kind of an idiot confuses "num-num" with "peekaboo"?

"Num-num!" she roared, grappling at the front of my blouse in a mad bid. That's all well and good for refrigerator doors, but when my breasts are to be served up in public, I like to control the presentation. I dug in my bag for the sarong.

"Okay, okay, okay, okay, we're going to do it, just shh, we're going to do it, but we're going to do it under here, okay?" I hauled Inky into my lap and draped the bright purple fabric over her head. Irritated, she ripped it aside just as I was stealthily reaching into my sports bra. "Yeah, I know. I know what you want to do, but we've got to be cool, okay? You can only num-num if we do it under here."

Duplicitous child! She agreed, ducking under the cloth only to yank it off the second I had exposed the feedbags. What fun! Perhaps num-num and peekaboo weren't mutually exclusive after all. I tried staring at Dr. Zizmor. An oft-repeated bit of public nursing advice says to look anywhere but down at your suckling child. If you're smiling at the skyline or studying the ads in the subway, nobody will notice you're breastfeeding, even if your child is squirming like a python in a pillowcase. I was making a hash of not calling attention to myself. The passengers politely averted their eyes from the spectacle, all flailing limbs, untethered boobs and tangled sarong. Perhaps they would have felt free to look if I had been a bit more deft.

As long as they're not wrinkling their noses in distaste, it doesn't bother me if people take in a bit of a free show. In fact, here in my mid-thirties, with badly cut hair and shapeless ink-stained clothes soiled with peanut butter and baby pee, I rather enjoy it. The ham-handed frat boys whose ogling felt like aggression have turned their attention to fresher flowers. The only whoo-whooing I hear from building sites are the hard hats' attempts to coax a smile out of Milo. "Aww, he's byootiful," the guys tell me in accents straight out of *GoodFellas*. "What is he, about six months?"

Isn't it funny? As soon as you start showing them your tits, they stop holding up the sign that says Show Us Your Tits!

Speeding down the street one unseasonably hot day last spring, late for nursery school dismissal yet again, I passed a graying Rastafarian gent. "You have nice breasts," he saluted as I galloped by with Milo on my back. I stopped dead in my tracks, afraid that I'd forgetten to put myself back after Milo's last meal. I often realize I've been wandering around the apartment with my T-shirt riding high on my clavicle, the cup of my sports bra pinned beneath the very object it's supposed to support. I am a sloppy girl, and motherly responsibilities have turned my brain into a rusty bucket. Was I hanging out? No, thank god. Both cows were back in their stalls and the barn door was closed. I looked over my shoulder. The courtly Jamaican was halfway down the block. "Thank you!" I called after him. "Thank you very much!" What a nice guy. Not too particular either. I weighed one of my melons through the thin cotton of my tank shirt. Milo must have just eaten. I can imagine a milk-swollen breast giving an unpracticed male eye a mistakenly silicone thrill, but after Milo had taken his turn, my rack was about as exciting as wrinkled zucchini.

Not everyone is as matter-of-fact. When I came for a visit with the infant Inky, my mother snickered, anticipating my stepfather's response. "He won't know where to look," she predicted, turning in a hammy pantomime of flustered Art casting his eyes toward the ceiling, the floor, the TV, his knees. Monkeyshines like these can send nursing mothers into the guest bedroom. A friend returned from seeing his newborn nephew, mystified that although his sister frequently discussed milk supply and sore nipples in minute detail, she required absolute privacy to nurse. "I'm used to you," my friend said, holding my margarita so I could help Milo tug away layers of sports bra and sweater. "My mother was so weird, tiptoeing around downstairs, whispering that my father and I weren't to go upstairs under any circumstance because my sister was *breastfeeding!*" I think families should regard nursing as an activity more akin to feeding the cat than passing night soil. At the moment of revelation, my stepfather more than took it like a man. I doubt he had given breastfeeding much thought before his slovenly stepdaughter undid the work of previous generations with one hike of the T-shirt. Up to this point, the women in his life had done an excellent job of shielding him from this inappropriate sight, just as they had washed his clothes and cooked ninety-nine percent of the meals he ate at home. But Art appreciates machines that work, and, for such a gruff guy, he's got a surpassingly gooshy spot for babies. He checked out the suckling action like he was admiring a particularly well-crafted hunting rifle. He asked intelligent questions.

Rarely have we been so clearly on the same page. Our previous interactions were undermined by the assumption that he knows how to do a lot of manly things well and I know how to lie in the front yard on a beach towel reading library books. I once demonstrated my mechanical aptitude by backing his beloved off-limits Thunderbird out of the garage and miring it in mud before reaching the alley or asking permission. It came as a great surprise that, outside of bizarre late-night theater in black-painted basements, I knew how to do something with such aptitude. My health insurance reimbursed me for a breastfeeding class. A mother of four had coached a dozen pregnant pupils in the technique, correcting us when we held our rubber baby dolls too tensely. I took notes, which I read out loud to Greg after class. With the authority of a recent graduate, I was able to answer Art's questions almost verbatim from the handouts. I told him the difference between front milk, which is what the baby gets when she first latches on for a feeding, and hind milk, the premium stuff that's the reward for staying at the same breast for ten minutes instead of switching from side to side. We still reward Inky with hind milk in the form of Ben and Jerry's. She gets it when she finishes an acceptable amount of her dinner in one sitting instead of flitting away to play with her cash register and her new ponytail holders. I told Art how I had no need for pacifiers because I was the human pacifier. Later my bias against pacifiers turned me into the human airbag, when, Greg driving. I dangled dangerously above Inky's car seat, waving to truckers. I presented data regarding childhood illness, IQs and sudden infant death syndrome. I flipped Inky around, demonstrating the football hold, the side-lying hold, and several unwieldy holds of my invention. I told him, as I still tell everyone who has half a grain of interest, that human milk most closely resembles that of a goat. Take that, Elsie the Cow. It felt good to be an expert, as easy as becoming an ordained minister on the Internet.

Several friends have had a devil of a time getting their babies interested in nursing. I once attended a roof party where the guest of honor, all of one week old, fed from a small capillary taped to her father's finger. It was one of the cutest things I'd ever seen, but it didn't feel so adorable to her mother. It's a slap in the face to a frazzled, sleep-deprived first-time mother when her newborn won't do the main thing for which she's allegedly programmed. That pinky-sucking baby required a lot of extra work. Her mother had a call girl's schedule with a breast pump, a loathsome device that sounds like a lawn mower and feels alarmingly impersonal at best. The capillary had to be rigged to a bottle and then taped to one parent or the other. Supposedly, if the capillary is taped next to the nipple, the baby will get suckered into effective sucking. Most babies who have trouble nursing don't have the tongue motion down. Hey, most teenage boys can't undo a bra strap but they figure it out, eventually. I think the real service lactation consultants provide is emotional, reassuring distraught mothers that they're not doing anything wrong. Their babies won't starve. Their milk is just as good as your average goat's. It's tough on the fathers too. It's like childbirth. Any man who attends his child's birth is a fan, cheering from the sidelines. He's not the linebacker. He's the Gatorade boy. The best he can do when his newborn won't nurse is fetch herbal tea, tape the bottle to his finger for the two A.M. feeding and persist in the belief that his woman is doing everything right. Sooner or later, he will pull a more experienced mother aside and pump her for tips.

Ooh, it's tempting to mouth off when these guys come around seeking breastfeeding advice for their wives and girlfriends. I rarely stick at anything long enough to master it. There's a reason people don't ask me to play tennis or translate something into French for them. What an easy way to pump up the old ego after a long Sisyphean day of rolling diapers and spilled crayons uphill! I could help some poor remedial breastfeeder to do it right like me! Who doesn't love an easy chance at gratification? But thus far I have demurred when an anxious father invites me to hold forth. Such restraint is atypical. I just have a hunch that the biggest insult to women whose babies won't latch on properly is that every other idiot leaking milk through her bra gets to think it's a cinch. They prance around with their shirts open, braying, "You just point your baby in the vicinity of your rib cage! What's the big deal?" Before I get all puffed up because my baby trounced another mother's baby in the proper tongue-positioning sweeps, let me take pride in something really unworthy, like my singing voice. It's unfair that some

women have to work their buns off to get their babies nursing properly, but the good news is that their efforts almost always are
rewarded. Some adoptive mothers not only have fed their babies at
their breasts using the capillary-on-the-nipple method, but also
have stimulated lactation! Who, except for every straight fourteen-
year-old boy in America knew that the human breast is so awe-
inspiring?

I'd never been much of a breast woman myself. A handful of
men out there might attest to the contrary, but thousands of things
give me greater pleasure than a mouth paying industrious attention
to my nipples. I was more than a bit worried about it in the months
leading up to Inky's birth. What if nursing a baby felt like a bad
date gone too far? I pictured myself stiffly cradling a famished
infant, grimly thinking of England while it satisfied itself.

I am pleased to report that feeding one's child is nothing like
enduring the attentions of an enthusiastic but unwelcome lover.
Before the nipples toughen up a bit, there is a moment of viselike
pain when the little eater chomps down for the twelfth meal of the
morning. It goes away. Only once have I experienced a blocked milk
duct. Never an alarmist, I immediately thought I was dying of breast
cancer. It hurt like holy hell to nurse then, but the good news is you
don't need chemo and radiation therapy to get through it. All you
have to do is line your bra with cabbage leaves. I swear this is not a
hazing ritual perpetuated by cool senior moms. If your breasts throb
like they've been suckling an asp, cozy up to a cabbage leaf. It works.

I'll never be able to describe an erection from the insider's per-
spective, but I can tell you that when the milk "lets down" it feels
the way your feet do when the ice skates are first removed. It tin-

gles. It happens in response to a baby's cries. Just as a shapely stranger crossing a sunny intersection without a slip can give a married man a boner, the lusty screams of an unknown baby are all it takes to activate the pins and needles. I saw an entire benchful of lactating mothers spontaneously darken their blouses with twin milk spots when a wailing four-month-old resisted his nanny's every effort to pacify him. When the milk lets down, you're locked and loaded. If somebody doesn't get busy draining the tanks, you'll be able to shoot a needle-thin jet for several feet, to the amazement of your horrified childless friends. For years I thought that kind of thing only happened in religious paintings, where a kneeling saint is nailed squarely in the eye by a statue of the Holy Virgin. I've heard that breast milk directly applied can cure conjunctivitis. I'm not fooling. It's a miracle on the order of cabbage leaves.

Breastfeeding is mostly like having pierced ears. You sort of forget the condition. One minute Milo's in the corner playing with a piece of string and the phone's ringing. Five minutes later I hang up to discover that the bib of my overalls is askew and Milo's chowing down to his heart's content. He must have started piping up while I was taking the call. Gathering him to my breast is second nature now. I walk from room to room with Milo casually attached, dangling even. I can open the mail, pick up toys and pay the bills. I have managed to steam the milk for cappuccino by propping him on the counter, leaving my hands free to operate the valve and pitcher. I can't weld or use the gas stove while breastfeeding, but I could rouse my nursing ass from the couch to put *Songs for Wiggleworms* on the stereo. I just prefer not to. I'm not above pandering to the stereotype of the nursing mother, nested comfortably in a sun-dappled rocking chair. Hey, if it means Greg gets stuck with the dishes, I'm all for it! When I'm seeking refuge from the constant household demands by giving Milo a snack in the butterfly chair, it does feel rather holy and womanly. Usually I'm equipped with a nice stack of reading material. Breastfeeding certainly has helped move my zine. An overwhelming percentage of subscribers seem to read it while their kids have their mouths full. A few have written to say that their partners also enjoy it seated on the toilet, which is where I tend to read it. On the rare occasions when I find myself nursing with no printed material, not even an old issue of my own zine in reach, it's not the worst thing in the world to bask in the baby. I can see why people stare. That trusting face, those heart-breaking sweat curls! What an honor to suckle the young of the species. I think it may be the best thing I've ever done in my life. It even beats giving birth, because it doesn't hurt.

Shortly after moving to New York, I decided I'd better make a plan in case I got pushed in front of a subway train. I'd read a grisly short story a former transit cop had published in *Esquire* on this subject (this is what my insomnia gets me). The woman in the story is a goner, not like the teenage survivor I'd read about years before in *Seventeen* who merely lost her hand. In the cop's story, the pressure of the train squashing the woman against the platform acts as a temporary tourniquet, keeping her alive just long enough to identify the purse snatcher who gave her that fatal shove. It was tawdry all right, but it stuck with me. Waiting for the train, I wondered what I would say if I were pinned between the train and the platform with just minutes to live. Not long after Inky's birth it hit me. If I ever had the misfortune to be flung into the path of an oncoming train, I could instruct the gaping herd to bring me my baby. "I want to feed her one last time. Don't bother with the sarong, boys!" Someone would put Inky to my breast. I would die happy. There would be a bidding war for the TV-movie rights. This anecdote may reveal a certain morbidity, but it also speaks to the joy of breastfeeding. What a sweet exit it would be, carried out on a wave of pure love. I replayed this scene often, sometimes while nursing. It was at least as moving as the end of *The Grapes of Wrath,* when the bereaved new mother permits a starving man to drink from her breast. (Oh Jesus, I hope I didn't spoil the book for anybody.) I never managed to explain why Inky hadn't gone flying under the train with me. Maybe her backpack came with a special ejection seat. It wasn't important. All that mattered to me was a good death and the chance to feed my baby one last time.

I felt really bad when it came time to wean her, what with my dying wish in the subway and all. As the babies in our crew started celebrating their first birthdays, techniques for kicking them off the boob were a frequent topic of conversation. We pushed the baby swings back and forth, pointed out the trucks rumbling down Avenue A to the boys and reviewed who was weaned, who was weaning and who would be taking Mommy to the junior prom to supplement the refreshments. "I want my body back," one friend said, shaking her head in fatigue. "I'm done."

I nodded in sympathy, inwardly rejoicing that I didn't feel that way at all. I was superhardcore, the soldier who leaps out of the foxhole with a grenade in her teeth. I was in for the long haul. My only fear was that Inky might wean herself spontaneously. It hadn't happened when she got her first taste of baby food. Some of her more robust cronies lost interest in nursing when they switched from the little jars to steamed vegetables and bagels diced to the size of croutons. I reluctantly offered her solids. Inky ate three peas, half a strawberry and a half-gallon of mother's milk. What a relief! Breastfeeding is wonderfully intimate, but it's also so danged handy! Kid did a triple gainer off the jungle gym? A hooter will fix what ails her. The balloon from the shoe store popped after a passionate but all too brief romance? Num-num num-num. Mom forgot to pack lunch again? May I recommend the breastfeeding?

I watched as her friends one by one spent less and less time at the breast. Some gave it up without a fuss. Others screamed in frustration, insistently tugging at their mothers' turtlenecks. I gladly would have bid adieu to her frequent nocturnal feedings, but how could I deny her the thing she loved best in the whole world? Inky would be one of the lucky few. The power was hers. We would not wean until she led the way. Fortunately, she showed no signs of doing so while I was attached so firmly.

"What if she decides she doesn't want to wean until she's six?" several charitable souls wanted to know, their jaws set at varying angles of challenge.

"Then she can nurse 'til she's six," I replied, standing my ground like Mother Courage.

Expect an earful if you nurse a child who's a bit too mature for one of those ridiculous Baby's First Christmas sleepers. The sight of a breastfeeding toddler can whip people into a frenzy. There was an article in a health-themed issue of *The New York Times* about a woman who breastfeeds her four-year-old twins. The story ran with an unimaginative shot of the bathrobed mother in quiet contemplation, suckling one of her big girls in a rocking chair. Brave woman, especially if her phone number's listed. Concerned adults have called the Department of Children and Family Services to report cases of abuse where none exists. It is as legal in our country to breastfeed children past babyhood as it is to bitch about it. People who want to protect children from harm would do better to fill up a grocery cart on behalf of a hungry family than to hassle mothers whose well-fed sucklings are too big for a high chair. In the land of plenty, breastfeeding women should be represented on a postage stamp, not in Family Court.

Once they've cut their teeth on breastfeeding toddlers, the scoundrels go after anyone nursing in a public place. A friend of a friend was asked to leave the children's section of a popular book-store chain where she sat feeding her baby as her older child browsed. According to the clerk, another customer had com-plained. Perhaps this other customer was in a neck brace and could not avert his or her eyes from the offensive display. Maybe the com-plainant was trying to protect an impressionable teenage son from copping a glimpse. A better parent would have trumpeted, "Jason! Stop staring at that woman! There's nothing unseemly about breastfeeding, but staring is impolite! If it's tits you're after, go to the art section!" As far as the clerk knew, the bookstore had no policy against breastfeeding. It had better not, as that would be illegal. However, given the complaint, the clerk and the manager felt that this nursing pair would be "more comfortable" in the women's bathroom.. At least the accused managed to rap out a snappy retort on her way down the escalator: "I don't shit where I eat, and neither does my baby." This woman lives in a distant city.

I never found out if the feed-in some people were trying to arrange via email happened. It sounded like fun. You get a bunch of women who were breastfeeding their kids all day anyway and relocate them to a comfortably furnished chain store. Their radical protest consists of nursing, drinking gourmet coffee and thumbing through magazines they have no intention of buying! That's my kind of anarchy!

At the heart of the matter is the breast. There's rarely trouble when a child drinks from a bottle in public. Occasionally I have seen a mother hunched over her child like someone caught shoplifting as a park bench of proud breastfeeders gives her bottle the hairy eyeball. To the best of my knowledge, the authorities never have been alerted because a four-year-old refreshes himself from a baby bottle. Nobody's ever been asked to leave the children's section because she satisfied her baby's hungry cries with something from her purse. There would be no hoopla if children nourished themselves via their mothers' elbows. So what if little Frances trots off the Little League field to have a slurp at Mommy's elbow? You can't expect to win the game without the breakfast of champions! I'm sure plenty of shy women would feed their children this way if the option were available. Chin, earlobe, even the silly old belly button would invite less reprobation and sniggering. I think I speak for all mothers when I say there's no naughty thrill in sticking our mammary glands between the lips of Healthtex-clad tyrants who have spent the morning demanding apple juice and unlimited access to the TV. It takes more than that to get me hot. Perhaps if we were more in touch with our animal selves we would find a shameless sexual element in the task. We're supposed to fear the pain of childbirth, hate our menstrual cycles and only recognize pleasure if it looks like a gift-wrapped salami. I'm all for breast-feeding feeling good! But it's an entirely different beast from an orgasm or even slow-dancing in seventh grade. From a child's per-spective, it's pleasure, the kind of unconditional love and reassur-ance we all crave. It's Mommy's lap. It's better than a Band-Aid when you fall off the swings. It's food. This is my best guess. Per-sonally, I never touched the stuff.

As her mother had hoped, Inky nursed for a long time. She stuck with it long enough to describe the experience in words, although she never waxed as poetic as the young ruler in Bertolucci's *The Last Emperor*. Enraged when his counselors send his surrogate mother packing, forcing him to wean cold turkey, he shouts, "Don't call her my wet nurse! She was my butterfly." Of course, the actress playing his butterfly was exquisite. She nursed the teenage monarch in an elegant boat adrift in an ornamental lagoon. I bore a closer resem-blance to a sag-bellied mule in a broken-brimmed sun hat. Then one day I became a wolf.

You'd think anyone who can remember tales of grisly subway maimings in lurid detail years later would retain the following information: It is possible to become pregnant while nursing. It's repeated ad infinitum in breastfeeding classes, postpartum checkups and every single book on conception, pregnancy and child development. It's as possible as getting pregnant in the backseat of a car or the first time you have sex. If a southern belle can find her-self in the family way after a bullet that passed through the testicles of a Union soldier lodges in her uterus, you can get knocked up while nursing. It's difficult to have sex when you're half dead from chasing after a breastfeeding two-year-old who sleeps between you and your mate, but sometimes you have an extra glass of wine at the picnic and start feeling pretty. I had all the contraceptive luck with breastfeeding that I've had with my diaphragm. A few days after I bought the home pregnancy kit that confirmed Milo's arriving flight, I hunkered down in Tompkins Square, nursing Inky on the spongy black asphalt. My breasts were killing me. That's what had led me to suspect I was pregnant, those familiar pangs like I was attached to cinder blocks by alligator clips. If it was bad going down the stairs at a trot, it was unbearable when Inky came calling. I was almost as miserable as Greg about this unplanned pregnancy when I considered that this wild punching-bag pain in my frequently used breasts might continue or even get worse over nine months of gestation. None of my playground buddies knew of my condition. I plastered my arms across my chest, trying to act normal. If it had been a speck of dust in my eye, I would have been bellowing for help and advice, but to tell the truth I felt a little chagrined. Breast-feeding wasn't supposed to hurt an old trooper like me.

The woman with four children was there too. She talks a lot, in the same way someone who's spent twenty minutes underwater tends to gulp a lot of oxygen. Usually my mind drifts. Her cheerful banter washes over me until we're interrupted by a child busting out of the gates or tumbling headfirst off the old brick drinking fountain. On this day, I couldn't have been more attentive if she had been telling an amusing story from my childhood. She had gotten going on pregnancy, how she and her husband had spent every penny on an expensive tropical vacation only to find out that she was up the stick with their first child. The other three appeared at intervals of two years. She nursed her oldest son while pregnant with his brother. She nursed her youngest son while pregnant with her oldest daughter, who now hung close by, eager for her baby sister's turn at the tit to be over. "I'm curious," I asked nonchalantly as visions of scorpions and venomous spiders danced in my head. "Didn't it kill your breasts, what with the hormonal changes and all?"

"Oh, no, I've never had a problem with stretch marks!" she tittered.

"No, not stretch marks. I mean like scorpions."

She looked at me blankly, momentarily stumped.

"Like a scorpion was stabbing you with its tail, stinging you over and over. Like you were bloating up with poison every time the kid started to nurse."

This would have been the perfect time for her to have said "You're pregnant, aren't you?" but instead she laughed again, in peals of amusement so silvery they practically were three-part harmony. "Oh no, it doesn't hurt at all! Scorpions? Yuck! Ooh!"

I wondered if she had some supernaturally high tolerance for pain. She did live in a one-bedroom apartment with four kids and a grown man. Maybe she was as gaily impervious to the bullwhip crack of a two-year-old's gnashers on her polluted punching bags as she was to squabbles over toy earth movers and the fact that she never could go anywhere without a full-sized duffel bag of Pop-Tarts, wiffle bats and plastic dinosaurs.

I hoped that the excruciating sensation in my breasts would go away like morning sickness or my favorite jeans. It didn't. I was beginning to show, Inky was as conscientious a milker as she ever had been and something snapped. That's when I turned into a wolf.

Maybe I'm flattering myself. I've seen Irish setters respond in the same way to their pups as I did to Inky. Whenever she latched on, my body went rigid. I had to grit my teeth so I wouldn't start barking. After the first rush of milk, the physical pangs subsided somewhat, but the ramrod mental resistance increased. What was I thinking? Nursing wasn't an intrusion! It was our great pleasure! It was my dying wish in the event of bisection by subway! Looking down at my daughter's voracious body, I was at pains to summon an ounce of sympathy. Instead, I felt a canine kinship with every four-legged mother who flashes her fangs at the pups who tarry too long at the nipple, snapping ferociously so they'll know she means business. I told myself that my reaction was purely animal. My inner dog, the poor woman's wolf, was telling me that it was time to wean.

I eliminated her first-thing-in-the-morning feeding. No more lollygagging around in bed for us. The instant I felt her jockeying into nursing position, I'd spring to the floor like an insane camp counselor enumerating all the fun in store for us that day. Still chattering, I bounded into kitchen snatching at the Cheerios. Her weak protests were drowned under a steady stream of wholesome Super Fun Mom badinage. Whenever a wave of nausea threatened to overwhelm me, I dropped to the floor, groping blindly for the crackers stashed on a low shelf. "Whoo! Mommy's just taking a little rest here," I croaked, splaying my fingers across my chest lest Inky spy an opening. As soon as the queasiness passed, I was back on my feet, brandishing bananas and soy milk.

The next thing to go was the bedtime feeding. This wasn't hard, as my condition had me so fried I barely could drag myself off the couch at seven o'clock to scrape up Inky's dinner. I felt like I'd been embalmed. I had been so robust when I was pregnant with Inky, carting huge bags of groceries for blocks and getting shot and thrown into walls in plays that didn't start 'til midnight. Back then, I thought that pregnancy's reputation as a depleting, delicate condition was a conspiracy propagated by right-wing extremists. Pregnant women were Amazons! Why was I so exhausted this go-around? The answer was right in front of me, demanding macaroni and cheese. Oh, those wonderful mid-morning naps when Inky was still a bun in the oven! The hours spent babying myself with good things to eat and read…all gone. Except for my howling breasts and the rapid weight gain that had me wheezing up the stairs like our elderly Ukrainian neighbor ladies, I barely remembered I was pregnant. I was too busy catering to the needs of my little charge. From the cruel moment she roused me for the Cheerios hustle to the highly anticipated sound of Greg's key in the lock after twelve hours spent scouting film locations, I was on duty. It made a first-year medical residency sound good. At thirty-two, I had taken long lavender-scented baths and prepared complicated herbal teas to ripen my body for labor. At thirty-five, I scavenged lunch from the leftover crusts of peanut butter and jelly on a compartmentalized plastic plate. It took every ounce of strength to roll out Play-Doh snakes or sip air from Inky's doll-sized tea set. My eyes burned like charcoal in my head. I think Greg feared for my health. I could barely work up the energy to glance at a takeout menu. By the time the food arrived, I had checked out for the night, a circle of drool widening on the couch cushion. Greg ate his orange beef in grim silence. He bathed Inky, put her in her pajamas and read upward of a dozen books to get her to sleep. He washed the dishes and put away toys. I sprawled like an alcoholic, dead to the world at an hour when other mothers were smartly shaking up martini number two as foreplay to the excellent meal in the oven. Oh well. At least Inky transferred her bedtime dependence on breast milk to *Goodnight Moon* and *The Lorax* as interpreted by her father. Even in the final months of my pregnancy, when I was feeling a bit more up to the task, Greg remained the featured reader. I didn't want Inky to feel there was any chance of nursing to sleep, not even for old time's sake.

Friends saw the circles under my eyes and realized that my endless tale of woe had some basis in reality. This was different from the insomniac's complaint that she'd only slept four hours in three days. They asked if Inky still napped. I told them that she did. Why didn't I do as mothers of newborns do and sleep when she slept? Maybe if I joined Inky for a siesta we could all stop hearing about my crippling fatigue. I rejected this sensible advice on the grounds that Inky's nap times were my golden hours. The second her eyes closed, I pounced, applying myself to the upcoming issue of the *East Village Inky* with a vigor I was amazed I still possessed. I couldn't sacrifice my tiny corner of creative time for something so unproductive as sleep. Besides, it wasn't just about my mental hygiene anymore. I had a couple hundred subscribers. If I didn't spend every nap time second on the zine, I might fall behind my self-imposed deadline. I lay awake at night imagining angry readers rifling through handfuls of mail. "It's April 18 already! It was supposed to arrive three days ago. I sent eight dollars to that liar! Where is it?!"

Inky napped because Inky nursed. She could have been weaned a whole lot sooner if I hadn't clung so tenaciously to those mid-afternoon comas. After two years of nursing her down to sleep, I couldn't very well order her to assume the recumbent position and expect it to work. Breastfeeding, cosleeping old Ma Wolf was suddenly jealous of working mothers who bragged about their nannies' magical nap-inducing powers. "It's incredible! She just puts him in his crib and rubs his back, and he's out before she's halfway through his favorite lullaby!" I wondered if I could hire a Tibetan baby-sitter to come sing me to sleep when I jolted awake at two A.M. with insomnia that threatened to stretch on for hours. I was far too cheap and financially precarious to pay someone an hourly wage to mind Inky, particularly if Nanny rendered her unconscious with some mystical baby-sitter's incantation. What would I have to write about if I farmed Inky out, even if only for the duration of this energy-sapping pregnancy? People who read the zine did so in good faith that Inky and I spent every waking hour in each other's company. That was okay with me as long as one of us was asleep for one, preferably two of those waking hours. I would do whatever I had to to ensure those naps continued. My breasts felt like boils that should have been lanced. Maybe she could learn to fall asleep without a drink. Recovering alcoholics do it all the time! I tried playing it cagey, stretching and yawning. "Hmm, I feel sleepy," I'd confide. "I think I need a nap. Here, let's lie down together. I'll read one book, and then let's close our eyes and see what happens."

What happened was I woke up with a start twenty minutes later surrounded by picture books and stuffed animals. Inky was in the kitchen. Not wanting to disturb me, she had fixed a snack by her ownself. A brand-new carton of orange juice lay empty in a puddle. She'd tracked it into the bathroom. Her pants were wet. With orange juice, I hoped dully. It was like being locked in a roomful of hay. I knew I had zero chance of spinning a single straw into gold, but I was expected to try.

She almost always conked out in the backpack if we went for a walk at a certain hour, but the transfer was increasingly dicey. She had a tendency to wake up as I eased the straps off my shoulders to lay her, pack and all, on top of the café table at which I planned to write for hours. The second those eyes flew open, the party was over. Also, the bigger her baby brother grew in my belly, the more burdensome the little passenger on my back became. I was going to give myself varicose veins carting her around like this. The only surefire method involved my ulcerous udders.

A lactating woman's milk is a matrix in constant flux. It subtly readjusts to meet the needs of the nurser. It's like those fancy pet foods with scientific ingredients suited to puppies, adolescents, dogs in their prime and farting, toothless old curs with urinary tract infections. If a breastfeeding mother becomes pregnant, her milk begins to change back, resetting the counter in anticipation of a newborn customer. It doesn't take into account the needs of the time-strapped zine-publishing mother who uses it to dope her constant companion. This recipe change doesn't go unnoticed by those accustomed to bellying up at the titty bar. Imagine if you'd grown used to a mid-afternoon pint of some rich amber microbrew only to have the bartender slip you a mug of Schlitz. That's how it went with Inky. Around two in the afternoon, she'd get that haggard look, stumbling around the playground, clutching a filthy pigeon feather like a talisman to ward off sleep. Licking my chops at the thought of her fast-approaching nap, I craftily swung into lullaby mode, hoisting her above my protruding abdomen for the half-block walk home. Odds were good that she'd fall asleep in my arms! I narrowed my eyes to slits, surveying the terrain for garrulous neighbors who'd been known to botch the job with such top-volume observations as, "Oh, looky there! She's going to sleep!" More often I was the guilty party, jostling her a bit too much as I pawed through every pocket and bag in search of keys. One of these days I'll standardize the location of my keys and wallet.

Okay, we'd made it into our apartment and she was still awake. Maybe a few pulls were all it would take to polish her off. I could weather five minutes of extreme irritation in return for a two-hour nap. I got us situated in the butterfly chair, took a deep breath and opened my shirt. I was determined not to turn into the exasperated Irish setter. But yogic relaxation techniques were useless. The second her mouth was on me I felt like my spine had been replaced with a metal flagpole. I ground my molars, twisting the chicken-print hem of Inky's dress. What was taking her so long? She rustled closer to me, her scratched, bruised legs swinging like she was conducting an orchestra. When did her legs get so long? She barely fit in my lap, what was left of it. "Go to sleep, Inky," I snapped. She sighed theatrically and slapped my sternum with an open palm. If I were a dog, she'd have earned herself a nasty bite. "I mean it. Go to sleep." Jesus, I sounded mean. I would never speak to her like that in public. She should be asleep. This was a travesty. She started making her outboard motor noise, the one she'd kept up for the entirety of Karen and

CJ's wedding. I had thought breastfeeding would guarantee a respectful quiet on our part during the ceremony, but all I ended up doing was flashing the groom's matron aunts.

"Urr-ruh urr-ruh urr-ruh," Inky idled, fiddling with one of my buttons. She was getting ready to tug. After two and a half years of nursing, I recognized the signs. My shoulders were frozen above my ears. I barely could remember what it was like to nurse a newborn, a sweet little swaddling no longer than my forearm. Goddamnit. Her eyes were wide open. I stared out the window, determined to make her fall asleep by ignoring her. After a few minutes, I sneaked a glance back down at her, expecting the coast to be clear. I had my pinky crooked, ready to break the vacuum seal her mouth was exerting on my nipple. Dog bitch shit ass! She was wide awake, her expression that of the diner who can't identify the prevalent flavor in a dish. Is it cilantro? She started chewing. That was the penulti-mate straw. Those who've never breastfed can make themselves cringe, imagining what happens when the baby gets teeth. It's not so bad. You get a couple of bad surprises, the kind that make you see stars, but the novelty of trying out the choppers on Mama wears off quickly. Milk has to be coaxed out. People who prefer to get their calcium from a bag of warm flesh know that. Ask a farmer, the old-fashioned overalled kind with a red barn full of friendly animals, not seven hundred Guernseys hooked up to a stainless steel milking machine. Even the kids who have difficulty nursing at first get the action down long before they sprout teeth. Nobody wants to bite the hand or any other body part that feeds them.

"Inky, I am getting to the end of my tether. If you want to nurse, you had better get down to it, because I am sick of this fooling around." This was Inky's first encounter with Bitch Mother. She thought it was a game. I always dealt with her as a buddy, like a best friend who incidentally wiped her ass, procured her meals and knew everything there was to know in the world. Instead of laying down the law, I played the part of the less daring girlfriend, forever trying to stop the prettier one from sneaking out the window to meet the handsome drifter with the bedroom eyes and the good pot. I recognized the punitive tone of voice, but Inky didn't. She smiled, tossed her head fetchingly and burrowed her nose into me. My breast billowed around her like a parachute on land. I used to be able to bounce her off, I was so round and full. It had been months since I'd experienced that tingly letdown sensation. Was there even any milk in there? I felt about as abundant as a dry well. She gave a couple of desultory sucks and then, without warning, clamped my nipple between her teeth and reared back as if reining in a runaway stagecoach.

I retaliated in a hot second, smacking the top of her head with an open palm. Instantly she was wailing in confusion and pain. I gabbled stricken apologies. She permitted me to rock her back and forth. I felt terrible. I recalled my high-minded promises never to touch my child in anger. I slapped myself on top of my head as hard as I could. It didn't hurt too much, but it made a great whopping sound. My prey had been unsuspecting, pursuing her favorite pastime in the bosom of her family. I had struck with a cobra's precision. Way to go, Supermom.

It almost broke my heart that she immediately settled in to nurse properly. Within two minutes, she had fallen into a hiccuping sleep. Her joking high spirits whacked out of her, she obediently consoled herself with the strange hot water that had replaced her mother's milk. She slept for a long time, but the nap was shot for me. I lay on the couch, whimpering, wondering what had happened to me. I had been such a groovy, uncomplaining pregnant woman in 1997, full of information about how cave dwellers and chimpanzees raised their young. I had dealt with the devil or possibly an incredibly gracious god in that Neonatal Intensive Care Unit, promising anything in return for my three-day-old daughter's health. What had happened to the gentle, good-humored mother of the cherished baby bathed as reverently as Jesus' feet? Did I intend to draw a funny little picture of me hitting my nursing child in the *East Village Inky*? You know I'm in bad shape when I put *Songs for the Inner Child* on endless replay so I can weep into a pillow without getting up.

I resolved from that point on to be Mother Earth. I would give without grudging. But the next time she snapped on, I seethed. I wasn't fit to nurse her anymore. I should be thankful that her naps had lasted as long as they had. A year earlier, when I had met a slender, intelligent and wealthy woman whose four-year-old daughter hadn't taken a nap since the age of six months, I considered myself the lucky one. It helped that her husband was an asshole of the first degree. Many mothers would envy my good long run. Maybe if she gave up her naps I'd let her watch the eensy weensiest bit of television. I consoled myself that the old reliable would have lost its power even if I hadn't metastasized into a snapping snarler. This new milk I was packing was a dud, lacking that all-important soporific ingredient. If anything, it caused her to shake off the mantle of drowsiness as she tried to nail down the mystery flavor. Was it dill? Forget the head smacking, the tense muscles and the vengeful mood. If this last vestige of nursing didn't yield a nap, it wasn't worth it.

A friend from the playground upgraded her stroller and gave me the old one. I was loath to use it, but for trips of more than a few blocks I had no choice. I couldn't carry Inky on my back or in my arms. Sometimes she could be cajoled into walking all the way to our destination, which was fine if we had six hours to get there. My cohorts in the playground had to show me the hidden levers that caused the contraption to collapse and reopen, like an umbrella. I was a slow learner. They demonstrated again, treating me with the elaborate, joshing solicitousness they would show to a befuddled father. I'm still not sure which way you're supposed to push the lever that sets the brakes. It was so elaborate compared to the back-pack. I hated needing it. When did I get to be so regular, pushing the child I couldn't wait to wean hither and thither in a navy plaid stroller? Inky found the hand-me-down as novel as a swan boat, a marvelous break from the routine. I had been sure she would turn her nose up at it, but she liked it as much as she like stuffed Tele-tubbies, store-bought cake and extra-long fingernails airbrushed with florid sunsets. We rolled around town, going much farther from home than I could have with twenty-five pounds on my back, even if I hadn't had an extra fifty on the inside. That stroller was the little engine that could. Inky fell asleep and stayed asleep! I could even tell when she was on the verge of cashing out mid-hike. Her right hand rolled palm up and the fingers slowly uncurled. With the backpack, I used to have to check our reflection in a store window to see if Inky was out, unless a helpful stranger hipped me, alarmed that my baby would suffocate with her neck at such a drastic angle. With the stroller, that pesky transfer from shoulders to table was moot. I could wheel her into a café, pull my rapidio-graph pen out of my bag and doodle away on the *East Village Inky* for at least an hour, sometimes two. She slept well without the threat of some bitchy wolf whapping her upside the head. Two days out of three she would nap in the stroller. On those third days, she didn't nap and she didn't let up until I permitted her to nurse. It was like being tied to a backboard in a Red Cross lifesaving course, one of the worst situations in which an extreme claustrophobe can find herself. Somebody once told me that pale green is a healing, antiseptic color to meditate on if you're feeling infected. When pale green failed to quell the heebie-jeebies, I tried glowing rose, elegant cream and a friendly sunshine yellow. Nothing could stop the navy blue plaid from seeping in, cementing my foul mood. Those third days always crept up on me.

One night, I realized we had gone three days without nursing. I made a successful bid for four. On the fifth day, Inky was covering the bench in sidewalk chalk when her coconspirator in this enter-prise took a break to nak-nak. It wasn't lost on her that her friend was indulged freely. She badgered me to nurse. "Want to go for a ride in the stroller?" I asked, burnishing the word with as much roller-coastery zip as I could muster. Mr. Nak-Nak didn't have a stroller. He traveled by grocery cart. Maybe Inky would make the connection. So what if her friend got an apple? She had a sexy, souped-up blue plaid orange! I rolled my eyes meaningfully toward our stroller, parked in a line of nearly identical models. Wouldn't somebody be jealous when he turned his head away from his mommy's breast? Inky scrabbled at me. I grabbed her hand and proposed a race to the slide. She snatched it back, staring at me reproachfully. "I want num-num and then I want num-num other side!" she shouted.

"Ayun, I'm so sorry," her buddy's mother whispered over the top of his contented head.

I waved my hand to show it didn't matter. I thought about what it would be like to strangle her, the way I dream about slapping the person who takes the last dryer at the Laundromat or blowing a whistle into the ear of the friend who telephones in the middle of *ER*. It's nothing personal. I'm sure she's felt the same toward me when Inky devours a dripping soft-serve ice cream cone in front of her sugar-free son. Inky shinnied up my leg like a monkey scaling a telephone pole. She seized the front of my shirt. This was the moment of truth. I could be a hard-ass or I could cave in, lose the ground we had gained. I could march around the East Village with my angry offspring or I could flop on the bench on a beautiful spring day. A grasshopper to the end, I chose the bench. Inky got to nak-nak on num-num, both sides. Flanked by other women and children, I didn't feel so wolfish. I forgot about strangling my friend. There are worse things than a last hurrah in the late afternoon sun.

Inky's final feeding slipped by unnoticed. I suppose it is the firsts that we celebrate. I have photos of her first rice cereal, the first time she ate from chopsticks and her first day of school. On her first birthday, I picked up a piece of beach glass on the Isle of Aran. Naturally, it is still gathering grime on the kitchen windowsill. She took her first step when she was precisely eleven months old. The first movie she attended was *Austin Powers* at the now defunct three-dollar theater on 50th Street, nursing through the entire thing, barely making a peep. The first movie she consciously attended was Austin Powers' unworthy sequel at the drive-in on Cape Cod. She ate her first ice cream sandwich from the refreshment stand. Her first real haircut, her first toothbrush, her first pair of underpants, I remember them all. But I have no memory of the last time she nursed. It must have been uneventful. I never got around to inventing a special ceremony, midway between a Masai puberty ritual and a Brownie Scout fly-up. Perhaps I'll have one ready for her first period.

The assurance that I would soon have another child to feed exterminated any lingering lumps in my throat. I had a reprieve of three months. The wolf slunk away. I reverted to being a crabby, heavy human with swollen ankles and listeria. When Milo came out nursing, everything was once again sweetness and light. Despite my only child's conviction that sibling rivalry is not a biological imperative, I wondered how Inky would react when her baby brother was permitted to farm freely the land from which she'd been displaced. What if she resented Milo for his claim on my breasts? I've heard tell of a mother who made a special nursing basket full of gift-wrapped quiet toys to appease her preschooler while the new arrival sucked up the private reserve. That sounds like the bullet train to Veruca Saltville. If Inky got it in her head that she was entitled to an Oompa Loompa every time her brother started rooting around, we'd all be in serious trouble. I hoped our old standbys—the purloined scissors, her father's camera and the litter box scoop—would provide ample entertainment while I attended to the baby. Maybe I could frame it in such a way that she would take to fetching as an important responsibility that only a very, very big girl, a big sister, can handle. She could bring me magazines and lemonade while I reposed, Milo arranged on my chest like a hot-water bottle. If she asked me nicely, I might agree to let her mop the floor.

Far from begrudging Milo's time at the tit, Inky seemed to find Milo's native know-how hilarious. It was even funnier than the time I flailed his tiny arms to a frat rock drum solo, realizing too late that this might be a bad precedent to set. Whenever he latched on, she'd shriek with approval. "Lookit little My-lee-moe! He want to num-num! Look at him!" Her shrill delight invariably woke the baby and got on her mother's dangerously frayed nerves. I consider these manic good spirits the humorous child's temper tantrum. Still, if it's a choice between her hornpipes of enthusiasm and pinching, slapping meltdowns, I say let the good times roll!

With the possible exception of the Barbies I'm forever refusing to buy, Inky loves nothing better than a good prank. She got me good one morning shortly after Milo joined our household. I was in bed with my husband and my son, trying to scavenge what sleep I could before Inky hit the floorboards yelling for vitamins. Baby brother had hooked himself up to feed several thousand times the night before. I was more tired than I had been when I went to bed. I have no trouble snoring through sirens, the telephone and practically every video Greg brings home, but usually I spring to attention at the slightest peep from one of my chicks. When something that felt like an anteater attached itself to my left breast, I allowed myself a half-conscious flash of irritation at my newborn son. Dang, hadn't he tanked up plenty between the hours of midnight and six A.M.? No wonder he was hoovering away with such intensity. I needed time to replenish. He would have to suck with all his might to get another drop. I figured I might as well get comfortable. Maybe if I bolstered myself with buckwheat rolls and sock monkeys, I could drift off for another precious minute or two. Crooking my elbow in search of the ideal nursing position, my right hand brushed against a foreign object, roughly the size and texture of a grapefruit upholstered in velour. What was it? Could I tuck it under my shoulder so I wouldn't give myself a rotator cuff injury hunching toward the baby? Wait a minute. How could Milo be going to town on my left side when his head was tucked under my right armpit? Oh no!

"I make a joke," Inky chortled, flashing a toothy grin an inch or so above my breast.

Good one. Laughing uneasily, I pulled the sheet to my chin before she could crack the joke again.

Knock knock.

Who's there?

Your older kid whom you had planned to tandem-nurse before you turned into some wolfy mongrel!

My older kid who?

To my immense relief, Inky's reappearance at my breast was not the alarming thud of a little girl falling off the wagon. I'd heard of a child her age who weaned himself from his pregnant mama's unappetizing hot water only to wring his newborn brother's hand in gratitude for bringing the milk back for both of them. I love that story and am so glad it's not mine. Inky will not require me to accompany her to the junior prom after all. I'm back in the saddle with Milo. I'm happy to be here. For another year or two anyway, I won't have to scramble for a wish if I end up pinned between the platform and the train.

The Chopping Block

My family has a highly complex relationship to amputation.

First there was the impending baby, my first child, known to be a boy because my ballooning body resembled an apple more than a pear. When not pregnant I resemble a pear. Since every hard-luck nutcase on the streets of the East Village agreed definitively and without solicitation that I was carrying a male, there was no need for a sonogram.

I forget where or when the circumcision argument began, but I can pinpoint the moment it blazed beyond our control. We were at the Odessa diner with Little MoMo and her short-lived new boyfriend. He, it's fair to say, was asking for it. "So," he inquired with the smirk people seldom employ when discussing the amputation of an arm or leg, "are you going to chop off his weenie?"

That's what passes for adult cocktail conversation these days, and, believe me, my banter is a lot less witty when I'm tanked up on plain tomato juice, no ice. After about a minute's worth of unamusing repartee, Greg and I were at each other's throats. Things escalated rapidly, as intimate high-stakes fights in front of someone you've just met do, and before you could say "snip-snip ha-ha," I was blinking back tears, aghast that Greg would so blithely mutilate our son. Greg, a third generation Jewish atheist whose great-grandfather was a rabbi, was dismayed to learn he'd married an anti-Semite whose hippie-dippy ideas would break a tradition dating back to Abraham and Isaac, if not further. We made a real scene. It's amazing we didn't tip over the table.

The fight continued for two days, until my red, swollen eyes trumped every argument in Greg's arsenal. I had stood firm and weeping when presented with such pearls as "his penis should look like his father's penis," "what if the other kids laugh at him in the locker room," and "it's unsanitary." I did research on the Internet and enlisted the support of Karen, who rallied her uncircumcised Scottish fiancé to email Greg, whom he had never met. CJ is a good egg, as they say. He is so soft-spoken and discreet that you would never guess that he'd email American strangers about his penis. The testimony of a satisfied, uncut Glaswegian notwithstanding, Greg held his ground. "You know how the Nazis identified the Jews, don't you?" he said. "He has relatives who died in the camps. I want him to be connected to that."

He almost had me there. At least I stopped thinking of him as the would-be baby butcher. A little more research on the Internet, and I returned to Greg with a Talmudic riddle. "If you can tell me why the Jews circumcise their male children, I'll do it."

It was my turn to have him. Greg's childhood religious instruction weighed in at zilch. I, however, had participated in a seder in my Episcopal Sunday school. Greg wasn't bar mitzvahed until his late twenties when he was pulled off a Lower East Side street into a Lubovitcher van. I had attended many bar mitzvahs back in Indiana. They were my first boy-girl parties. "Do you give?" I asked.

"Well, it's to show, it's because of, when you become a man…" he stammered.

"No, it's a covenant with God," I told him. "Who you don't believe in. We can take him to the Holocaust Museum. He will know about his relatives who died in the camps." The non-atheist Jews' covenant with God sealed the deal my red, swollen eyes had brokered.

We still had the problem of the cat. I have known Jambo longer than I have known Greg, and he has never once behaved like anything other than a foul-tempered, ungrateful, violent little murderer. I saw the jigsaw remains of many mice trapped by his swift and steely claws. God only knew what he could do to a baby's finger. "It's an amputation! It's like cutting off their fingers!" rang the words of a strident, hulking veterinarian I once knew. She had favored harsh penalties for barbaric pet owners who prioritized their upholstery. An eye for an eye, a finger for every declawed paw. I didn't like her much, but I couldn't shake her low opinion of people who whacked off their cats' extremities as mindlessly as cutting crusts off a sandwich. It wasn't that far removed from my anti-circumcision platform.

Greg and I know where we stand with Jambo. We love him, but he doesn't love us back. The only thing he loves is that mangy rag doll he has humped at least three times a day since adolescence. I didn't buy into that old wives' tale about cats sucking the breath from a slumbering infant, but I know from experience that Jambo never "uses his words" when he can swipe and bite. We couldn't give him away because his reputation preceded him. Some friends claimed allergies or asthma. Others laughed in our faces. Even our mothers refused. A friend of Greg's had baby-sat Jambo for six months while we were traveling in Asia, but we hadn't seen him since our wedding, he lived halfway across the country and there was the matter of the hammer. When we got back from Asia, Josh had returned Jambo with one of those little rubber and steel hammers doctors use to test reflexes. "He likes to play with this," Josh told us. I'll bet.

With my due date looming, Jambo was going to lose either way. Your fingers or your life. The vet who performed the amputation had no problem with declawing, though he did take me to task for neglecting to schedule the operation during Jambo's infancy. "If you knew you wanted children, you should have had the procedure done at the same time you had him neutered." (Oh yeah, before we took his fingers, we took his jewels, which didn't put a damper on his relationship with the rag doll.) I felt sufficiently chastised that I didn't tell the doctor that the few motherly fantasies I'd entertained seven years earlier rarely strayed beyond adorable baby clothes.

Anyone who tells you that declawing is not painful has not seen her pet hobbling about, long stitches trailing from his foreshortened paws like busted guitar wires. His confusion upon finding his litter box filled with shredded newspaper nearly broke our hearts. If nothing else, Jambo's suffering convinced Greg that his reluctant decision to leave our son's foreskin as is was a good one. We spent our final childless days following Jambo around the apartment, apologizing to him and putting his doll in easy reach.

Imagine our surprise when I gave birth to a three-thumbed baby girl who required a spinal tap within forty-eight hours of delivery. "Don't worry, she won't feel it," a young resident assured me. Yeah, right, that's what they tell the anxious mothers of boy babies right before circumcision. I was sitting beside Inky in the Neonatal Intensive Care Unit when a little boy was circumcised one bassinet over. He arched his back nearly double and screamed as if someone were cutting a piece of his penis off, which indeed someone was. Sharp things applied to soft tissue cause pain. I'm sure if Doberman pinschers could speak a language humans understood, they wouldn't hesitate to lobby for the aesthetic merits of unbobbed ears.

As Inky underwent all sorts of medical intervention in those first two weeks, the extra thumb became a rallying point. When told of our baby's minor abnormality, a friend getting her master's in gender studies at NYU rasped, "Wonderful! She'll be a feminist and a witch!" The third thumb came to represent an extra resource, proof that our baby had strength in reserve. The nurses wisely treated it as a nifty surprise, like an antique ring that flips open to dispense a pinch of arsenic. Toward the end of our hospital stay, the pediatric cardiologist offered to refer us to a hand man to have the thumb removed in an easy procedure. I would imagine that it's a refreshing change of pace for a pediatric cardiologist to discuss something so elective and unimportant with parents. But by that point, all three of Inky's thumbs were as precious to me as my own. The miracle of birth still fresh in his mind, Greg conceded to the mother's etched-in-stone wishes.

The family was less convinced. No doubt relieved that the circumcision decision would remain hypothetical, Greg's mother began to play that old song, "Children Can Be So Cruel." I happen to think adults can be much crueler. The jury's still out as to whether a certain three-thumbed teenager will give the finger to her freakshow-loving mother for ruining her chances for a normal life. For all we know, she's going to be the cruelest kid in class, hectoring the kid with the hearing aid, the fat kid or the kid whose father died. I hope not. I think I'm raising her to be pretty compassionate, to stick it to the twerps who jeer at differences that elicit curiosity. Children invent ways to be cruel without the prop of physical abnormalities.

I came home from first grade crying because some bad boy had called me "pantyhose."

"Baby thumb" came in handy when Inky and every other child at a party noticed that one young guest had a large purple mass on his neck. Our hostess had told me that the little boy's mother was sensitive about her son's appearance. It must make every children's party a nightmare for her, as one piping voice after another demands to know what that thing is and why he has that thing and look at that thing, Mama! When the little piping voice was one I recognized, I was ready, maybe a little too ready. I deftly reminded Inky of how her baby thumb was something special she had been born with and her new friend had something special he had been born with, yak yak yak. My explanation exceeded the term limits of her interest. It hit home that our position is one of luxury. A cute little thumb-bud will in no way inhibit my pretty child's career as a surgeon or a concert pianist. I doubt the mother at the party would use the eggplant-like sack growing from his neck to satisfy his questions about my kid's dinky thumb. She might draw his attention to it when he notices a kid born with just one eye. In the grand scheme, I can't imagine that Inky's deformity will cause her much more grief than her brother's foreskin will bring him.

"It looks like an aardvark's nose," Greg commented while

changing Milo's diaper. The circumcision decision of 1997 held for the child born in 2000. The old name was dusted off too.

The cat is still declawed, his temper just as foul.

Of our children's male cronies, I would say about half are circumcised. If a diaper change is in progress, we look, just as curious as little boys in a locker room. Nobody accuses anyone else of barbarism, though we all have our thoughts.

No one outside the family has told me that I'm crazy to leave my daughter's baby thumb in peace. Actually, a French mother on the playground did, but she thinks all Americans are crazy, particularly the ones who circumcise their sons. I like her. I bet she was a cruel child. She gets a lot of mileage from how I dress my baby boy, in hand-me-down leopard-print bonnets and loopy crocheted sweaters. "Are you trying to turn zees child into a fairy?" she laughs.

"I wouldn't mind it," I tell her as we watch her son charge the length of the playground gripping a fallen tree branch like a battering ram. "But I think it has to be something you're born with."

These Parts

My introduction to sex came courtesy of my father's anthologies of *New Yorker* cartoons. The references to FDR and cubism went over my head, but it's pretty clear that a rich old man with a naked lady perched on his lap is up to something, especially if she's pretty, with breasts like basketballs. Even a four-year-old knows that. My suspicion that naked people were naughty predates memory. In my earliest recollections I checked that the coast was clear before pulling my playmates behind the wing chairs to peep at the fat capitalists and their nubile secretaries to our hearts' content. Once I got busted. A child visitor told her mother that she had seen naked ladies at my house. The woman phoned my parents. I wasn't punished until I was a teenager, when my father trotted out the anecdote to anyone who would listen.

I think now would be a good time to move our collection of underground comix to the highest shelf. Inky has inherited my graphic tendencies. She can't get enough of big-nosed Buddy Bradley screwing his girlfriend in Peter Bagge's *Hate,* which is child's play compared to the explicit fantasies of R. Crumb. The lascivious swells in vintage *New Yorker* cartoons are koala bears compared to this stuff. My old co-worker from the hippie clothing store was horrified. "I just don't understand how you can be a feminist and like these. I mean, God! Look at this! He's forcing this woman to bend over backward so she can deep-throat the heel of her own shoe. While he fucks her from behind! Doesn't that seem like rape to you?" She regarded me soberly from behind wire-rimmed granny glasses.

"I know. I know, it's terrible! It's just that he draws so well! It makes me laugh."

"That's really disturbing."

"I know. It is. I don't know. I like the way he draws himself as so puny and powerless compared to these massive women with their big butts and their clunky shoes."

"Ayun, he's not powerless. He's trying to subdue them by humiliating them. It makes me sick. Put it away."

I put it away, but every time I take it out I laugh. Inky laughs too and wonders why I snatch the book out of her hand. She always starts at the first page, which puts a buffer of a minute or two between her innocent eyes and the hard-core calculations of Fritz the Cat. I know what's going through Inky's mind as she pulls one of our comic anthologies off the shelf. Finally, an adult book that isn't boring! It's got pictures! Some of the people are naked! That's funny! Nudity always gets a laugh. Inky learned that lesson the summer she turned two. Riding home from the beach on her father's shoulders, she threw off her beach towel, shouting, "I'm naking!" The house went up for grabs. A star was born.

It's hard to keep Inky in her clothes. She's always led the nudie pack. It keeps me on my toes. I know funny old men peer through the wrought-iron bars of the playground fence. One looks just like Santa Claus. It baffles me that some people are sexually aroused by the bodies of four-year-olds. I'm relieved that R. Crumb doesn't go there. Still, when I saw an ad for an underground comic starring the hired hand from *Charlotte's Web,* I laughed. His tormented face prickles with sweat as he writhes on his narrow cot, dreaming of Fern. It's sick, I know. It makes me laugh. It's drawn well. I'll put it way up high, behind the oven cleaner and the X-Acto knife. When she gets to junior high, I'll burn it. I can imagine her squealing to her girlfriends, "My father is so gross! Look what he squirreled away on the top shelf. I don't know how my mother can call herself a feminist, sleeping with this guy!"

Inky wears her birthday suit well. Unless she's angling for a laugh, she doesn't even think about it. She's still in the garden. I was never that way. At around age five, I was sitting in the bathtub improvising a pious discourse between Moses and Jesus as played by washcloths draped over my feet. They looked like shepherds in long headdresses. This meeting of Old and New Testaments, as entertainment, was only a slight improvement over *Timothy Churchmouse,* a local religious program in which a trunk full of poorly manipulated, expressionless puppets traveled to see such secular personages as the Gnome King. Their boring adventures never failed to teach Timothy and his sister, Kathleen, a faith-based moral lesson. In my play, Moses and Jesus talked about manners and loving each other, the standard Barney line with a little bit of God thrown in. When my mother walked in on me I was so mortified I could have slipped right down the drain—I was naked. This might be what turned me off to Sunday school early.

I knew I had these parts. I didn't know what they were called, only that I should resist when Joey Pearson offered to show me his if I showed him mine. Why did I have to go first? Experience led me to suspect that he had no intention of fulfilling his end of the bargain. As trusting as a lamb, I'd sat fully clothed in a wading pool on a cool spring day when some older neighbor kids tricked me with that "you first" jazz. They hadn't joined me. They'd pointed and laughed, their Toughskins bone dry. I'd caught all kinds of hell when I went squishing home. I was interested in the bait Joey promised to dangle. I knew our mothers wouldn't like it one bit. Why was Joey nervously hunkered down behind the brick wall where my grandmother burned trash? Why me first?

Inky stripped minutes after a friend from out of town arrived with her son, a year older than Inky. The last time they saw each other Inky was too little to be much of a playmate. The grown-ups had had to amuse him by transforming Inky's bumblebee-shaped teething rattle into a gun that fired lethal rounds out its hind end. The bee-butt gun. On this visit, the kids dumped every book and toy onto the floor of Inky's room before starting on the tackle boxes that hold my art supplies. When we heard a crash, my friend's boyfriend went to investigate. "They're okay," he reported. "But I think Manny is a little embarrassed that Inky's naked."

"That's something new," his mother whispered, so the children wouldn't overhear. "This time last year he'd have beaten her to it. He used to hate his clothes. Now he's so modest. My little baby's turning into a prude." We laughed.

Maybe it's part of human development. They start out naked, then they lock the bathroom door and wear gym shorts under their dresses, and then they get a boyfriend. I have the most trouble imagining Inky in Phase Two. Recently she streaked past me at a picnic attended by hundreds of women and children. Hot on her heels was an eight-year-old girl, picking up the abandoned clothes and pleading, "Will you please be normal?" Delighted by the ruckus, Inky wagged her naked heinie in the big girl's face.

I would never have done that. Inky's shameless. She loves fart jokes, heinie jokes, any word that rhymes with "bukiluki." That's the word I've been using since she was born, when a nurse brought me an ice pack for my throbbing stitches. "You know what to do with this, babydoll?" she asked. Nodding vigorously, I told her that I wasn't sure. "Stick it in your underwear, right up against your bukiluki. It's time you got you some relief!" I'm eternally grateful to that woman. Should I be worried that Inky says "bukiluki" instead of "vagina"? Maybe we should expand the pool of users.

Would you mind using "bukiluki" so that my daughter can continue to be as healthy and uninhibited as she is at four?

I can't remember when I first heard the word "vagina." The most open discussion of human reproductive organs in which I participated was initiated by David Sykes, who held my second-grade class in thrall every afternoon at milk lunch. Teacher at a safe distance, we'd gather around him with cookies and half-pint cartons, rendered slack-jawed by his stories of stunning dirtiness. These tales invariably began with a classmate eating some enchanted snack that caused his or her body parts to grow to gargantuan proportions. For a boy, the mutating part was a "dick." I knew that a dick was a "penis," a shameful word that I never uttered in public. Sometimes I said it in private. Now that I think about it, Moses and Jesus might have talked about penises in the bathtub. David's brazen use of "dick" marked him as a bad boy as surely as did his short attention span and his wild teenage brothers. A good boy like George Otis, the class math whiz, would never use that word. George listened though, guffawing at the part when a girl got hold of mutant French fries, her "boobs" rocketing out from her flat chest like Play-Doh through a template. For all the daring information at his disposal, I guess David didn't know what a vagina was either. Maybe he just couldn't figure out what to do with one. Maybe breasts presented smuttier opportunities. They were evident under the sweaters of our teachers and the upper-school girls who read stories to us once a week as part of their Civic Club duties.

In Inky's world, breasts belong to the little children who drink from them. They're useful. She's impatient to have the economy-sized models. She plants herself in front of the bathroom mirror, grousing, "Why come I got boy num-nums?" If only she had access to one of David Sykes's special brownies. Just think how many babies she could feed with a fifty-foot rack.

School was a prime source of information. A copy of Judy Blume's *Are You There God? It's Me, Margaret* made its way around our sixth-grade class. I can still see its creased purple cover. I really can! All I have to do is go to Inky's bookcase. Inky couldn't even roll over unassisted when my old friend Angela mailed her a copy from a used bookstore. It's an important gift, like the beauty, wisdom and narcolepsy the good fairies presented to the infant Sleeping Beauty. Reading this book ranks high above that first bra as a rite of passage. It was unusual in that it told it like it is, or was. Its frank discussion of girls getting their periods seemed practically pornographic. We didn't have to hunt for the sensational paragraphs. A hundred preadolescent thumbs had ensured that the book opened to the most explicit passage. When it was my turn to take it home, I devoured it crouched behind my twin bed. I was prepared to chuck it under the dust ruffle the second I heard my mother coming upstairs. I knew the biological facts of menstruation because Anna Garcia had found an article about it in one of her mother's magazines. Huddled in a tent in her backyard, I read the article out loud to her by flashlight. It was the same night her dog Prince chewed up my mother's lice comb. I worried that Anna, whose mother was European, might know more about this matter than I, who knew nothing. I pronounced the word "menu-stration" and sometimes worry that I still do. My mother never caught me with the communally owned copy of *Are You There God? It's Me, Margaret* nor did she ever sit me down for a womanly chat. I never even got a pamphlet! I was a late bloomer. I didn't get my first period until the summer after seventh grade. I was at camp. At thirteen, I was old enough to be in a cabin without a counselor. There were four of us living in the "Hornet's Nest," including my best friend from school and a new friend named Kristy, who'd learned a whole bunch of neat stuff from her older sisters, like how to play guitar and what French kissing is. When I discovered what was happening to me in the camp bathhouse, I tried to ignore it. I still do that when I want to forestall the inevitable. I'm plagued with health insurance billing problems that go to collection agencies because I'm loath to deal with snafus apparent from the moment I open the envelopes. I took care of myself at camp using the material I had on hand, toilet paper. I'm sure Kristy would have helped me. No doubt she had an ample supply of feminine hygiene products in her footlocker. I was too shy. I'd been doing my best to hide all evidence of blood for four cycles when my mother finally offered to buy me some sanitary napkins, to my horror and relief. Laundry doesn't lie.

Once I was reasonably straight about what to expect from a human body on its own, I had to start from scratch. Rumor had it that naked bodies could rub up against each other in the service of romance and baby making. Again, Judy Blume put the ball into play. Sally Augenblick got hold of the infamous teen novel *Forever*. We read the sex scenes out loud in the shadow of her dollhouse. Some of it made sense in a dangerous spine-tingling way, but other parts were no clearer than if they'd been written in Sanskrit. Our best guess was that when a boy "comes," he pees inside his partner's body. Sally had it on the authority of her older sister, a dangerous teenager who once lured us into an old playpen in the basement. As soon as we climbed in, she covered it with a piece of plywood. While we yelled and yanked on the net, she lounged atop the board with her teenage girlfriends, tabulating the foxiness of various guys from the boy's academy. It was very educational for an only child and possibly was the origin of my claustrophobia. Sally's sister tortured on a regular basis, but the tradeoff was a wealth of classified information obtained by eavesdropping. Sally was a year younger than I was, but she knew about pierced ears, rock music, keg parties and making out. Compared to her, I was a babe in the woods.

Not every only child is so dim. For a couple of years, I was friends with a girl named Casey Malone. She was an only child too. I was a regular fixture in her family, the kid who accompanied them to Benihana and hockey games so that Casey wouldn't get bored. Her parents were mild souls who liked candy. Casey never got in trouble. She whined for what she wanted. Nine times out of ten, she got it, and so did I. We got souvenir programs, quarters for video games and as much fudge as Casey desired. In seventh grade, she ditched me for some fast girls who'd gone to a different elementary school. I was too babyish. I damaged her chances with the in crowd. It was a shock, because I'd considered myself slightly superior to her. She had an exercise bike, pink shag carpeting and a Mylar poster of Sylvester Stallone as Rocky, but any blind man could see I was much more mature. I didn't have tantrums like a two-year-old. I never had to be removed from my own birthday parties. Plus, I was skinny where she was chubby, not to mention a much better artist. One day, we were holed up behind her bureau drawing naked ladies. Casey decided to get fancy, giving one of her reclining female nudes a naked man in the background. Not to be outdone, I did the same. I should have taken a closer look at Casey's picture before embellishing my own. When I showed her the fruits of my labor, she shrieked, "Where are his balls?!" She kept it up while I furiously dissembled. What could she mean? My man had a penis, a banana-shaped appendage dangling between his legs. "He doesn't have any balls!" It was clear she enjoyed having the upper hand. Alerted by the sound of a possible skirmish, Mrs. Malone trundled across the bright shag, asking to see what we'd made. Casey wriggled like a worm on a hook, but you'd have thought I had Anne Frank hidden behind the bureau, so desperate was I to conceal. At least Casey's had balls! In truth, our drawings were no dirtier than Renoir's. Picturesque, slightly romantic nudes. I can't remember whether Casey's mom forced me to hand my master-piece over. She was so pliant and pillowy, I'll bet she was swayed by my tears. Eventually I found out what balls were.

As I got older, it was a drag being an only child. Sure, I got a lot of presents at Christmas, but I sure could have used an older sister when the time came to go on the Pill. I had a steady boyfriend, a modest, well-mannered fellow whom I had to push into everything. We'd been fooling around in his car for months. Coming up for air one evening, I suggested that we should go ahead and pick a night to have sex for real. He took a little convincing. He was disap-pointed that we weren't both virgins. We were, but I let him think that I had gone all the way with a boy who had taken me to the drive-in the previous summer. I drove myself to Planned Parent-hood and got a prescription for Ortho-Novum, taking into account the two weeks necessary for the drug to become effective. I took the pills with me when Marnie Stahl's family took me on to Arizona for spring vacation. Marnie asked me to keep the telltale plastic case buried in my toiletry bag. The mothers I grew up around had a tacit don't ask, don't tell policy, heavy on the don't tell. When on the eve of my departure for college my mother sarcastically reminded me to pack my birth control pills, I felt humiliated. I was not unlike the little brown hen, with no help for the hard parts. After I'd taken care of everything, she might not have been entitled to a spiteful little joke. She was probably just out of sorts because her baby was leaving the nest.

Inky says that she wants to live with me when she grows up. It troubles her, the idea that I'll kick her out. She exacts frequent promises that I'll keep her around forever. Even if she's driving me out of my gourd, I promise, suspecting that the day will come when I'd give anything to enforce this contract. Maybe I'll be so exasperated that I'll think, "Fine! Beat it! You and Ronnie deserve each other, you ungrateful little brats! If his van breaks down on the way to California, you can finance the repairs by selling your eggs! But you know that, because you know everything!" The second the door slams, I can go to pieces over her baby book, snapshots of that adorable little body splashing around in the bathtub.

I'm struggling to remember what it was like to be a young girl, aching for an embrace. It's not that I have trouble recalling my adolescence. Enormous amounts of my mental hard drive are occupied by the outfits of the popular girls, the preparations for dances and parties that never panned out and a handful of songs from the earliest days of MTV. Apparently I forgot to hit save on the file containing trigonometry, physics and eleven years of French. The all-consuming hormonal melodrama of those years has not grown cloudy. Even if it had, I've got pages of torment, carefully set down in a journal decorated with an adorably encephalitic urchin. I daydream about moon rituals to honor her first period. Walking home from the grocery, with Milo on my back and Inky in the granny cart astride a throne of cereal boxes, I can joke that the young neighbor making erotic pretzels on the stoop with her boyfriend is Inky in ten years. Their clinch is defiant, seemingly postcoital and accomplished in the after-school hours while their parents are at work. Hey, I'm cool with that. Inky's four. I've got a while before I'm served my eviction notice from never-never land. It must be tempting to pretend that your child prefers the familiar comforts of bubbles and puppets to boys with wispy facial hair and man-sized hands. By the time I hit seventh grade, my longing for romance was all snarled up with the need to keep it from my mother. It was awful. The swoony glow of holding hands with Godfrey Neff every morning for two weeks was offset by the extreme anxiety that this intimate connection to a boy, so proudly displayed in school, might follow me home. My mother moved in the same social circles as some of my teachers. Maybe they'd spill the beans at a party, laughing about it the way they laughed at my interest in *The New Yorker* anthologies. I'd be subject to my mother's extreme pejorative: boy-crazy.

The private school I had attended since second grade advertised its "tradition of excellence" in the symphony orchestra program. No one was ridiculed for academic achievement. It was expected. Studies came easily to me. The openly boy-crazy girls didn't get very good grades. Most were transfers from the public elementary schools. My mother didn't approve and neither did any of the others who'd been pruning their kids to bloom late. They didn't mince words when it came to cutting down the fast girls with C averages attributable to their interest in the opposite sex. We heard all about it at the dinner table, then we went upstairs and did our homework. The boy-crazy ones were out slow-dancing at the popular boys' bar mitzvahs. Not only did they get to walk around with big combs stuck in their back pockets, but they got invited everywhere.

In high school, I got hold of a weird older boy whose frayed oxford-cloth cuffs were too short to accommodate his bony wrists. Unkempt and sardonic, he was way too bizarre for most of my friends. It was the height of the preppy craze. Stewart had nothing but contempt for it. He and Greg would have hit it off. I wonder where he is. He was hardly a catch. He was more like the strange suckerfish that you're supposed to throw back in the canal. Not knowing any better, I baited my hook, reeled him in and ate him. I liked him. He made me nervous. He was not very *Seventeen*. His lips were far more decadent than those on our star linebackers. Not that I ever kissed a football player. I attempted. It was a requirement of *Oklahoma!* in which we both had parts. We marked through it for the first few rehearsals, the director sensitive to the time-bomb quality of the material. Finally, with opening night fast approaching, we were instructed to proceed with the big moment. I closed my eyes and parted my lips. He reared backward as if stung by an asp, shouting, "No! You don't really kiss me! You do it like this!" He situated himself so that the audience's view of my face would be blocked entirely by his blond feathered hairdo. Tenderly grasping my upper arms with his big mitts, he simulated passion by wiggling his head an inch away from my inflamed cheek. It was very hot. Mission accomplished, he let go of me with less care than he lavished on the towels that he used to sop the half-time sweat from his brow. He turned to smirk at his teammates, who slouched against an upstage fence in lesser roles. "God, man, she tried to kiss me!"

Stupid puka-shell-wearing football jerk. Thank god for the freak boy. He wasn't afraid to kiss me, as long as there were no strings attached. I figured the strings would take care of themselves when he fell in love with me. He stoked my hunger for skin on skin with pot and whiskey from his older brother. I got the feeling that there weren't many secrets in his large artistic family, churchgoing Catholics, freaks all. The smell of vinyl station-wagon seats is still a big turn-on for me. If his mother hadn't lent him her car, we wouldn't have had any kind of relationship at all. Throughout our summer of love, he remained stalwart that the only thing he was interested in was fooling around. I hoped fooling around was proof of love. I was ready to go all the way, but he declined. He liked me too much to take advantage of my fabulous offer. What a gentleman, in his own heartless way. He had spent the previous fall having sex daily with the Peruvian exchange student. "Carmela was okay," he told me. She entered the bargain with both eyes open, and nobody cried when she went home to Peru. I nestled closer, content that he liked me better than the Peruvian exchange student he'd been "fucking," the cold-blooded term he used for their affair. If it were me he'd say "making love," but he wouldn't have to, because he liked me too much to fuck me. His fondness did not prevent him from plenty of oral gratification. His mother probably worried that he was going to get me pregnant.

I don't know what my mother thought we were doing. In retrospect, it would have been a wonderful time for a mother-daughter chat. It gets harder the longer you wait. We're still waiting. I'm going to assail Inky with the facts of life early and often. Not only can she live with me forever, she can ask me anything. It will keep me young. I have a friend who went home for Christmas and took her mother to a sex-toy store. Her mother never had been before, but she was game. All the women in the family bought the same vibrator—mother, daughters, cousins, aunt. It sounds like fun, the way stumbling on a cottage made out of gingerbread, peanut brittle and chocolate sounds like fun. The closest my family's ever gotten to a sex talk was the time my mother plucked my denim prairie skirt from the laundry pile. I'd worn it on a date with Stewart. We'd spent an hour at a street festival before we retired to the station wagon. Her face pinched with anger, she'd gestured angrily at a whitish stain. "What is this?" she demanded. I shrugged. Gratification of the flesh had made me just the tiniest bit defiant. She looked at me expectantly, her eyes as bright as a mother bird's. I leaned against the washing machine, wishing that I were an emancipated teenager with my own apartment and no one to boss me around. Man, that would be cool. Infuriated by my silence, Mom took it upon herself to answer her own question. Correctly, I might add. "This is sperm!" she shouted, almost triumphant in her disappointment. I told her it was white clam sauce. With no independent prosecutor to follow up, the matter rested in uneasy silence, not quite the same thing as being off the hook.

I'm not insensible to the fact that millions of other Americans have grown up in an environment of sexual repression and shame.

Like lemmings, most of us managed to grope our way to the sea without the encouragement or blessings of our parents. I still feel ripped off. Once upon a time, I was as fresh and delicious as a nectarine, but I was bred to let it go to waste. It's not that I wish I'd been auctioned off, the way Susan Sarandon sold Brooke Shields to the highest bidder in *Pretty Baby*. I just wish I hadn't been forced to expend so much energy hiding everything. I wish I had been allowed to go a little bit boy-crazy. My mother took it as a great compliment when her friend, the artistic director of the Indiana Repertory Theater, confided that I had been passed over for a part because I wasn't sexy enough. She repeated this information to me as soon as she hung up the phone, probably thinking I'd be glad to know there was nothing wrong with my acting chops. I was fourteen. What if she had snapped, "Not sexy enough? Are you out of your mind? She's a fourteen-year-old girl! She can't help but be as fresh and delicious as a nectarine! Listen, tell me if you think she can't act. It may save us a useless degree in theater down the road."

Wandering the streets of New York with Inky and Milo, I am an anonymous mom. I can't quite believe it. Only now is it sinking in that I don't get a second chance to be fourteen. I could stare for hours at the young girls, the undisputed queens of the sidewalk, blocking the intersection, laughing too loud. They're so beautiful, even the dumpy ones, the pimply ones, the ones those midriff-baring tops will never flatter. Greg and I always pick out the prettiest one, the one the midriff top does flatter, the one flaunting it with a temporary tattoo circling her belly button like the rays of the sun. "That's Inky," we whisper to each other. We shudder like we won't be able to stand it. It feels a little fake to me, one of those things parents are obliged to do, the way we're supposed to move to the suburbs and own a sports utility vehicle. I'm committed to forcing myself to feel differently about Inky from how my mother felt about me and my grandmother almost certainly felt about her. I am lucky to have parents who provided for me, sought out cultural activities I would enjoy, read to me and supported my ridiculous choice of career. They tolerate with good humor my bile-driven attacks on their support of the Republican Party. They paid out the nose for my education. I traveled all over Africa and Asia in my early twenties, and my mother's only meager request was a monthly phone call to let her know I was alive. I've had a lot of freedom, but they sure dropped the ball when it came to sex. I want to be there when Inky emerges from the cocoon as a glorious, sexy butterfly. She shouldn't be made to act as if she were still a caterpillar, no matter how much I might miss the good old days of her four-year-old self in the bathtub. I remind my future self that that little devil splashed her brother's eyes, tweaked my tired breasts like she still owned them and refused to let me shampoo her hair unless I sang "Glow Little Glowworm." It might be a relief to hang out with a teenage girl, a responsible one who uses birth control, never drinks to excess and bitches intelligently about conservative politics in her own zine.

Inky's a fundamentally different child than I was anyway. No shit, Sherlock. At a Christmas get-together, she amazed our close friends by marching up naked, her labia held back for inspection. She showed about as much concern for her exposed clitoris as a dog caught licking his glistening red erection. "The white stuff makes my bukiluki smell bad," she announced. Amen to that. No need to obscure the hard facts of feminine hygiene with wildflower meadows and maidens in filmy white gowns. I used to think I'd die whenever a douche commercial interrupted a program I was watching with my mother.

As for my baby boy, well, he's got balls. I know that much. Right now, he's sweet and girlie in his sister's hand-me-downs. The mothers of Inky's male cronies breathe down my neck, their anticipation as humid as an orchid show. They lick their chops, eager for Milo to erupt in a geyser of testosterone. Watching him caress the marabou puff on a pink dress-up sandal, it's hard for me to imagine him ever braining another little boy with a toy dump truck. Maybe he'll be a gentle artist type with no interest in emergency vehicles. "Just you wait," the other mothers say, winking as their sons bombard one another with sidewalk chalk. The battery of sound effects they produce is impressive. These three-year-old boys lob whistling bombs and pitch-perfect machine-gun volleys with an expertise far beyond my grasp. My gun noises sound like footsteps in gravel. I'm sure Greg will pass this mastery along to his son. I guess it's a good survival technique for a boy, but I'm not-so-secretly hoping for Milo to turn out like Ferdinand the bull, who loved flowers more than fighting. Greg insists that Milo will learn the manly art of organized sports. Fine with me, as long as Greg doesn't get any fancy ideas about tarting my boy up in any of that Li'l Slugger baseball drag. I'm pretty sure that will never be a problem. Greg can put a severe crimp in my hippie-dippy ways with his insistence on logic and precision, but he's never been one to get his Y-fronts in a bunch over the faintest wisp of homosexuality, like a male infant in tulip pink. He's even a big boy when it comes to hot man-on-man action displays of homosexuality. Either I'm the last one to know that my husband's gay, or I was so charmed by his willingness to weather Uncle Monkeybutt's tales from the gloryhole that I married him. Any way you slice it, we've got Milo covered. I've never lived with little boys before. I'm willing to concede that the majority do seem to prefer cockpits to ponies with long, brushable hair, but I still have some feminist designs on how Milo will treat women. All women, not just the ones he lives with and his boyfriend's mother. He's going to learn about girls. If our bank account continues to swell as rapidly as it has since we moved to New York, he'll be sharing a bedroom with his older sister until she leaves the nest. Oh, I forgot, she's going to live with us forever. Maybe he will too. I could see this throwing a wrench into their plans for masturbation or heavy petting with football players and the freaky kid from the large Roman Catholic family. Maybe the two of them can work out a schedule or something.

Hot Dates

December 25

Danged if it isn't true: You really can't re-create the Christmases of your childhood. I can't even re-create the Christmases of my teen years, which were orchestrated by a friend with a predisposition toward entertaining. She would have made an excellent caterer. Her tree-trimming parties could have come straight from the pages of *Seventeen* magazine, as long as the models were a little chubby and dorky and one of them, I'm not saying who, was swaddled in inappropriate vintage clothing and purple gauze harem pants.

As you get older, the grandparents who used to arrive an hour before the agreed-upon time bearing three bags of presents from L. S. Ayres department store dwindle, then disappear. You lose track of the high-school friends you once made passionate plans to meet the second you were excused from family obligations. The holiday begins to feel a little hollow. I don't know if other only children of divorced parents share this problem, but I have spent too many Christmases on the interstate shuttling back and forth between the one I'm staying with and the one with whom I'm eating dinner. My early religious instruction never took hold, but I've found myself at midnight mass sniffling during the first strains of "Silent Night" because it reminds me of when I was little and didn't have to limbo through all these emotionally underwhelming get-togethers.

Long before I married Greg, he made it absolutely understood that he was a Christmas-hater. Greg and his brother had been raised in the woods of Cape Cod by two Jewish atheist New Yorkers. Not surprisingly, when December rolled around, their mother feared that her boys might feel a bit left out of the prevailing reindeer games. Since she wasn't constrained by any personal religious beliefs other than "it's all a bunch of bullshit, really," she was free to provide a real old-fashioned Christmas for Greg and Sam. They had presents and a tree with all the trimmings except for the manger scene. She accomplished this without any assistance from Greg's father, who showed his disapproval by staying in his room listening to NPR. When he was a child, Greg enjoyed the gift-wrapped bacchanal. As an adult atheist Jew, he realized how much he resented Christmas's stranglehold on America. He wished he had never been coerced into inadvertently celebrating the birth of Christ in such a consumeristic frenzy. He had allowed himself to be corrupted by a childish desire for Matchbox cars and baseball gear. Too bad his mother didn't suspect he would turn out this way. She could have saved herself a lot of trouble.

Given our respective backgrounds, were we doomed to spend December in a snow globe straight out of Kafka? Was there to be no holiday cheer for a seething Jewish atheist, an infantile, party-loving former Episcopalian and a foul-tempered cat who could be counted on to devour and regurgitate any greenery that crossed the threshold? Our first few Christmases together were pretty lame. We exchanged presents and then I drove from Chicago to Indianapolis to put in an appearance with my family. Greg accompanied me on a couple of these trips, enduring my mother's Spode plates and the inevitable socks, ties and Harveys Bristol Cream our family bestows on males outside the bloodline. Once he even went with my father and me to the services at All Saints. I reasoned that we had attended various Hindu and Buddhist ceremonies while traveling around Asia, so it wouldn't kill him to feign an anthropological interest in my tribe of origin. He went, but he was in hell. He looked at me in wild-eyed panic every time the congregation knelt in prayer or sprang to their feet, booming Christmas carols that made no mention of Santa Claus, Frosty or Rudolph. The next time Greg made the trek to Indiana, I begged off mass for both of us, transferring allegiance from my father to my beloved. It was like an exchange of wedding vows, except it didn't occur in a church.

When we moved to New York, childless and engaged, we lived for a year near a well-attended, active synagogue. Never before had I been so aware of the Hebrew calendar as devout young families trooped past our window on their way to worship and socialize. Greg had no interest in joining them; in fact I had to tell him which holiday was being celebrated. Just after Yom Kippur, our Dominican doorman filled us in when we wondered why the congregation had built a shed in the cement breezeway where our building's garbage cans were stored. The Jewish families dined there noisily every night for the week. I suggested that we go join them in their Succot. Juan had assured me that we would be welcome, but Greg insisted on keeping his distance.

When December rolled around, I was delighted to discover Christmas in abundance on every street corner, even the ones near us. Every Korean grocer had slapped some 2 -by-4s together to support a display of wreaths and Christmas trees. Jewish mothers not much older than myself directed their children to walk straight down the middle of the sidewalk to keep from getting pine sap on their Saturday best. It smelled like Vermont. Aggressive merchants wired loudspeakers and lights to the front of their stores. Anticipating tourist hordes, I didn't go see the huge tree in Rockefeller Center, but I liked knowing it was there. I would celebrate the season on the heavily decorated streets of New York! Every time I left the building, boom, there was Christmas (and to a lesser degree, Hanukkah). Greg could stay in the apartment with Jambo, doing whatever he wanted to express his opposition. One year, when I returned solo to Indiana, he'd rented a double feature of *The Sorrow and the Pity* and *Rosemary's Baby*.

So I was fit to be tied when Greg told me that his family expected us to spend the holiday with them. What holiday? Greg and Sam were big boys now. I couldn't believe they'd feel left out if they were the only fellows who didn't get wallets and machine-knit pullovers on December 25. Of course it would be nice to visit with Sam and Beth and their one-year-old daughter, who had recently moved to the D.C. area after several years abroad, but why did we have to do it on Christmas Day? I was going to commune with the unsold

Christmas trees, marvel at the absence of traffic and buy eggnog at Korean groceries that never closed. If it snowed, I would go sledding in Central Park. I wanted to have dinner in Chinatown and I planned to get Greg to go with me by telling him that it was a New York Jewish atheist tradition.

Instead, our presence was required in suburban Alexandria. There would be an exchange of presents. My obliging sister-in-law, the only religious Jew in the immediate family, called, worried that she might fail to provide some necessary Christmas element. "Please, Beth," I told her, "please do not knock yourself out on my account. I just want to spend time with you guys. Please. I'll kill you if you go out of your way to make it seem like Christmas."

I worried that Greg's family saw me as a big Christian baby who had to be pacified with meaningless holiday traditions. I wanted nothing to do with it. I had wanted to get away from empty exchanges of gifts and the requisite heavy meal that forces someone to spend all day in the kitchen, trying to figure out how the hell you get the metal things to come out of the electric eggbeater. My hopes for a Woody Allen Christmas were dashed. Who knew, maybe there would be opportunities to sneak away from the weekend celebration and scribble tearfully in my journal about how Christmas never measures up to my old childhood expectations. Isn't it the pits when those women's magazines are actually right? The holidays are stressful. With luck, Beth's cabinets would be stocked with cookies and M&Ms so I could go all the way, caving in to the temptation to overeat rather than nibbling sensibly on carrot sticks without the French onion dip.

I actually do have pleasant memories of that freezing Christmas in Alexandria. If the temperature rose above zero, it was a miracle akin to a virgin giving birth in a barn. As such, we were house-bound. Sam and Beth's daughter, Sarah, was running a high temperature and her face was chapped from swiping her runny nose across her cheeks. Her only relief came lying on her parents' bed to watch *Barney* videos and reruns of *Seinfeld*. Sarah's discomfort was rivaled only by that of her grandmother, who lobbied continuously for medical attention for the child. Sam and Greg had remained friends with a high school buddy whose misfortune it was, at least on this day, to grow up to become a physician. Every time the good doctor was disturbed, he stuck to his guns: Sarah had caught a minor bug. Give her plenty to drink and, if it makes the grown-ups feel better, some baby aspirin. Merry Christmas again. Sarah's Nana Paula allowed herself a minute's comfort in this reassuring diag-nosis before resuming the campaign to take the child somewhere, a hospital, there must be someone who can see her on Christmas, look at her, she's obviously sick, something has to be wrong, would it kill us to see a doctor?

Goddamnit, those women's magazines were right again! It didn't take long for everyone to take up their respective family roles, Sam and his mother screaming at each other while Greg, too old now for model airplanes, tuned them out with a biography of Stalin. Despite our status as relative newcomers, Beth and I were already familiar with the drill. She attacked the kitchen counter with a sponge, cleaning up the mess that others had left. I disap-peared at regular intervals, staring at myself in the bathroom mirror for so long that eventually my mother-in-law interrupted herself to inquire as to my whereabouts. At least Beth had taken me at my word, dispensing with any plans she might have had for wassail and a dramatic reading of *The Night Before Christmas*.

After her fifth phone consultation with Sam's doctor friend, Beth drew me aside. "What do you think about Sarah?" she asked. "Duncan says that we shouldn't worry, that it's just the flu. She's not that sick, right?"

Pregnant with my first child, I was not only an expert on discipline and juvenile psychology, I was a veritable encyclopedia of pediatric health. "I think she's fine, Beth, just a little under the weather is all. I can't imagine that she'd feel any better sitting around an emergency room for hours on Christmas."

"That's what Paula wants us to do."

"Well," I said, shrugging.

"Screw it. Pardon my French, but Sam can watch his child for an hour or two. She'll be fine. Where are my keys?"

It felt good to burst out into the fresh air. Greg came along for the ride, leaving Sam with their mother and his feverish toddler. Beth piloted her Hyundai like a sleigh across the frozen tundra. We cruised alongside a tree-lined reservoir. "This is where I go jogging," Beth announced fiercely. We wound up at the gates to Mount Vernon, George Washington's estate. To our surprise, it was open. Beth asked us if we wanted to go in or if we thought we should go back home. I could see historic reenactors in capes and tricorn hats clustered around a bonfire. "Let's take a peek," I said.

Getting out of the car, I could hear sleigh bells. The bonfire smelled wonderful, not unlike the fireplace in Zionsville, Indiana, where I charitably imagined my mother and stepfather entertaining my grandfather for a quiet early dinner. "A happy Christmas to you, travelers!" a high school science teacher–type in wire-rimmed glasses and knee socks sung out. "Won't you join us for some gingerbread and hot cider and warm yourself at the fire?"

I seized Greg by the elbow and dragged him into the colonial midst. We took the complete tour, following heavyset ladies in mobcaps trimmed with holly through ascetic rooms fragrant with real bayberry, not scented candles. Never in my life have I been so interested in horseshoeing, butter churning or the Father of Our Country. I wondered what drove these volunteers to leave their comfortable homes on Christmas Day to stand shivering in the stables and usher strangers past the velvet ropes protecting George and Martha's bedroom. Was it patriotism, a mad desire to dress up like a late-eighteenth-century blacksmith or something else entirely? I could have stayed longer, but Beth was starting to feel anxious about Sarah. Mount Vernon isn't exactly a hotbed of pay phones.

After a couple of years in D.C., Sam's family moved to the Middle East. We were sad to see them go, but I was excited at what it portended for Christmas. Although Inky is a seasoned traveler who actually breaks up the monotony of airports in a pleasant way, Milo is miserable in his car seat. He allowed me to feign immobility. I had watched my stepbrother and his wife drag their two children all over kingdom come as they made the Christmas circuit of divorced grandparents. I always assumed they would have preferred to stay at home in their pajamas, sipping coffee while the kids covered the living room floor with the 125 choking hazards that came with their new Fisher-Price Gas Oasis. I know I would have. I begged off Indiana and my mother-in-law's apartment 150 blocks north, blaming it all on the children. I didn't feel too bad about it. In my day, grandparents dug their Buick out from several inches of accumulation if they wanted to see the expressions of rapture on their little darlings' faces.

Inky was deep into Santa Claus. Every time we passed a creepy window display in which Santa and Mrs. Claus rotated their rosy heads like replicants, she screamed with excitement. Her enthusiasm must have been infectious because Greg came home with a six-foot fir he had bought on the corner from "Jose's Xmas Trees for the New Milleniom." Jose spends January through November drinking beer in front of the auto-repair shop down the block, but his sign stays up year-round. I contributed a heavy-duty metal tree stand I had bought at the same thrift store that yielded Milo's bee costume for Halloween. None of that flimsy plastic stuff for us.

Immediately, we had a discussion over where to place the tree. Greg, for some baffling reason, had assumed it would go in the bedroom. "No, man. You've got to put it in the living room, so everybody can admire it!" I had gotten my fill of entertaining guests on my bed when we lived in that chairless, couchless East Village dive. "Put it here in front of the windows, so the neighbors can see it too." I swatted the lights out of Inky's hands, telling her that she had to be patient. Jambo came in to assess the size of the feast he would enjoy later that night. "Inky, I mean it. Get away from those lights. Mommy and Daddy will do the lights. You see that plug on the end of them? Do you know what electricity is? It's like fire. It can burn you right up on the inside and then we'd have to go to the hospital."

"Why do you not ever let me do the stuff I want to do?" Inky grumbled, moving on to the fragile glass balls from the 99-cent store. I had squandered precious preschool hours embellishing them with bizarre stickers from an East Village store that caters to Japanese club kids. My attempt at handicrafts didn't look like much, but I was pleased with the effect just the same.

"How much did you pay for the tree?" I inquired, smelling the tinsel garland. It lacked the ambrosial aroma of the tinsel garlands of my youth.

"Thirty bucks," Greg said uncertainly. I fingered the garland and said nothing. "Is that too much?"

"Oh, I don't know," I said. There was not a doubt in my mind that we could have saved ourselves fifteen dollars by driving into Chinatown. "Maybe, probably, but who cares? You only buy a Christmas tree once a year! Why not splurge a little? Besides, you picked out such a handsome one. Doesn't it smell good? Inky, did you smell the tree? Admit it, Greg, the tree smells good."

"Oh wondrous odor!" Greg rhapsodized from beneath the bottom boughs, where he was attempting to screw the stand into the trunk.

I squeezed past him into the kitchen, on the prowl for baking soda. "Don't let me forget to pour some of this in once you've got it up," I announced self-importantly, waving the box in Greg's face.

"Why?"

"Because otherwise the tree starts to smell like vomit after a couple of days."

"Vomit? What? How long are we going to keep this thing up?"

"Don't worry, we have baking soda. Hey, do we have any rope?"

"Rope? What for?"

"Because I think you'd better tie the tree onto something. My father always tied the tree to the handles of our French doors, so it would stand up straight."

"I think it's straight enough." Greg crawled out from beneath the tree.

"Daddy, now we do the lights okay? We do the lights now. I want to do the lights!"

"In a second, honey, Daddy needs a beer first."

"Greg, I'm serious. All it would take is Inky or one of her cronies tugging on one of the ornaments and the whole thing could come crashing down on top of Milo. We've got Jambo to consider too. Cats are a real nightmare around Christmas trees. I think we should tie it to the window guards."

Greg's chin rested on his chest for the duration of a spectacular exhalation. When he had recovered, he grabbed the top of the tree and rocked it from side to side. "Look, this tree isn't going anywhere. I understand your concerns, but I think we'll be okay here without having to lash the thing to the windows. It is December, after all. I think it would be nice to be able to close our windows all the way, which we can't do if your graven image is lashed to the child guards. Look, it's snowing out there."

"Ooh, white Christmas!" I squealed, rushing past him. "Inky, look! White Christmas! White Christmas, Milo!"

"Yes, white Christmas!" Greg trilled ominously from the kitchen as he popped the cap off a beer. "Very white! And now to round up some Jews!"

"Easy with that. We have some little pitchers here who don't understand that you're being ironic."

"Ah, but who says I'm being ironic?" he said, flopping on the couch with the current *New Yorker*. "Ah ha! Ah ha ha ha ha!"

"Okay, Inky, now we can do the lights."

Inky had divested herself of her woolen schoolclothes while Greg wrestled the tree into position. Naked now, she executed a little entrechat, barely able to contain her excitement. She threw herself on the light strings, yanking them free of their bristly plastic rack. The spiky plastic sleeves surrounding each bulb looked about as child-friendly as razor wire, but I bit my tongue. I didn't want to "no" her to death on Christmas. It was my own fault for buying the second-cheapest kind from the 99-cent store instead of going with a quality product from Rite Aid or Tony's Hardware.

"Greg, you have to hold Milo so Inky and I can do the lights." Greg grunted and lifted his magazine a few inches higher to accommodate his five-month-old son. "Do you mind if I put on some Christmas music?"

"That would be wonderful, simply wonderful!" came the reply from behind *The New Yorker*.

Inky and I began winding the unplugged lights around the tree. I had tested them earlier at the store to make sure they worked. When I was a child, the arrangement had always been that my father would cantilever the tree into position while my mother offered grimly gay commentary from the sidelines about how putting up a Christmas tree was grounds for divorce. He would fix himself another drink while she tended to the prosaic chores of lights and tinsel garland. I got the good part, the ornaments: Victorian-clad mice and Styrofoam gingerbread boys, crocheted bells from my grandmother's bridge-club friends and the sinister candy-cane hobby horse my father had picked up in college. My personal favorite was a blond baby Jesus in a walnut-shell cradle. I had purchased him from L. S. Ayres Holiday Sparkle Shop with the money I earned feeding a vacationing neighbor's fish. I realized that Inky at three hadn't had much time to amass many ornaments or forge allegiances toward particular ones, but I did find her determination to be so involved in the traditionally maternal domain of the lights unsettling. As I am so often tempted to do when she insists on helping me cook or fold the laundry, I tried to make it sound like the most insignificant responsibilities were crucial to the enterprise. I handed her the plug end and told her to hold it while I festooned the branches.

"You lift me up. I wanna do it."

"No, you're the plug holder. You've got to make sure that Milo doesn't get the plug."

"Milo's sleeping."

"Yeah, he might wake up though."

"His eyes are closed."

"Okay, Jambo then. It's very important that Jambo not think the plug is a mouse and try to eat it. Keep up the good work."

"I want to do the lights! Why do you not ever let me do the lights!" She stamped her foot, glaring at me. God, she was pretty.

"Okay, okay, I'll tell you what. I'll wrap the lights up top here and then I'll hand the cord down to you. You walk around to the wall and pass the cord back to me."

"Yippee!" she shrieked, leaping about at her good fortune. The old wooden floor rippled beneath her like asphalt in an earthquake. Our poor downstairs neighbors. They never say a word.

"Watch out for needles, the green things. They're sharp. They'll bite your heinie if you get too close," I said, willing myself to keep calm. There are so many times when I'd love to snatch something out of her hands, so strong is the impulse to accomplish a task within an adult time frame. Too frequently I succumb, but this was Christmas, after all, Christmas in my own apartment in Brooklyn. Even the atheist Jew showed signs of getting into something resembling the spirit. This would be a bad time for Commando Bitch Mother to seize control.

"Bite my heinie?!" Inky burbled, yanking on the cord with all her might. "Bite my *heinie?!* Daddy, did you hear about that? Mommy said the Christmas tree was going to bite my heinie!"

"She's not jacked up at all," Greg observed wryly.

"Inky, shh, let's not wake up baby brother. Here, pass the cord along the wall. No, that way. No, the other way. This way."

"I can do it my ownself," she protested. When I reached for the cord, she hopped away. "I do it! I do it! I do it! Bite my heinie? That's silly!" How I wished I could be watching a rerun of *ER* on an early June night at this very moment. I hoisted Inky into my arms, helping her reach the branches so she could do the lights by her ownself. Satisfied, she took five agonizing minutes to clump them all in a single-square-foot area. I set her down and she scampered away.

"Wait, Inky, don't you want to see me plug it in?"

"You do it! I need to play with my Madeline blocks now!"

With Milo down for the count, that would usually be my cue to drop everything immediately to work on the upcoming zine. This was Christmas though. You don't trim the tree with three strands of lights just to leave it dark when the kid loses interest. "I'm plugging in the tree now."

"Oh, sweet Christian miracle! How it blinds me!" Greg remarked affably, his glasses now off and his eyes closed.

I plugged it in. Two thirds of the tree blazed, but the middle section remained dark. It looked like it was wearing a bra and panties.

"Shit! Fuck!" I pounced into the branches, joggling electrical connections and individual bulbs. That's the way it worked when I was a kid. If one bulb came loose, the entire cord went dead. Of course, when I was a kid, there were no such things as VCRs and the closest thing I had to a car seat was a beach towel my grandfather stapled to a board to keep me from falling through the space between the Buick's front seats. "I checked them! I swear to god, I checked them in the store. I can't believe it. Fuck! Shit!"

Greg opened his eyes wearily and swung his feet to the floor. "Take the boy," he said, transferring Milo to my arms. "You have the receipt, yes?"

Gratefully, I dug through my wallet. As Greg thumped down the stairs, defective lights in a plastic grocery bag, I helped myself to a beer and settled into the spot he had just vacated. It was still warm.

I wrapped presents while Inky was at preschool, grumbling over this waste of my valuable time. I could have been working on the zine or indulging in that pedicure I'm always threatening to get. Instead I was chained to a roll of wrapping paper. Milo backed himself into a paper bag full of ribbons, where he remained for almost an hour, chortling at his great accomplishment. I know that there are women who love to wrap presents, but I am not one of them. I resent it, particularly since every man I've ever lived with, including my father, stepfather and husband, has hornswoggled me into wrapping his gifts too. They think I can't see through those lavish compliments regarding my superior abilities in the gift-wrap department? Yeah, and I know how to clean the toilet really well too, fellas. Even when I replace the schmaltzy Christmas music with the Ramones, I still detest the task.

The presents needed to be hidden in a bag at the top of the closet, on top of the medicine that's supposed to stay out of children's reach. I had envisioned a bountiful display piled underneath the tree, showcasing my efforts in the gift-wrap mines, but Inky had put a stop to that. I had been so proud of myself, purchasing presents for Beth and Sam and their kids well in advance of the overseas shipping deadline. I wanted the parcel to get to the Middle East by December 25, just in case they were keeping up the charade we'd started when they lived in D.C. Everything was neatly wrapped and stacked on the dining room table. In the time it took me to locate some strapping tape and a Sharpie marker, Inky managed to unwrap every single one, the little criminal.

"Oh, Mama, look what I found!" she breathed, wide-eyed. She was ankle-deep in the remains of my festive wrapping job. "Inky, no! That's for Cousin Sarah! Not every present you see has your name on it, you know. No, don't touch. Didn't I just say that this is a present for Cousin Sarah?"

"I just want to see it," she scowled, petulant as a teenager.

I flashed the Barbiefied sparkly autograph album at her for all of three seconds before whisking it into a plastic bag.

"Hey, no fair!"

"No fair? You unwrap other people's presents and you're calling me unfair? Think again, pal."

"I just really really really like to open presents," she wailed plaintively, taking herself to her room to wallow in a self-imposed time-out. Grumbling, I set to measuring fresh squares of holly-print paper. It occurred to me that the apple doesn't fall far from the tree. The friend who'd ridiculed me for not knowing what men's balls were once goaded me into opening one of the presents my mother had arranged under the tree in anticipation of the big day. Disappointed that the box I'd selected contained a sweater, we clumsily retaped the package and cracked open another. We continued in this vein until we finally hit upon something that merited the transgression. When my mother observed that it looked as if a little mouse had gotten into the presents, I got huffy, believing my innocence beyond reproach. I was much older than Inky, too, old enough to know better. When I was Inky's age, I arrived home from a shopping trip with my father and announced, "Daddy and me just got your birthday present. I can't tell you what it is but I sat in it and I rocked in it!"

The sequestered presents were joined by several handfuls of stocking stuffers. Milo and I had collected them from locations all over the East Village while Inky was playing at Abby's. Apparently, Santa has a soft spot for Japanese candy, the kind with really funky individually wrapped packages. My mother generously offered to send us a couple of our ancestral stockings prestuffed, but I refused to delegate this responsibility. Although I hate wrapping presents, I like wandering into and out of stores where I ordinarily have no business, purchasing a trinket here, a doodad there. Also, I was attached to the idea of filling the stockings once the children were down for the count on Christmas Eve. This seemed like one of the few nondepressing rites of passage left for a married mother who's long since gotten over the thrill of voting, driving and buying booze. Think about it: Kids spend the first two and a half years of their lives sort of out of it and then another three or four believing that most of their presents were delivered down the chimney by the fat man from the mall (or in Inky's case, from ABC Carpet & Home, a deceptively named emporium where silk organza Christmas stockings fetch upward of $85). Nothing can shake that belief, even if the presents have price tags and come wrapped in the same paper your mother uses for her mother-in-law and the neighbors who took care of the cat while you were on vacation—but then another Christmas rolls around. Something has happened to you in the New Year. You have found out, through osmosis or the crew-cut troublemaker next door, that only babies believe in Santa. You spend the rest of your life not believing in Santa Claus, though from time to time, in the right mood with a couple of drinks in you, you may believe in reruns of *Miracle on 34th Street*. You have this knowledge, but can't really do anything with it, unless you're given to torturing younger kids, which I certainly hope you are not. The only people who get a payoff for not believing in Santa are the parents of three-year-olds. Oh man, is that ever sweet. You get to be Santa Claus. There's really nothing to it. You stuff the stockings and eat a plate of cookies. If you don't plan to go whole hog in a fake beard and a fat suit, at least try to make sure you've got something decent set out for yourself, something better than the stale fortune cookies left over from your last hundred Chinese carryout meals. Try a little bit harder than that for Santa.

I once heard Isabella Rossellini describe in an interview how she once coaxed a male friend to put on her red terry cloth bathrobe and a beard made from cotton balls. Her children, unsurprisingly, were not fooled in the slightest as this familiar man pranced around in an outfit he had obviously thrown together in the upstairs bathroom. While they were jeering at the sorry Saint Nick, the professional Santa Claus their mother had also engaged arrived in crimson velvet robes, belly and beard his own, every bit as real as the other was fake. As a result of her theatrical ingenuity, Isabella Rossellini's children continued to believe in Santa Claus well into their teens. If I remember correctly, David Letterman thought this constituted child abuse.

There was no need to get elaborate on Inky's behalf. By the time Christmas Eve finally arrived, she was exhausted. Leafing through a kid's guide to New York City, I had learned about the holiday lights in Bensonhurst. According to this book, a couple of residential blocks in this working-class section of Brooklyn decorated the outside of their homes so extensively, the department store windows around Rockefeller Center paled in comparison. The author delicately hinted that the kiddies weren't the only ones in for a treat. Adults with a kitschy streak were sure to be dazzled by the sheer gaudiness on display: five-hundred-watt reindeer landing atop an army of choirboys, snowmen packed like sardines in yards the size of twin mattresses. I began petitioning well in advance of the event. "Greg, I know it's the kind of thing you hate, but it really means a lot to me that we drive to Bensonhurst on Christmas Eve to look at the lights as a family. It's very important to me. My parents used to take me around to look at people's decorations and I'd like to make that a tradition with Inky and Milo. Okay?"

He looked up from his cereal bowl. "Uh, sure. Wait. What's in Bensonhurst now?"

"Lights. Christmas lights and, you know, reindeer and stuff like that. I want to take the kids on Christmas Eve because that's something I always enjoyed when I was little." I wasn't 100 percent sure on this actually being an ancient Halliday tradition, but I felt it could only strengthen my case. I do remember driving alongside a darkened canal in our wood-paneled Country Squire one year, marveling that Roselyn's Bakery was still open, selling their distinctly Protestant cookies on this holiest of holy nights.

Every couple of days I would remind Greg about the holiday displays at Bensonhurst. I wanted to make it impossible for him to feign ignorance when the big day rolled around. Christmas Eve morning, I found out that the mother of one of Inky's cronies had been to see them the previous year. "Oh, you'll love them," she laughed. "They're really tacky. It's right up your alley. But you don't have to go all the way to Bensonhurst. Just drive down around President and Union. There are a couple of houses there that give me a migraine just thinking about them. You can't miss it."

Greg arrived home at sunset, which in New York in December occurs at 4:30. Like a soldier set to storm the beaches at Normandy, he would not shirk his duty, but neither could he pretend to look forward with any lightness of spirit. When he learned that the holiday display was much closer to home than originally reported, he suggested that we swing by Met Foods on the way and fill up the trunk with groceries. That sounded like a good idea, as in the excitement of the season I had let our pantry dwindle to several cans of chickpeas and a refrigerator door's worth of exotic condiments. Besides, I always leap at any scheme that involves getting ten bags of groceries home by some means other than me single-handedly hauling them six and a half snow-covered blocks and up three flights of stairs with a baby on my back and a small child who is suddenly too weary to walk.

I forgot what it's like with all four of us in the grocery store. When it's just me and the kids in the subway or a restaurant or Met Foods, Inky and I have a highly ritualized, idiosyncratic understanding that allows us to take care of business safely and somewhat efficiently. Greg reports that they have a similar deal when I'm not around, although it must play out differently since Inky has often remarked that Daddy doesn't let her pick up discarded MetroCards from the subway station floor. Sure, they're dirty, but frankly, so is the hand that I expect her to hold as we step with no nonsense aboard several tons of meat-grinding metal. If you want to get, you've got to give a little, right? I give discarded MetroCards. I'm not sure what Greg gives. When we're both present, neither of us stands a snowball's chance in hell of controlling our child. With Santa's much-anticipated visit looming nigh, Inky bombed around Met Foods like a speed freak. She lurched for produce, dived in the path of oncoming carts and danced away from us when we tried to rein her in. If it hadn't been Christmas, our disconcerted attempts to play good cop/bad cop would have deteriorated quickly into bad cop/bad cop. Approaching Inky's favorite cashier, a gentle Latina woman who always treats her like a big cheese, I worried. What if Gloria was thinking, "That stupid yuppie and her crazy, ill-mannered brat. I would like to be home with my son tonight, but no, I must be here ringing up soy milk and premium orange juice for idiots like this."

"I swear she's not like this when you're not around," I told Greg, smiling helplessly at Gloria as Inky attempted a kamikaze raid on the candy rack. "I bet your little boy's really excited for Christmas too."

"Oh, yes," Gloria agreed, swiping a can of coconut milk over the electronic eye.

"Is he deep into Santa Claus and all that?" I inquired, immediately regretting my slangy, lazy speech. No wonder the Spanish-speaking cashiers and bag boys mostly smile and nod when I attempt to make casual chitchat with them. The only time they're called upon to converse in English is when a baboon like me comes into their workplace, gumming away at them like we're old friends.

"Oh, yes, Santa Claus," Gloria echoed pleasantly, no doubt thinking, "no, my son is deep into the miracle of his Savior's birth, you spoiled, godless fool!"

"Okay, well, thanks a lot, Gloria. Merry Christmas! We'll see you next week!" I prepared to hustle Inky past the gumball machines as Greg looped the circulation-destroying handles of five plastic bags over each wrist.

"Oh yes. Merry Christmas. Merry Christmas, Inky. Merry Christmas, My-love." I never adequately cleared up Gloria's mis-hearing of the newborn Milo's name. After a few months went by, it seemed rude to correct her. I wondered what was going through her head as she smiled and waved to us through the big plate glass window. "What kind of loca names her son My-love?"

"Are you sure you still want to do this?" Greg couldn't help asking as he glanced dubiously at Inky, who was practically humping a parking meter.

"Yes, I'm sure." If I hadn't been so certain he didn't want to do it, I probably would have voted to cut our losses and head home.

The transfer from sling to car seat roused the slumbering Milo, who immediately realized where he was and retaliated with an ungodly racket. I think those old yarns about babies being pacified in cars or on top of washing machines only apply to babies living in places where you have to drive to every place except the Laundromat because you have a washer and dryer in your basement.

"I want to go home." Inky spoke up over Milo's screams.

"Don't you want to see the pretty decorations, honey?"

"No."

"You'll see. You're going to love it. You won't believe your eyes in just a minute. Greg, what are you doing? Nancy said President Street! Why are you turning down Carroll?"

Silently, Greg gestured toward a one-way street sign and continued to navigate. I wrenched my arm backward in its socket, hoping that Milo might pacify himself by sucking on my pinky finger. This might have worked better if I'd trimmed my nails in two weeks.

"I want to go home," our little stick-in-the-mud reminded us. "Milo's crying. I think he wants to go home."

I dug around under the seats. "Here, take this, honey. It's that magnetic slate thing you used when we drove to Cape Cod last year. Why don't you draw me a picture of Milo?"

"But it's dark. I can't see."

"Well, you can see when we drive under the streetlights."

"I don't want to draw. I want to go home."

We had arrived at a crossroads. One way led toward the promised splendors of President Street. The other led toward home. Greg peered down the block. "I don't see anything," he said hopefully.

"Turn anyway. Oh, Inky! Look at the lights! Greg, slow down so she can see it!" Greg obediently came to a stop so I could point out the small illuminated snowman in somebody's second-story window. "No, the other way. Inky! Look the other way! Out Daddy's side! Yes, but up. Look up. No, not in the trees, look in the window of that building."

Imperiously, she turned her head toward the opposite window again, stonewalling. "I want to go home."

"Okay. Okay, we'll go home. Let's go home. But, Greg, just humor me, turn left here and see, let's just see, if there's anything worth looking at."

Bingo. In the middle of the block a brick row house was lit up, weighed down and wired for sound. Several Santas crowded the three wise men to get a look at Baby Jesus. There was a police lineup of Winnie-the-Poohs and Mickey Mouses wearing molded plastic Santa hats. There were seraphim, cherubim, giant candy canes, fake snow and hundreds of dollars worth of that Christmas supernumerary, the tin soldier with dots for eyes. A team of reindeer and a sleighful of presents balanced precariously on the roof of the tiny porch. A strobe light had been set up on the chimney with nary a sign to ward off people with epilepsy and heart conditions. I'd seen full-body Christmas displays before, but never squished into such tight quarters. It must've taken at least a week to lug all this stuff into position, more if it had been accomplished without the help of a crane. I wondered if they had an agreement with their neighbors to power down at a certain hour. "Jesus fucking Christ, Tony, turn that shit off! My kid's got to get up early and open presents, and he can't sleep a wink with all those pa-rum-pa-pum-pums you got coming out of your speakers. I'm calling the cops!"

When I turned in my seat, eager to reward myself with the expression of openmouthed wonder on Uncle Crabcakes' face, I learned why she'd gone quiet. She was asleep. She looked the way she had as a sleeping baby, not so much innocent as disapproving and mildly dyspeptic, like Queen Victoria. Her brother had cashed in his chips, too, gulping raggedly around my captive pinky.

I looked back at the house. One thing was certain. The mastermind behind this spectacle did not have little children at home. I wouldn't be able to outline a single window frame in lights with Inky and Milo underfoot. I can barely manage to make toast! This display must be the work of a local grandpa, a retiree driven to heights of excess with which no neighbor could compete. Indeed, a few doors down, another house twinkled and flashed, but compared to Grandpa's, its decorations were strictly sophomore level. As Greg shifted into drive, I dashed off a mental screenplay about a kindly old man who stashes the preteen victims of his once-a-year rampage in the four-foot hollow plastic figurines crammed onto his property. I'd never rent it at the video store, but I bet it could make millions, or at least enough to send both kids to school out of state.

Inky resumed consciousness as we unbuckled her from her car seat, but she was so sleepy it was easy to hustle her into pajamas and herd her toward bed, with just one pit stop to lay out milk and cookies for Santa. I felt a bit tawdry, filling a saucer with the store-bought cookies Inky takes to nursery school in her lunchbox. One really ought to bake for Santa.

Our bedroom has a fireplace. When our landlady bought the

place, she was told it didn't work. Before our movers' truck had pulled away, Jambo had already tried to make a break for it by jumping straight up the chimney, showering himself with bricks and a century of old soot. The handyman who was sent around to make sure all was in order stuck his head up the chimney and saw sky. He told me the fireplace was operational. I immediately embarked on a fantasy in which, pregnant, I spent cozy winter evenings sipping soup with Inky and Greg in our new king-sized bed, watching the embers instead of TV. Greg couldn't kill that idea fast enough. I had to admit that perhaps he was right. I once ignited a plastic shower curtain by falling asleep in a candlelit bath. I am a liability around fire, and our fireplace opens right onto a creaking polyurethaned wood floor. One spark and the party's over. Our fireplace became a display case for some of the junk we've picked up traveling: ankle bells, unlit novena candles and an Indian miniature of two cat-faced demons slyly screwing each other in public. We housed these treasures in an old crate to block access to the chimney, should our own cat-faced demon take another crack at escape. Inky, who showed no concern for her fireplaceless friends in the East Village, voiced anxiety that an old Canada Dry crate might prevent Santa and his bag of toys from gaining entry. "Santa's magic, Inky. He'll just kick it out of the way or I'll wake up and help him." When she looked like she might perk up to offer some argument, I removed the box, hoping that Jambo would not seize the day. He'd already complicated Mother's Day by rolling out the unscreened third floor window onto our landlady's flagstone patio. I didn't want Inky to creep into our room Christmas morning only to discover the stiff carcass of our undeservedly beloved pet, his skull crushed by a loose brick.

After Inky had crashed, Greg and I stuffed the stockings and arranged the presents under the tree. We were very excited about Milo's present. In my worldview, Santa subscribes to the Waldorf School theory of creative play, trafficking in wholesome wooden blocks, elfin dolls and bright silk scarves that can be draped into just about anything a child can imagine short of a gun. Milo's exersaucer, a primary-colored nightmare of molded plastic and tinny battery-operated tunes was a stretch for Santa, but he was willing to bend the rules as long as it did what it was supposed to do and occupied the baby for hours. It was as big as a coffee table. The infant Inky never had an exersaucer or any of those baby accoutrements that are promoted as so indispensable. Instead, she had the broiler, which provided many happy hours of playtime fun.

Just as we were getting in bed, I remembered. "Greg, the cookies!"

Greg wrinkled his nose looking at the small saucer in front of the fireplace. "I just had two beers. I don't want to eat those."

"I don't want to eat them either. You eat them."

"We could just throw them away."

"No, she'll see them in the trash. Eat them. Put them back in the bag." I slid under the covers, abdicating responsibility. "Or throw them away if you want to, but shove them all the way down under a diaper or something."

Greg went into the kitchen and returned with the saucer, empty except for a few carefully arranged crumbs. Jambo had at the milk. I got back out of bed to rummage for a blank videotape. The bride who banned all video cameras from her wedding slept with the equipment in easy reach, ready to hit Record at the first stirring, which came all too soon.

"Greg! Wake up! Inky's up." He mumbled and rolled onto his stomach. How could he be so lax about witnessing his three-year-old child's six A.M. glee? I sprang about like a two-bit choreographer jacked up at the notion of showtime. I was much livelier than Inky, who lay in bed stretching and rubbing her eyes, her father's child. "Merry Christmas, baby girl!" I piped. "Good morning! Good Christmas morning!" She eyed me like an exhausted mother whose toddler has roused her much too early. I tickled her. She smiled indulgently and then rolled on her side, protecting her ribs and closing her eyes. "Guess what? Santa came! Don't you want to see what Santa brought you?"

At the mention of her god, Inky snapped to attention, hitting the floor with a thud. I could barely keep the video camera trained on her as she streaked toward the fireplace.

She stopped dead in her tracks, gaping at the conspicuously empty saucer. "Ooh. He eated the cookies," she intoned reverently. That had been a close one. My stepfather later told me that that's how he figured out the truth about Santa. Before he went downstairs one Christmas morning, he overheard his mother asking his father if he'd remembered to eat the cookies.

Inky clamored onto our bed to open her stocking at warp speed, screaming with approval at every ordinary item rendered wonderful by Santa's touch. She ate several days' rations of chocolate and moved on to Milo's stocking. She seemed thrilled for him and by the opportunities his stocking booty provided for her. She could feed him his new cereal with his new spoon after tying him into his new bib! She could slather him in seven-dollar diaper cream! She would force his tiny hands into the ridiculous red-striped mittens

Santa couldn't resist at the Salvation Army! She would do it all simultaneously and without adult assistance. "Coffee," Greg groaned as a box of rice cereal conked him on the head.

It took less than an hour to rid the house of wrapped gifts. I was glad to see Inky tearing into her presents with gusto. When I was little, I was unduly influenced by my grandmother's thrifty desire to reuse pretty paper. By the age of four, I had learned how to slit Scotch tape with a fingernail, shaking the box free like a pillow from a pillowcase. I loved presents, but I never experienced that savage abandon. It was satisfying to see my child make a hash of my careful wrapping job, but then I became fixated on stuffing the papers into a box for organized cleanup. I don't know why. I'm not a housekeeper by any stretch of the imagination. Maybe I was afraid we'd lose Milo in the melee. He'd logged about two minutes in his exersaucer before issuing an SOS.

What did Greg and I get? Nice things, thoughtful things. I forget. What did Inky get? Wooden puzzles and a wooden stovetop with lots of plastic fruit from the 99-cent store. Feathered wings, books, and the "regular" headbands she'd been agitating for since Halloween. A little wooden chair and a fancy dress. Her father gave her a book of fables illustrated by underground comic artists. It was a very good Christmas. We sat around assembling the dinosaur puzzle, Inky naked except for her wings. I looked at my new Vietnamese cookbook and pretended that I am the kind of woman who is content to spend her time shredding green papaya and making her own hot sauce. Greg made coffee and waited a suitable amount of time before ducking out for *The New York Times*. Milo permitted himself to be decked out in a quantity of ribbons and bows and

Jambo hid until we left for my mother-in-law's place up near Central Park. An hour before she was due to arrive at our place she had called to see if there was any chance we might bring the party to her. Why not? It was Christmas. I relented. The second the door closed, I could hear Jambo yowling as he mounted his rag doll. It was Christmas. It had been an ordinary day at home. Wonderful.

February 14

Valentine's Day was a pretty big deal for us girls back in high school. Every year the senior class raised money for graduation by delivering carnations for a dollar apiece on Valentine's Day. The flowers were routed to the lucky recipients by red construction-paper tags on which the purchaser could write a romantic message of his or her choosing. If you received a carnation you could carry it with you to your classes or leave it in your locker, affixing the tag to your clothing as proof of your worthiness, sort of like wearing one of those paper flowers the veterans give you in return for donating to their charitable collections. The cheerleaders and others of their ilk were covered with red construction-paper tags. One young lady memorably tied these trophies all over her braids, lest anyone fail to notice her popularity. The people who received no carnations slid along the corridors trying to attract as little attention as possible. I would have hated to be a teacher on that day. I think my heart would have broken, looking out at all those hopeful, smug and crushed faces, that vicious little microcosm.

My small group of close friends served as buffers against the unkind world, ordering carnations for each other. We wrote cryptic messages on the tags, alluding to whatever secret unrequited crushes we happened to be harboring. Thanks to these trustworthy late bloomers, I always survived Valentine's Day with a respectable four carnations. With great relief, I pasted the tags into my scrapbook. I entertained fantasies of one day hooking up with a man who would cover my bed with roses.

By senior year, I had a boyfriend, a real boyfriend who ate dinner at my mother's house and paid for my movie tickets. Finally, I would get a real carnation instead of just the ones my girlfriends and I sent each other as insurance policies. A group of us seniors stayed up half the night, tying the tags we'd collected onto five-hundred-some stems. Coyly, I refrained from reading the sentiments on any of the ones addressed to me, lest I spoil the surprise of my boyfriend's message a day early. Instead, I peeked at the tags of classmates who were suspected of having sex.

We delivered the carnations during the next morning's assembly and our free periods. By lunchtime, I had received quite a few, but none from my boyfriend. Perhaps he was holding back so he could deliver it himself during a shared class. Maybe his had gotten lost. Some did every year. At least that's what we told ourselves. When the dismissal bell rang, I couldn't believe it. He hadn't sent me a carnation. We'd peddled the damn things for weeks beforehand. He'd had plenty of opportunities. I knew he had a dollar. I collected my books and carnations and headed toward the parking lot.

"Wait up!" It was my skinny, preppy boyfriend. "Here, I got you this." He handed me a carnation, but not the kind we'd sold to raise money for the senior class. For whatever reason, he had failed to send me one of those, the badge that I could have displayed to my classmates all day long. At some point, he must have realized the egregiousness of his error and run out to the florist a couple of blocks from campus. Instead of buying something wonderful—*how could I give you a lowly carnation when you are as exotic as a bird of paradise?*—he bought me a single stupid stem of the exact variety he was supposed to purchase at school to pay for his own graduation.

Of course, I would rather have died than let him know it mattered. What I had hoped was that, after sending me ten carnations at school, he would present me with an enormous chocolate cupid or a heart-shaped locket, the secondary school equivalent of filling the bathtub with rose petals. The dumb ox. I accepted the flower casually, wishing I hadn't been so mushy filling out the tag on the one I'd bought him the first day they went on sale.

"Uh, thanks for sending me a carnation," he said, stumbling along beside me, an awkward teenage boy in Docksiders and a crewneck sweater. Maybe in *Seventeen* magazine the boys were men, conducting themselves with ease at picnics, football tailgates and holiday parties where the girls wore floor-length plaid taffeta. Not in my world. In my world, the boys were duds. What a rip-off.

I remembered what Valentine's Day had meant in elementary school. My mother always came up with good ideas for the homemade valentines I laboriously assembled on the dining room table, one for every classmate. Only one year did we miscalculate. That was the year we baked heart-shaped sugar cookies on which I signed my name in pink icing. As I was loading them into a box to take to school, I realized I'd forgotten to make one for myself. If everybody else was going to get one, it didn't seem right that I wouldn't get one too. I mentally sorted through the kids in my class. We didn't have any bullies that year, no obese smart kids or new kids with bizarre parents. Finally I settled on the Jehovah's witness. He was nothing to me, right? For the next eight years, until we graduated and went to different colleges, I gave that boy a wide berth. When others referred to him in conversation, I cringed.

Given the charged nature of the holiday, I expected Inky's pre-school to send her home with a memo requesting that parents steer clear of the whole business. Instead, they promoted it! They approved it as a way to acknowledge friendship! The memo they sent home described the classroom activities that would culminate in Valentine's Day, when the children could deposit cards in the heart-shaped mail pouches they'd made to adorn their cubbyholes. I started freaking out.

There was the issue of the cards themselves. They still sell those lidless boxes of goofy valentines, twenty-four to the pack, with a special one for the teacher. Naturally, Ms. Has-Be-Special-Has-To-Be-Homemade couldn't stand the thought of those. The cartoon characters may have changed, but the jokes are just as lame as they were back in my day. If some smarty-pants Hallmark exec had thought to reissue a bunch of kiddie valentines from 1929, I'd have bought those. Nobody had though. I checked surreptitiously when Inky was in the next aisle worshipping a bottle of children's shampoo that came topped with the disembodied head of one of her pals from *Dragon Tales*.

In theory, I liked the idea of cutting hearts from red construction paper, covering the table with newspaper so we could decorate them with glitter and glue. I always enjoyed the unfamiliarity of the paper doilies my mother brought home to trim my homemade valentines, but I haven't forgotten the drudgery of the assembly line. After the third unit, it's just grunt work. I wasn't keen to spend an afternoon pasting together sixteen little cards after Inky got bored. Also, I know I have a bit of a tendency to be an aesthetic control freak, and involving a three-year-old in the process was courting disaster. I don't want to be one of those mommies who snap at their children for doing it wrong; neither can I stand to see a big glob of glitter glue squirted where it doesn't belong. Glitter glue should be distributed evenly, to form a pleasing shape. Actually, glitter glue should not be distributed at all. Please do not give glitter glue to people who have children, even if they are artsy. If you have given glitter glue to Inky in the past, please refrain from doing so again. It turns her mother into a bitch.

I had my own valentines to think about as well. I never got around to making Christmas cards last year. Like many parents of small children, I view Christmas as an excuse to send a photograph of the little wieners to every living person in my address book. When I realized I wasn't going to make the deadline, I plotted to send valentines instead. It ended up being a particularly good idea, given Milo's pulchritude at seven months. It seemed to me imperative that nobody miss out on his unbelievably endearing fat rolls. If I stripped him naked and gave him wings and a bow and arrow, he would make a fine Cupid. This was a much better plan than just sending out photos of the two of them seated on the couch. Let it never be said that I am a garden-variety braggart.

You don't send out a picture of one kid and not the other, right?

Beats me. I'm just an only child, doing my best to head sibling rivalry off at the pass. We could have two cupids. I decided to make a postcard featuring both of them. Naked and scraggle-haired, Inky was only too glad to get in on the action, balancing on one foot while Greg and I challenged one another's knowledge of archery positions. Having no actual bows and arrows, we were taking the blue screen approach. I would draw them in later.

Greg squatted on the floor, looking through the digital camera he used for work. Inky mugged, flashing her teeth and rolling her eyes so far back in her head, they looked like peeled grapes.

"Inky, look at Daddy. Look regular, honey."

"She should hold her arm out straight. How can you shoot an arrow if your elbow is bent?"

"Okay, but the other arm has to be cocked back like this. Inky, can you pull arm back like this, like you're holding something next to your ear?" She squeezed her eyes shut and toppled over as Greg snapped her picture. We waited for the results to upload. Not so good. "Greg, don't take it from the front, take it from the side."

"Well, you want her to look like she's shooting an arrow, right?"

"Yeah, but from the side."

"Why don't you tell me exactly what you have in mind?"

"You know, like she's shooting an arrow. Like Arjuna."

"Who's Arjuna?"

"Arjuna, you know, from Indonesia. The guy who shoots the arrow. The prince."

Greg shook his head and muttered, squatting again. Inky rolled her eyes back and hopped up and down. Her legs looked exceptionally bruised and scratched, even for her.

Could I send this through the mail? What if the authorities came looking for me, the mother of the naked, unwashed little girl with the marks on her legs? "Greg, make sure her bukiluki's not showing."

Inky dropped her archer's pose, examining her vagina like someone hunting for a quarter in her change purse. Greg sighed and crawled over to show me the results. "I'm not wild about her expression," I said.

"Ayun, if I don't leave now, I'm going to get a parking ticket. Is this really worth a hundred and fifty dollars to you?"

"No, but if we don't take the picture now, I can't get the cards made in time for Valentine's Day."

"Okay, okay. Inky, one more picture, okay?" Greg's enthusiasm for Valentine's Day rivals his enthusiasm for farmers' markets and fund-raising carnivals. He knelt for the last time.

"I want Karakushka to be in the picture." Inky held up a filthy stuffed animal with a scary rubber face. A friend had given Karakushka to Inky a couple of years ago as a souvenir from Moscow. He said it was either that or a Russian Barbie, who he described as looking like a cheap hooker. Karakushka is supposed to be a magpie. It sort of looks like a black snowman with a beak and disturbing, penetrating eyes.

"Oh, no, honey, Karakushka can't be in this picture. This one's just you."

"Why?"

"Because this picture is going to be our valentine to our friends and they don't want to see Karakushka. They don't know Karakushka. They want to see you.

"But I want Karakushka to have her picture tooked."

"Karakushka can have her picture taken, just not in the same one as you. Daddy will take your picture and then he'll take Karakushka's picture and then you can both have your picture. Won't that be fun?"

"Ayun," Greg warned, pointing to his watch.

"Inky, you can use my camera to take a picture of Karakushka after Daddy goes. Okay?"

"Wellllll . . . Okay, I guess I can take a picture of Karakushka later," Inky conceded grudgingly, as if she were canceling plans to attend the opera because her ailing mother's home health aid had phoned in sick.

Greg got the shot and clattered down the stairs, late for work and just barely ahead of the parking cop.

The card turned out pretty well. Milo at his plumpest sticks his fingers in his mouth in the foreground while Inky minces smarmily in the background. I inked feathered wings onto their shoulders. Greg's criticism of the bow I drew in Inky's hand was not unexpected; it was like the time he made me draw him as an Iron Age hunter, brandishing his atlatl. But the implausibility of my bow didn't matter. Love was the message, not accuracy of hunting implements! Assuming the U.S. Postal Service didn't confiscate them as porn, our friends would have something nice to magnet to their refrigerators. I started thinking that maybe the card I made for our friends could do double duty in Inky's school exchange. It didn't say anything dirty on it. It would save me from having to fool with doilies and glitter glue. The only thing was, I wasn't sure about setting my daughter up to glad-hand naked pictures of herself to her classmates. (I had a hunch that I was the only mother dealing with this particular valentine dilemma.) I devised a way to draw a bikini over Inky. I tried to interest her in this activity, but she preferred to fill in Milo's image with a dark purple pencil. When she was done with him, he looked like he was wearing one of those Thneeds the bad Once-ler made from the Lorax's Truffula Trees. It sort of destroyed the intended effect, but at least it smacked of collaboration. If anyone at school bridled over the nature of our card, I didn't want to be implicated alone.

On the big day, every child except one was dressed in shades of red and pink. "Oh, is it Valentine's Day?" little Brown Shirt's mother asked as her unconcerned son dive-bombed the sandbox. "I completely forgot."

"Oh, yes, I nearly did too," I replied, shaking my head jovially as I guided Inky to her friends' mail pouches. Dutifully, she stuffed a valentine in each one, even the one belonging to the kid who pushes and bites.

When I picked her up after school, her own pouch was full of tiny envelopes, the kind that come twenty-four to a pack. We sat on the couch, opening them one at a time. "Look, Inky, this one's from Sophia. It's got a little mouse kicking a ball and it says, 'Have a ball, Valentine!'"

"Sophia," Inky agreed solemnly, holding the card in both hands.

Some of the little cards bore evidence of children just learning how to write their own names. Others were signed in the parent's hand. I wondered if they had sat together, the cards spread out on a table before them, slowly choosing which valentine should go to which friend. I'd probably be a much healthier person if I could just bring myself to show Inky a box of storebought valentines. "Look, I got these Pokémon cards for you to give your classmates on Valentine's Day. Do you like them? Good. Now go watch TV while I address them to the kids in your class." I'll have to try that sometime.

The only other homemade card came from the pusher-biter. It was a really appealing assemblage of red feathers and tiny Styrofoam balls. Looked like a lot of work for a three-year-old.

Valentine's Day was months ago. The pouch is still thumbtacked to the wall above Inky's bed. All the valentines she received at school are inside, as are some risqué ones that came free in *The Village Voice* as an advertising ploy from Altoids mints. Once a week or so, Inky takes the pouch down and shuffles through its contents, examining each little card as reverently as she did on the day she received them. Adult visitors are amazed to hear her correctly identify the senders. Sophia. Daisy. Theo. They assume she can read.

It both breaks my heart and pleases me that these tokens from her nursery school classmates are accorded such respect. I wonder if they'll stay tacked to her wall forever. What will I do when my teenage daughter comes to me in exasperation, pleading, "Mom, can we please get rid of those valentines I got when I was three? I'm afraid that someone will see them!"

Conversely, I can imagine a smitten junior high boy tormenting the secret object of his affection with a childhood keepsake his own mother couldn't bring herself to throw away. The day may come when a certain reformed pusher-biter boasts that he has a picture of Inky naked. Despite the presence of a colored-pencil bikini, he

won't be lying. I just hope she won't be mad that I made her sign
her name with love.

April 15

By Easter, I needed a break from all this holiday jazz. Valentines, Halloween costumes, Santa Claus. I was fatootzed, as my
mother-in-law would say. I felt ready for a nice somber bank holiday, where you take the kids to the cemetery to weed the graves of
long-dead veterans. No presents, no special food or songs, no articles on how to help your child handle holiday stress.

Unfortunately, Rite Aid had other plans. Why couldn't they be
like the little Polish pharmacy in the East Village, where I used to
go to make five-cent Xeroxes? No matter what the season, their
window display was utilitarian, an inventory of sitz baths, athletic
supporters and rentable toilet chairs. Judging from the bacchanal
that Rite Aid set up the day they marked all unsold Valentine candy
down to half price, Easter would require at least five hundred
dollars and a week off from school to celebrate properly. The long-
time Italian residents in our neighborhood apparently agreed, decorating the tiny cement yards in front of their brownstones with
banners, egg trees and carefully arranged groupings of rabbits,
lambs and chickens in spring outfits. Enormous pastel eggs
appeared at the feet of a crucified Christ who stays up year-round
outside the church a few blocks away from us. This only reinforced
my adult impression of the Easter bunny as a heartless corporate
shill. I could picture him hopping around the church grounds late

at night, so concerned with shitting out his gaily colored eggs that he wouldn't take a second to rescue Jesus from the cross.

Of course Inky didn't see it that way. She doesn't know Jesus from Adam, but somehow she had gleaned a few important facts about the Easter bunny, the wonderful creature without whom none of this cellophane grass and molded chocolate would be possible.

"Does the Easter bunny exist?" she asked me on the subway one morning, frowning over the top of her juicebox.

"Uh . . . what do you mean?" I parried, stalling for time. Greg and I hadn't broached the subject of the Easter bunny. We had no parental position on him whatsoever. I had a strong suspicion that if his existence were given our thumbs-up, it wouldn't be the atheist Jew out trolling the aisles of Rite Aid for Marshmallow Peeps and packages of dye.

"I mean is he real?"

I flashed on an Easter Sunday of my youth, remembering how grown-up I felt, having been entrusted with the responsibility of running around the side of the house, hiding colored eggs in patches of melting snow for my little cousins to find. There were other memories too: the lemonade-colored vinyl pocketbook and matching mary janes to wear to church; the year my grandfather dressed up like the Easter bunny to entertain at a children's party and was nearly busted by two starstruck little girls when he retired to the host's bedroom to remove his uncomfortably hot papier-mâché head. The cross-shaped bookmarks my grandmother sent without fail to every member of the family. Devouring all the Godiva chocolate from the three-tiered holiday centerpiece my wealthy best friend's mother left unattended on their dining room table, knowing that her skinny daughter didn't care for them. Greg couldn't relate to any of this.

We'd already stricken the Christ from Christmas, which was okey-doke by me. As far as I was concerned, Christmas had much less to do with the little Lord Jesus than with the tree, the lights, my own childhood and the way the ornaments smelled. (I swear to god, that lumpy treetop angel's fragrant vinyl hair is more familiar to me than the sweaty scent of my own children's heads.) But I felt bad about cutting Jesus out of his other big holiday. As a child I'd spent many Easter Sundays marching up the aisle of St. Paul's to donate my pennies on behalf of a roofless church in Haiti. At the start of Lent, we were issued flame-colored cardboard boxes, and every day my father would give me a penny to deposit in mine. On Easter, we were excused from Sunday school so we could offer them up in a special ceremony. Midway through the service, we children were invited to the altar to stuff our boxes into a giant wooden cross with slots in neat rows, sort of like those things you can buy for cassette tapes. Once we'd disposed of the boxes, we processed from left to right—or gospel to epistle, as I believe it's called in the Episcopal church—to poke flowers from our mothers' gardens through the chicken wire front of another towering cross.

Does this sort of thing still go on? I haven't thought about it in years. Recalling it now, it almost feels like my parents were part of some bizarre devil-worshipping cult, cleverly disguised as Episcopalians of the gin-and-tonic, polished-loafer variety.

I was disturbed by the theological implications of Inky's question. I, the great explainer who had observed the twentieth anniversary of John Lennon's murder by making sure my child knew more about it than any other three-year-old on earth, did not have the energy to open this new can of worms. *Well, you see, Inky, it's like this. A long time ago, a little baby was born in a manger and then he grew up and was nailed to a giant cross by some bad men. Do you know what a cross is? It's the same shape as that cake in the Puerto Rican bakery that you always think is a T. Anyway, he died, like John Lennon, but then he became alive again three days later and went up to heaven, which is where you go if you don't believe you just turn into food for the flowers and animals after you die. So then a lot of people worshipped this guy because he was so nice and they wanted to be like him, presumably. They still do. Your grandfather goes to church every Sunday. So, that's one religion, Christianity, and then there's another one called Judaism, which is like your daddy, but not really. Like your daddy's daddy's daddy's daddy who was a rabbi, like those guys with long beards and black hats on the F train. And then there are a whole bunch of other religions too, like Islam, which is what all those little girls in our neighborhood who wear veils are. And then in India, there are Hindus. They have lots of gods. Like Hanuman, right, your brother's middle name? He's a monkey but he's also a Hindu god. So, anyway, in our country, you can be any religion you want to or no religion at all, except a lot of people are Christians, so Easter is sort of a big deal at places like Rite Aid in a way that Diwali or Ramadan aren't, even though those days are really impor-tant to you if you're Hindu or Muslim. Where the Easter bunny comes from is, I guess people wanted to make it more fun for kids than just a big cross, so they figured, well, Easter is in the springtime and there are lots of baby animals in the spring, like kitties and puppies and also bunnies, which are the cutest of all, and then, uh, eggs, too, there are*

a lot of eggs, and people dye them pretty colors so they'll look like
flowers. So, in answer to your question, the Easter bunny does not
exist, but you are free to believe in him if you want to, and I will go
to Rite Aid and get you some chocolate in support of that belief, but
not a big flag with a chicken on it, or a stuffed rabbit that plays music,
or a bunch of plastic crap that we don't need.

It came out that what really mattered most to her was the
basket. The Easter bunny could be a hologram on the back of a
driver's license for all she cared, as long as she got a basket with a
long handle. I offered her the one that I use for bread when we
have guests for dinner, but she said it wasn't the right kind. We
headed to Rite Aid. They were charging a fortune and all their
baskets came preloaded. We found an empty one that met both of
our standards at the 99-cent store. Rather than add the Easter
bunny to our family pantheon, I worked it out with Inky that we
could take turns being the Easter bunny, hiding small toys
around the apartment for the other to practice finding. Inky
loved this game. Every night I found a handful of plastic fruit
shoved under my comforter from when it had been Inky's turn. I
told her that we would hard-boil a dozen eggs on Saturday afternoon and dye them. On Sunday morning, I would don bunny
ears and hide the eggs. Inky would cover her eyes, just like she'd
been doing during our dry runs. "Daddy can take pictures," I told
her. "Karen and CJ are coming to visit from Chicago this
weekend, so they'll be here too." She would have an audience.
Once she'd filled her basket with the eggs I'd stashed, she could
redeem them for some Easter goodies, specifically a jump rope
she had seen at Rite Aid. This sounded good to her: The Easter

bunny was fluid, someone you pretended to be. You got stuff.
You bought more eggs than usual.

Karen and CJ arrived on Good Friday. Being a fun, childless
couple, they had a long list of obscure record shops, cool cafés and
edgy performances to check out during their forty-eight hours in
New York. I was exhausted just hearing about all the wonderful
things I wasn't going to be doing with them. By Saturday evening,
the only thing I was good for was stretching out on the floor,
nursing a beer and the baby. Inky had roped Karen into a game
they'd made up while waiting for me to go into labor with Milo the
previous July. It involved racing back and forth from Inky's bedroom to the table at the other end of the apartment, alternately
snoring and bolting down great stacks of invisible pancakes. To do
it right you have to shriek, "Good morning! Good night!" over and
over at the top of your lungs. I'm sure Karen was delighted that her
little shadow had not forgotten this game of wits in which
everyone's a winner. Inky was so intent on it, she seemed to have forgotten about the eggs we had hard-boiled that afternoon. She
hadn't breathed a word about the dye. I hadn't managed to get the
bunny ears either. Maybe we could just forget the whole thing.

Even before I had children, I was too chronically fatigued and
ultimately conflicted to celebrate holidays with all the bells and
whistles blueprinted by *Family Circle* and Martha Stewart. That
said, I can't let them slide entirely. I tell myself it's for Inky's sake,
even though I've heard plenty of mothers claim that their families
couldn't be happier since they went cold turkey for Christmas. Their
kids have learned firsthand that there are things more satisfying
than presents. They really look forward to the Yule log and all those

solstice candles. But my kid looks forward to whatever hybrid notions I have planted in her head, both deliberately and by accident. She also takes into account the traditions she picks up from her playfellows and the windows of Rite Aid. I couldn't not do Easter.

I hauled every teacup out of the cabinet, filled them with water and vinegar and dropped in the fizzy tablets of pigment from the Paas egg-dyeing kit. I found myself feeling very hostile toward the little octagonal wire that still comes in a packet of Paas, just the way it did when I was a kid. How could Inky be expected to balance an egg on that thing? This was sure to end in tears. Actually, she did quite well, dipping the eggs with her fingers. Removing them from their teacup baths, she dropped no more than half. "Hey, that's a good one! Look how pretty!" I squealed, pointing to the spiderweb pattern of smashed shell with one hand. With the other, I held the back of Milo's overalls like the choke chain of a pit bull. The child was suddenly into everything. What would we do with him the next time Christmas rolled around? The tree, the gift-wrap—I didn't like to think about it.

It took five minutes to dye a dozen eggs. It would take several weeks to clean up. After Inky had gone to bed, Karen got it into her head to blow an egg as a surprise for her. Greg, who still expects to be lynched by anti-Semites every time we go to Indiana, was unfamiliar with this heathen ritual. He watched skeptically as Karen applied her lips to a tiny hole she'd made in the shell of the last raw egg in the refrigerator, exhaling with such force that her eyes bulged out. "No, what are you doing really?" he asked, certain he was being set up. Karen blatted against the egg like Louis Armstrong.

"She's blowing the egg," I told him. "You didn't do this in school? We always did it in French class, except we made the holes too big and they never worked out right."

"Jesus, how weird. You really called it 'blowing' an egg?"

"No, Greg, we called it sucking an egg's penis. Of course we called it blowing an egg. That's what you do!"

"I've never heard of it. CJ, do they do this in Scotland?"

"I can't say as I recall. It's the sort of thing my mother would have taken care of," CJ answered politely. He is constantly called upon to verify Scottish tradition for interested Americans. He says shortbread, bagpipes and kilts never came up in daily conversation until he married Karen and moved to Chicago.

Karen came up for air, massaging her cheeks. When the egg was empty, she mixed up a couple of quarts of the blood-colored Greek dye I had bought at the Middle Eastern grocery. We all watched as she pushed the fragile orb around in it with a chopstick, turning it over and over until she achieved the desired hue. "Now I have to polish it with olive oil to make it nice and glossy. Do you have any olive oil?"

"Sure," I said, banging a large metal can of it down perilously close to the egg.

"Look what it did to my fingers," she remarked as she oiled her masterpiece with a paper towel. "Turned them bright red. Oh no! Shit! The oil's making the color come off! Now it's all ugly. I have to put in back in the dye." This cycle repeated itself until midnight, at which point the egg was an un-Eastery shade of brick and Karen's fingers looked like dried cherries.

While waiting for our guests to finish with the bathroom, I did a mental run through the following day's Easter bunny routine. I should have tried harder to get those ears. Maybe I could make a pair out of construction paper. It should feel a little more ceremonial than the practice hunts Inky and I had rehearsed all week. The whole exercise struck me as pointlessly elaborate when I could just spend five minutes heaping the prizes from Rite Aid into the basket from the 99-cent store and have done with it. That's what any sane parent would do. It might be nice to enjoy a leisurely breakfast with our friends instead of hopping around the apartment like a moron. I'd already made it clear that the Easter bunny was just a charade, a construct of the imagination. If Inky had a full basket of goodies to keep her occupied, chances were I could make it through an entire bagel in peace. I retrieved the Rite Aid bag from the top shelf of our single closet. Once the contents were transferred, I centered the basket on Inky's vinyl place mat. The effect was rather charming, especially since I'd sponged off the sticky coin-sized splashes of dried soy milk and dehydrated Cheerios in an attempt to impress our company.

What about Milo? I might have forgotten about Milo, but the bunny couldn't. Luckily, we still had a bag of never-used stuffed animals, gifts left over from the birth of the infant Inky. Back then, I was adamant about not acquiring a menagerie until she was old enough to understand what one was. I'd always had it in mind to give the toys to the Hell's Angels to distribute to needy children some Christmas, but then Christmas would arrive and I'd be too busy running around the city on my own last-minute missions to brighten an unfortunate youngster's holiday. Really, I was no better than the Easter bunny who refused to come to Jesus's aid. I excused myself by picturing a deprived ten-year-old boy who'd spent the better part of a year praying for a Game Boy unwrapping a teddy bear clad in chintz pajamas.

Fortunately, one of the animals was a rabbit. I remember writing the thank-you note for it, telling a sweet older couple I barely knew how much our one-month-old daughter was enjoying their thoughtful gift. A little resurrection for Easter. How perfect. It went straight into Milo's high chair. I went to bed.

The next morning Inky, who had given up her bed to our guests, started prodding me with her foot at six A.M. "I need covers," she announced peevishly, yanking the comforter off my naked body. "I need space! Give me Kleenex." She reached over me to pinch Milo's cheek. "Ha ha! Milo's awake. I want breakfast. Mawwww-meeee, I want to get up. I want breakfast. I said I want to get up. I want to make my breakfast. Get up! Get up! Get up now!" Ah, how lovely were the days when I could burrow back into the pillow and sleep until mid-morning. I had not appreciated them nearly enough.

"Okay, okay," I mumbled, coming to life with the vigor of someone recently hospitalized for hip-replacement surgery. "I'm getting up, but you've got to be more quiet because Karen and CJ are trying to sleep. Come on, Milo."

"I need my stepladder! I need my stepladder!" Inky trilled as she raced ahead of me, hell-bent to spill milk all over the counter in the name of help. I heard her gasp and apply the brakes. She had noticed the basket.

" I told you so!" she shouted. "I knew it! The Easter bunny does so exist! I told you he does too exist. Look! He bringed me the jump rope! Ooh, he bringed me a red egg and lots of stuff. Milo! You don't get a basket. You get this bunny. Mawww-meee! Milo's pulling on my Easter basket! No, Mi-lee, no!"

I ate my bagel on the fly, guarding a 99-cent straw basket from the advances of a nine-month-old baby. Strange to think he'd been outside my body now as long as he'd been in it. Already he knew enough to protest when a jump rope was yanked out of his hands. Karen defused the situation by playing Easter bunny with Inky, taking turns hiding eggs for the other to find. As we were leaving to go jump rope in the park, Karen alerted me that there were only eleven eggs in the basket. I told her to check under my comforter, but apparently Inky had gotten a bit more sophisticated. A week later, I discovered the missing egg in the snack cup of Milo's exersaucer. Actually, Milo discovered it, slurping at its sky-blue shell as if blowing it in reverse. Easter eggs meant nothing to him. It was just another object to cram into his mouth. He didn't know jack about no bunny either. By the time he's old enough to ask that kind of existential question, I'm sure his older sister will be happy to clear things up for him. For now, though, the Easter bunny, who I once dreamed of marrying, is once again alive and well, shopping at Rite Aid, eating bagels when he should be at church, the sole reason for the holiday that bears his name.

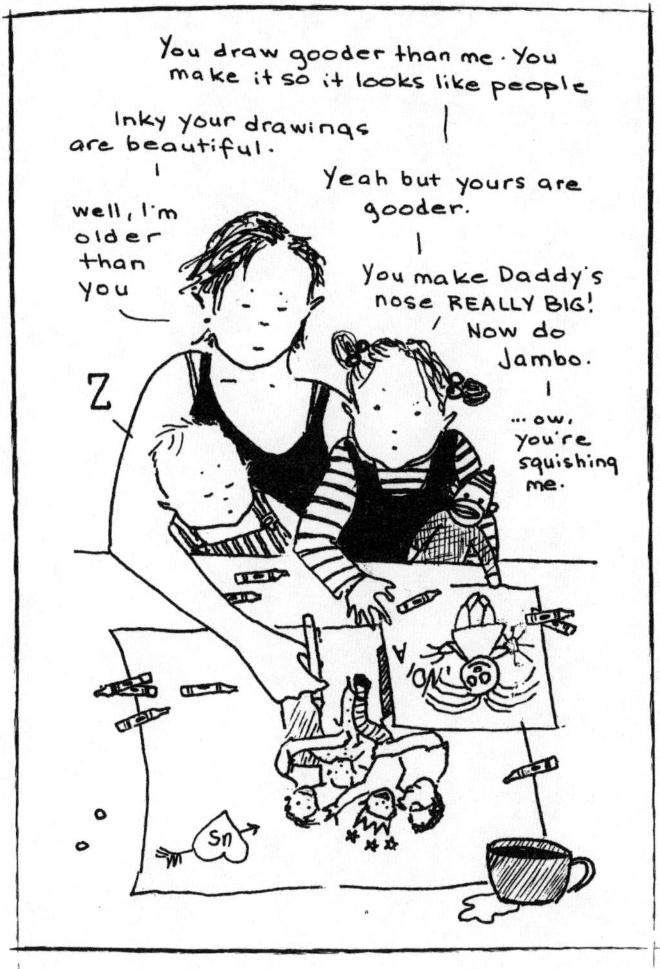

The Extremes

Spare Us

Here's the fear: that they will die. Which they will, as will everyone else we love and hate and regard with indifference.

Here's the real fear: that they will die before I do and I will be left without my children.

I seem to be exempt from a condition that affects many new parents. I don't mind thinking about the unthinkable. It doesn't bother me when children die in the movies or on television. It bothers me when they die in the newspaper, but not so much that I can't finish the article. I read every word and I never forget.

I collect stories of dead children the way I used to cut pictures of furniture out of the Sunday supplement, pasting them in a book of wallpaper samples, imagining a grand house with a hundred rooms in which I never expected to live. I collect stories of dead children in the hope that it won't happen to me. Please don't let my children die, like my friend's nephew who drowned in a swimming pool, like another friend's two-year-old godchild who drowned in the swimming pool at her parents' house in the Bahamas, bought so that they could live in Paradise instead of the Midwest. I guess that's one plus about New York apartment living. There's very little chance that my children will drown in a swimming pool belonging to me. I eye the pond on my friend's property, an hour away from us. Every summer there's a terrible headline as the currents claim another couple of ten-year-olds, cousins, best friends who thought they could outsmart a heat wave. I look up their mothers' names in the Brooklyn phone book, but I've never sent the lovely notes I compose in my head. Neighbors invariably describe the bereaved mothers as honest, hardworking women juggling three jobs to send their daughters to parochial school. The mothers are at work when the tragedy occurs. I ache, wondering if someone was supposed to be keeping an eye on the girls. I add all my friends' children to my own. Please don't let my friends' children die in my care. Don't let them die while their mothers are off doing whatever they do during their hotly imagined two hours away from the children. Coffee and shopping are meaningless. Working on the zine is nothing. The children are everything. Please don't let Milo or Inky wander into the pond on Sarah and Jesse's property and die.

Not every story concerning a dead child is told well. I'm an aesthetic snob, and there are far too many endlessly replayed shots of charred teddy bears for my taste. The producers of reality programming or prime time newsmagazines or whatever that tripe is called get rich by exploiting others' tragedies. If I could stomach swelling string sections and blurry snapshots of kids with red retinas in party hats, I would join the avid millions who tune in weeping. I always wonder why the parents didn't come up with a better photo. I consider which photo I would give if it were Inky, if it were Milo, and I swear I will never throw away another out-of-focus or unflattering print of them again. If the unthinkable happens and they die, I will spend the rest of my life pawing through the shoeboxes that serve as our family album.

When Inky was born, I used to say I would kill myself if anything happened to her. This was no idle threat. At least, I don't think it was. You go around saying, "If anything happens to my child, I'll kill myself," and then you hear about some grieving mother whose child really did die, fell out the door of the subway car, ran the wrong way around the ice cream truck, got some weird bug that looked like the flu and killed her in a handful of hours. Sometimes it takes another woman's tragedy to realize the arrogance of claiming to know what you'd do. When it was just Inky, I was all set to kill myself, and then I had Milo. And now I think, "Please don't let one of them die so I have to stay alive for the other one." Please don't let either of my children die.

Please don't let the Christmas tree catch on fire and kill them both while Greg and I try to douse the flames.

Please don't let them slip between the slats of the Golden Gate Bridge while we're on vacation.

Please don't let anything bad happen to them at the zoo.

The new millennium's umbilical stump had yet to fall off when Michael Atkinson, a film critic for *The Village Voice* crowned parental anxiety the "new great theme of modern culture." I know I'll pay good money to see a busload of schoolchildren crash through the ice into the lake. I'll pay for the young girl discovered raped and murdered and I'll pay for the rapist's mother visiting him in jail on the eve of his execution. It's the only form of prayer of which I'm capable. I witness these stories and pray, "Please don't let it happen to my children. Please don't let it happen to me." Perhaps this is what was running through every ancient mother's head as the sacrificial lamb's blood spilled over the altar. Michael Atkinson correctly identified the fear that plagues us from the moment our babies are born, but it's nothing new. I have read *Macbeth* solely for the scene in which assassins murder Lady Macduff and her children. For me, *Macbeth* isn't about a Scottish killer and his ambitious, tainted wife. It's about the moment when Macduff learns the fate of his wife and children:

> ...All my pretty ones?
> Did you say all? O hell-kite. All?
> What, all my pretty chickens and their dam
> At one fell swoop?

Shakespeare articulates this howling loss in a way five thousand charred teddy bears never will. Please don't let anything happen to my pretty chickens.

Of course, with two little kids in the house, I don't get out to see as much Shakespeare as I'd like, and it's resulted in a serious addiction to a popular prime time hospital drama. I credit this program with my putting the iron supplements on the highest shelf. My kids might suck on the plastic outlet covers I left on the floor the last time I plugged in the vacuum, but they'll never be brought into the emergency room with iron poisoning. I hope. Please don't let my children die from eating my vitamins. Please don't let my baby choke on a plastic outlet cover. My beloved hospital drama caters to parental anxiety with all sorts of nightmarish motor vehicle accidents, science lab explosions, drive-by shootings and premature deliveries. Sometimes the kids die. Sometimes the parents. Rarely both. Someone has to ask the nurse what happened to the person in the passenger seat. My friends know they're not supposed to call during my fix. When the phone rang the other night during a commercial, Greg answered before I could stop him. It was Jesse. "Is Ayun crying?" he giggled. "Because Sarah is." Of course I was crying! The child's wounds were very serious, and despite the doctors' best efforts they were unable to save her and she died. That's the little speech they give the parents, at least on TV. May I never hear it in real life.

After the men had a manly laugh at our expense, they passed the phones to us. Sarah and I had about two commercials to talk. "Did you see that?" she wailed.

"I know! It was so sad," I spluttered, trying to modulate my voice.

"It was so sad," Sarah echoed. Then we both burst out laughing, because our children were safe in their beds and we had had a wonderful catharsis, for free! It was like a pretend time-out Inky gives herself. The mundane concerns of potty seats and glitter glue and spilled juice were shelved for the time being.

I also cry whenever an actress manages to pull off a labor scene. Greg doesn't laugh at me then. He's seen for himself how hard it is to bring a baby into the world, but he hasn't felt it or he'd be crying too. I know a mother of small children who hates this show. She has decided there's karmic power in refusing to watch it. She calls it pornographic, the fat paychecks everyone takes home for depicting children in pain. Another chimes in that it purifies the soul to turn off any news report in which a child is reported dead. I would argue that our country is suffering from a severe shortage of bards and messengers, people who serve as repositories for the stories that awaken a cold, eyeless creature in the pit of every parent's stomach. In a dream world, every artist lucky enough to have his or her work produced in the public square could carry it off with complexity and respect. Charred teddy bears would be incomprehensible as shorthand. Nobody's children would die.

In the spirit of full disclosure, I must divulge that despite some close calls no one close to me has suffered a violent, unexpected end, not even when those twin towers collapsed on a gorgeous September morning. I am lucky. Perhaps I collect these stories out of ignorance, using them as prayers because I foolishly believe that someone who is not God will spare us. Whatever you want, just don't take the children. I might well be that ardent opponent of capital punishment whose mind changes the instant a brute lays his hands on her child. Or the Christmas tree catches fire. Or something awful happens at the zoo. Knock on wood. Knock on wood. Knock on wood. Knock on wood.

• • •

Mash Note to Milo

Dear Milo,

Let me be the first to write you a love letter.

You are plump and delicious, as fat as a ham. I count the creases on your thighs and feel rich. I remember meeting a friend's baby when she was about two months old. The baby's white legs were unbelievably fat, like unbaked bread sticks or grubworms. My friend was so proud of those legs. She dressed her baby in revealing diaper covers so that everyone could admire those meaty stems. Inky, who had seven months on that baby, was crawling hard, burning the fat off everything but the ripe fruit of her cheeks. I looked at my friend's daughter's legs, bulging out from the elastic bands of her colorful briefs, and thought, "Oh man, of course Patty thinks they're cute. Patty's her mother. But Jesus, look at them! They're really fat! It looks like she's been pounding those deep-fried peanut butter and banana sandwiches Elvis Presley loved." I told Patty that her daughter was adorable but secretly preferred your sister's lean drumsticks, scratched and bruised from those early attempts at mobility.

At your pudgiest you were at least one crease fatter than Patty's baby ever was. I loved you beyond reason. I am drunk on your pulchritude. I love you now, and I'll love you two months from now when you've run yourself creaseless.

I love you the way I loved my boyfriends, if memory serves, except I know I won't find you boring and offensive in a year and a half. I love you the way I loved them at one o'clock in the morning, when I pedaled my bicycle through the dark streets of Chicago, my skin electric with anticipation after an eight-hour shift in the restaurants where I worked. I love you the way I loved them before I got to know them, before I met their parents and grew weary of their casual farting. I love you like I loved the one with the beautiful hands and the calfskin jacket, but more. I love you like I loved the one from that endless happy summer on the front porch of my dilapidated undergraduate house, the one who quoted Shakespeare, but more. I love you more than the guitar player, the only one whose penis I could pick out of a lineup. He had a little something extra on it, like your sister's tiny third thumb. This leads me to wonder if I could pick your penis out of a lineup. If I thought I would be called upon to do so, I would study it more carefully, but I have to say I think I could do it only if it were attached to juicy darling you. And I'll never know it better than I do now, wrestling you into a clean diaper as you struggle to flip onto your belly with the strength of an eel. I don't write these things to make you squirm in high school. I write them because I love every inch of your body. Your breath is pure banana. I am completely infatuated.

This Christmas your sister was consumed with Santa and the stockings he comes down the chimney to fill. We hammed it up now that we have a chimney. I got presents for your stocking because I didn't want Inky to get the impression that it was all about her. As if Inky, nearly blind in a frenzy of chocolate, puzzles and the "regular" headbands she had been agitating for since Halloween, would have paused to consider the implications.

While she was at nursery school, you and I spent a December afternoon trolling the aisles of an overpriced health food store in Brooklyn Heights. Santa saw no reason to add to your heaping basket of rattles and small stuffed animals. Instead, Santa prepared to fill your stocking with an eye toward practicality. Not much of a one for babyproofing, he selected several glass jars of solid food, if yams and butternut squash milled to the consistency of a frozen margarita accurately can be described as such. Intended for your stocking, this was just one more present for your sister. She looked forward to the day you'd start eating almost as much as she looked forward to Christmas. I was ambivalent. All that hassle with bibs and tiny spoons and Ziploc baggies, not to mention the horrible pooh.

"Milo, I'm getting this fancy diaper rash cream for your stocking," I whispered. "Don't tell." God bless Christmas for providing me with the excuse to slather your heinie from a seven-dollar tube of crushed marigolds and beeswax. "Meadowsweet," your father and I croon, octaves above our normal speaking voices. "We call you Meadowsweet because you smells so meadowsweet." I suspect that one day when your buttocks are covered in pimples and coarse hair, I will shell out another seven bucks so I can snort your infant scent to my heart's Proustian delight.

I love your hair, especially when it's rumpled from the leopard print pilot's bonnet you've almost outgrown. "Your hair is a mess," we tell you tenderly, your father and I. Your sister thinks this is hysterical.

"Your hair is a *mess!*" she screeches, jumping up and down on the couch, barely able to contain herself. You swivel your head back and forth, smiling obligingly, toothless and utterly uncomprehending. I cling to the desperate fantasy that your hair always will be as it is now, insubstantial as a newborn duckie's fluff, that I never will need give you one of those straight-banged little-boy cuts.

I love the small twigs of wax in your ears. I love the grimy triangles I trim from the edges of your finger-nails, always too late to stop you from scratching a red divot across your plump cheek. I love the dirt between your toes. I'm so proud. I sit you down on the filthy blacktop of the playground and you come away as grubby as the big kids racing too close to you on tricycles and infernal metal scooters, lobbing balls at one another's heads. I was wrong at Christmas. There's nothing so horrible about the little patties you pump into your diapers. The exact color of whatever you've been eating, they prove that your innards are performing at the peak of their abilities. I love your father, but when he goes to the bathroom I want him to flush and light a match.

A friend whose only child is one day older than Inky can't get enough of you, a living reminder of how sweet and without guile her little boy once was. I hand you over reluctantly, wishing that she would continue wrangling the three-year-olds so that I could have you all to myself a bit longer. Back when milk was your only food, she would nuzzle your cheek only to wrinkle her nose in reproach. "P-U, Milo, you smell like throw-up!"

What could I do? You needed a bath by 9:30 every morning. Your rump smelled like new mown hay, but the rest of you was a bit sour. Still, throw-up? To me, your reek was as inviting as an expensive French cheese.

Now you stand. You stand, and you are so short that I have to check your legs to make sure that you're not sitting down. In a few weeks I imagine you'll be walking. Inky took her first step on June 3, 1998, fifteen years to the day I graduated from high school, one month shy of her first birthday. You are a July baby like your sister. I put away our wool clothes knowing what is in store for me. I only packed up your heavy footie pajamas when I fooled myself that you might fit in them come Thanksgiving. For good measure, I left a few pairs crammed into the corners of your drawer. Maybe one night in August, when temperatures fall below freezing, I will see you in that nappy pale blue fleece

with the zipper up the front once more. When the mer-
cury soared past ninety degrees at the end of spring, I
put you in the calico shorts you had worn as drawstring
trousers throughout your infancy. The waist used to sag
far below your diaper even with the string cinched as
tight as it would go. Now the waist fits perfectly beneath
your fat belly, and the hems come to your knees as
intended. In your sky blue flowered shorts and a
midriff-baring newborn-sized Keith Haring T-shirt,
you are still the girliest boy in town, mine for a little
while longer.

I fear for the next school year. Good baby, you
crawled like a puppy at my feet while Inky was off
making hand turkeys and paper plate Valentines. Will
you continue indulging me with your long morning
siestas? Promise me you'll spend hours amusing yourself with the cord to the vacuum cleaner while I type
furiously, glancing at the clock. Will we waste the valuable hours spent away from your sister on the playground? How can it be that you will seize others' toys,
shouting, "No no no no mine!" Baby, you are doubly
sweet because I know what you have in store for us. Too
soon I'll be staggering in your toddling wake. I think we
humans are too evolved. I'd like to dispense with the
vocabulary, the small bags of Cheerios, the exhortations
to share and the insipid plush creatures you'll crave even
if you never see the TV programs that catapulted them
to fame. I would prefer to teach you how to pluck fish

from the river with your sharp claws. My cub, I swear
I'd never let the predators get to you. I'd never leave you
wounded to follow the rest of the herd. I'd carry you in
my pouch 'til it dragged along the ground.

Milo, my Meadowsweet, you are getting big. Second
baby, it goes by in a flash. I hope you will be loved this
madly again, perhaps first in high school and then again
in springtime and again and again until you find a mate
with whom to share your precious life. For a few ecstatic
months, your mate will love you unconditionally, as I
have for a year now. After that, you will learn to nego-
tiate and compromise, loving through aggravation, disappointment and anger. Your father and sister have
taught me that it is worth it.

Sooner than we think, I will be ready to share you.
May the issue of your bowels never find an admirer so
ardent as your mother, but, boy of mine, I hope life will
net you your fair share of love letters.

Your humble servant, I remain,

Ma ma ma

About the Author

AYUN HALLIDAY is the sole staff member of the quarterly zine the *East Village Inky*, which has been nominated for three Utne Reader Alternative Press Awards. She has contributed to *Bust* and *Hipmama* and her essays have appeared in the anthologies *Breeder, A Woman Alone* and *The Unsavvy Traveller*. As a member of the Neo-Futurists, she wrote and performed in several full-length solo works as well as hundreds of short plays for *Too Much Light Makes the Baby Go Blind (30 Plays in 60 Minutes)*. She lives in Brooklyn with her children and husband, the man responsible for *Urinetown (The Musical)*.

Contact Ayun at thebigrumpus@hotmail.com.

Selected Seal Press Titles

Breeder: Real-Life Stories from the New Generation of Mothers
edited by Ariel Gore and Bee Lavender, foreword by Dan Savage. $16.00, 1-58005-051-4. From the editors of Hip Mama, this hilarious and heartrending compilation creates a space where Gen-X moms can dish, cry, scream and laugh.

The Mother Trip:
Hip Mama's Guide to Staying Sane in the Chaos of Motherhood
by Ariel Gore. $14.95, 1-58005-029-8. In a book that is part self-help, part critique of the mommy myth and part hip-mama handbook, Ariel Gore offers support to mothers who break the mold.

Young Wives' Tales: New Adventures in Love and Partnership
edited by Jill Corral and Lisa Miya-Jervis, foreword by bell hooks. $16.95, 1-58005-050-6. This bold and provocative anthology captures the wide range of responses and lived realities of young women, whether they are trying on the title "wife," deciding who will wear the gown in a lesbian wedding or demanding the space for solitude in a committed relationship.

Body Outlaws:
Young Women Write About Body Image and Identity
edited by Ophira Edut. $14.95, 1-58005-043-3. Essays filled with honesty and humor by women who have chosen to ignore, subvert or redefine the dominant beauty standard.

Listen Up: Voices from the Next Feminist Generation
edited by Barbara Findlen. $16.95, 1-58005-054-9. The voices of today's young feminists are brought together to explore and reveal their lives.

Sex and Single Girls: Straight and Queer Women on Sexuality
edited by Lee Damsky. $16.95, 1-58005-038-7. In this potent and entertaining collection of essays, women lay bare pleasure, fear, desire, risk—all that comes with exploring their sexuality.